Ghost Stories from the Ghosts' Point of View Trilogy Vol. 3

Tina Erwin, CDR USN (Ret)

Ghost Stories from the Ghosts' Point of View,
Trilogy Vol. 3

Copyright © 2012 Tina Erwin
Third Edition Published 2022
Second Edition Published 2016
First Publication 2012

Published by Tina Erwin

ISBN-10 : 1732267332
ISBN-13 : 978-1732267336

All rights reserved. No part of this book may be reproduced or transmitted in any form or by any means, electronic or mechanical, including photocopying, recording, or by any information storage and retrieval system, without permission in writing from the author at:
Tina@TinaErwin.com

Cover Photography by Tina Erwin
Cover Location: The village of Castle Combe, Wiltshire, United Kingdom

Works by Tina Erwin

The Lightworker's Guide to Healing Grief

The Lightworker's Guide to Everyday Karma

Ghost Stories from the Ghosts' Point of View, Trilogy, Vol. 1

Ghost Stories from the Ghosts' Point of View, Trilogy, Vol. 2

Ghost Stories from the Ghosts' Point of View, Trilogy, Vol. 3

Soul Evolution, Past Lives and Karmic Ties

Karma and Frequency

The Crossing Over Prayer Book

Special Notice to the Reader:

WARNING

Due to the mature nature of the content of this book, which may deal with tragic and/or violent death, reader discretion is advised. These true stories are intended for mature audiences only.

Acknowledgments

Tremendous effort is required to put forth the information you are about to read, and no successful author accomplishes anything alone. I am blessed to have wonderful people supporting me as I share this critical knowledge of how the living can help the dead.

My loyal and loving husband has earned my undying gratitude for supporting all of my psychic efforts and for his conscientious editing work on these books.

I would like to gratefully acknowledge the support and critical assistance of my entire publishing team: my daughter, Jeanne Marie Erwin Coronado, my daughters-in-law Amee Erwin, and Monica Lane. A special thanks to my sister Andrea, and her daughter Marisa Harris for all the efforts to help the dead in all the locations we have visited over the years. Also, a very special thank you to Marisa for the house she spent helping me to format this book!

Thanks to all of your dedication, hard work and attention to detail, the world will get to know the true stories of those ghostly souls who will now live in our hearts forever.

Dedication

This entire book series is dedicated to all of my friends who, over the years, have taught me so much.

This dedication is also intended for all of those brave souls who asked for help in assisting many a ghostly soul to cross over.

And finally, I am deeply grateful for the Spiritual Beings who unfailingly assist us all to guide lost and lonely souls to the Heaven World.

Preface

This book is the third volume of ghost trilogy stories. However, the stories you are about to read in this volume are not merely ghosts telling you their stories. No, this book also shares with you my own personal journey into learning how to help the dead. Some of the events were terrifying for me. Some of them seemed to shred my very soul. Others opened me up to concepts that, at the time, seemed unimaginable.

This is my life. This journey of learning how to deal with my psychic ability took me down many, often chilling paths. Yet I am simply a person with psychic ability trying to figure out how to use this skill to help others, both living and dead.

If you see or sense ghosts, if you want to help, perhaps there will be lessons and ideas within these pages that will empower you to use **The Crossing Over Prayer©** at the end of this book, to help those souls. You can also use The *Crossing Over Prayer Book©* available on Amazon. Once you read this book, once you can fully understand the challenge of being dead but believing you are still alive and needing help to understand what happened to you, then perhaps you can understand why *Crossing Over Prayer Book©* is such an important companion book. People die by so many different methods, that it is important to provide all types of prayers to help them and that is what *Crossing Over Prayer Book© does.*

Spiritual service is the most important critical element on all of our spiritual paths. Whether you are reading this book for the pleasure of a good set of ghost stories or you want to learn more about helping the dead, I hope this book is of service to you.

Tina Erwin, CDR USN [Ret.

Testimonials

"I have known Tina Erwin through her books and guest spots on my Internet radio shows for several years. She is a truly compassionate person and I feel her dedication to her mission as a ghost helper every time I interview her. She works very hard to help lost souls that haunt this world to cross over and find their way to heaven. She is always an interesting guest and very good at looking at a haunting from the ghosts' point of view."
Ron Mills Host of "Journey into the Paranormal"

"My wife and I had heard some unusual sounds late in the evening coming from the kitchen. It was a rustling sound like someone squishing leaves, a crunching sound. We did not think much of it because we have heard it before, but we still wondered. One day my wife got up early and had TV on and heard what sounded like a rocker rocking. We have one in the next room, which can be seen from where she was sitting.

When she heard it for a second time, she turned and saw the rocker going back and forth. We knew then that we had a ghost visitor. We did not care who it was or why. We just wanted them gone. I had heard about the Crossing Over Prayer available at Tinaerwin.com and found the Crossing Over Prayer Video. I played it and turned up the speakers because Tina says the prayer out loud. After that morning and playing that video all the strange noises stopped completely! Thanks Tina, for your help in removing the ghosts and allowing us some peace and quiet. The Prayer works!"
J. Paul, Boone, North Carolina

"I have worked with Tina for quite some time now. I have come to know that often when I am feeling yucky or just not my real self, there are spirits and beings trying to attach to me. Tina is strongly connected with the ghost world and is able to handle the darkness and help it move towards the light. She has helped me tremendously not just in my personal life but for our business as well. She is a compassionate, strong, connected medium that helps those who need crossing over. I am so grateful to have her in our lives. She has the ability to explain things rather than just follow her lead, she puts my mind at ease and has suggestions that I can actually implement in my world. Her work is a service to many like me on this earth and those who need it beyond this space."
Vaishali P. National City, California

"Several years ago, Tina helped me cross over my brother Matthew who had been murdered. Prior to that time, I had an unsettled feeling when I thought about him and what happened to him. His crossing over was emotional, beautiful, and comforting. Afterwards I finally felt at peace that he was safe and I had an indescribable sense of relief."
Heather D. Poway, California

"This book has tremendous value for everybody. Tina Erwin's Crossing Over Prayer© has become an integral part of my work with helping deceased people to move smoothly out of this life. Her book - all of her books, truthfully - contains gem after gem of extremely helpful and practical information for living life and for exiting this life, and for dealing with those who have become stuck in a repeating pattern after their death. By applying these techniques, she describes, I've become more effective and definitely clearer in my work, both as a medium and with my energy healing practice. Reading and studying this book can result in freedom on many levels, for the reader and possibly for the one who crossed over."
Rev. Bonnie Willow, Director, The School of Peace

"Saturday night our four-year-old daughter came into our bedroom around 3am. She said that there was a scary lion under bed. She slept with us that night and then Sunday, we

asked her if it was still there. She said it was, so we played The Crossing Over Prayer video twice and she said it was still there so we waited about 10 more minutes and I asked her again and she said it was gone! It's great to have such a simple tool to help our daughter. Thanks!
James and Suzanne E. Mission Viejo, California

Foreword

My name is Pat Baccili. I am the host of The Dr. Pat Show and founder of Transformation Talk Radio. For nearly 15 years, I have personally had the privilege to interview over 6,000 of the most brilliant, fascinating, visionaries, authors, and change catalysts in the world and that doesn't include the hundreds of interviews done by some of the incredible hosts on Transformation Talk Radio. So, it is my honor and privilege to share with you my own heartfelt words about the extraordinary Tina Erwin.

As I sat at the microphone preparing for my show with Tina, I had no idea where this interview would take the listeners so for a bit of fun I asked my producer Benny, "Are you ready for what's to come?" Are you ready for some, "ghost helping?" He smiled a sly smile, but little did either of us know the real depth of my question and what was to come across the airwaves that day.

What I can absolutely say to you is even after all the amazing interviews I have done; I am continually in awe of the magic that is in this beautiful world we live in. And, with that, I can tell you without a doubt, we never know when someone will show up and take us on a journey beyond our wildest imagination, sharing the most mystical jaw dropping experiences. Tina Erwin is that someone.

Her gifts and stories will touch your heart, enlighten your soul, offer answers, and bring some peace to your deepest questions about what happens to us when we get to the other side.

In her stories, Tina invites you into a new realm of thinking where you will discover that your pre-programmed Hollywood visions of ghosts and the make believe. What Hollywood does package up and sell us is nothing remotely close to what is real, as Tina knows and many of us may intuitively know but are afraid to admit. This book will break every stereotype you ever had about ghosts.

Tina will challenge each of us to not only open our minds but to also open our hearts and to be open to going deeper than we have ever gone before. She shares her journey of helping lost souls that are seeking witness, crying out for validation, and assistance for release from this earthly dimension to the next unknown destination. These moments are both heartwarming, heart breaking and mind blowing at the same time and can only be expressed by someone who has first handedly assisted many souls to their freedom. That person again, is Tina Erwin.

Tina calls forth that part in each of us who questions our own soul's journey and fears that maybe; just maybe; it could be our own soul that wanders endlessly in limbo and daunting confusion seeking peace. After reading this book, each of us will find comfort and inner peace knowing that Tina's calling will be able to give each of us some guidance and answers to our own questions. Tina has embraced what anyone would agree is a mega resume of service, achievement, and resolution in modern day times that transcends the physical nature of our lives into a world of wonder and surprise. She is in service to answer the calling on her life to empower and assist souls to take that final step to freedom and graciously shares these stories with us in hopes of giving us a better understanding of this ever-mysterious process that will occur in all of our lives. Then suggests to all of us, we too, can help. Are you ready for that?

It would be too easy to simply say this is an amazing book and how fascinating the stories are because they are. As you begin to read the book you will find Tina and her stories of the soul's transitions will raise us all to a higher level of consciousness and deeper understanding of self.

This book will have you wondering how many of us have had experiences that we thought no one around us could validate even if we even wanted to tell someone. And so, with that, what do we do, where do we go, how we understand? We most often can't. Thank goodness for Tina. She is a witness, facilitator, and conduit for all of us. When you finish this book, you will realize that we are not alone. You will know that those interactions you had that you thought were unexplainable are now very believable.

Tina's trilogy, "Ghost Stories from the Ghosts' Point of View," take us above and beyond our humanness as we follow the stories of searching from the perspective of the soul's journey and not our own. Tina removes our human bias and projection from the conversation and will make us laugh, cry, and hang on to every sentence as we learn how powerful and compassionate Tina's process is. The book touched me so much so that I was able to re-examine my own childhood ghostly experience and make much more sense of it.

Tina validates our unexplainable experiences, intuitions, and connections not as exceptions as we are so conditioned to believe, but as tangible real experiences. Humans have been seeing ghosts for as long as we have been on this earth. In this book, Tina will show us how to take the mystery out of this subject and open doors to a new understanding of all our ghostly encounters.

Think about what we could really understand if we were to actually believe our children (or friends for that matter) when they so clearly and honestly talk about their invisible friends? What if they were no longer just "ghost stories" but acts of "spiritual service?" Tina asks us to contemplate these possibilities and her attention to detail makes that request easy as each story is so vividly presented with color, movement, and emotion.

Tina Erwin has integrated years of military service as a Naval Commander, guiding others in full accountability and integrity. Each day during her service, without question, she held the lives of so many in her command synthesizing information, needs, and action as each life on a submarine so expected her to do and she did it with quiet service and honor. When capturing her remarkable success as with so many, you will discover that her innate way, her intuitive nature, and her ability to apply her keen insight led her to become the psychic medium, healer, paranormal expert, that she is today. As was then, she still bears witness to grieving relatives, doubting naysayers, and individuals who think they are losing their minds by what has been revealed to them. Just as she guided the souls on each submarine to safety, Tina guides the many lost souls who have been left in solemn contemplation and struggle to find their way home to the light.

Throughout history, humans have been obsessed with the "unknown" which lends to the idea that there must be a deeper truth as to why we all feel so drawn to try to understand what will become of us when we leave the earth. Just as we all long to be heard and to tell our stories and express our purpose as we live, as our souls have the same desire to be heard as they embark upon the mysterious journey, beyond life, as we do know it.

This is a journey that often may require some assistance to accomplish. This is Tina's remarkable gift. A gift bound by spiritual law. It is undeniably clear to me that Tina's work in bringing forth these messages and stories will help each of us find our own way to separate the real from the fiction of what it means for us to pass over to the next dimension.

As I interviewed Tina after Volume 2 launched, I asked her if she questioned, "Why me?" Tina replied, "Well I believe that everyone is psychic. I felt the Navy was preparation because to do this work you must be very disciplined, you must be very logical, you must be able to use emotional anesthetic because you are going to hear things, that make you weep or rip your heart out. You must be disciplined enough to get yourself out of the way and help them and follow spiritual law. This is my mission until I take my last breath. And the ultimate element of the mission is to empower every person to feel that they can do this themselves because Pat, this is going to be the compassion that all of us will want for ourselves."

In "Ghost Stories from the Ghosts' Point of View, Trilogy, Vol. 3," Tina reminds us of the gratitude of the dead to the living, as they cross over. These are stories of healing and hope.

Tina's life is no ordinary life and this is no ordinary book! As you open the pages you will not be able to stop turning them as Tina shares the process of making connections with so many souls from any distance. Her work is simply beyond enthralling. Many of us will find it nearly impossible to comprehend how she is able to connect with these tortured souls and how she is able to help them. You are in for a life-changing experience as Tina shares the conversations between her and the ghosts who travel endlessly seeking the way to the other side. You will be on the edge of your seat as she vividly describes the scenario of a mother who has carried the burden of guilt as a parent, as you hold your breath praying for a happy ending. These stories open us up to healing on a personal nature as you discover that these souls are just like us.

"Ghost Stories from the Ghosts' Point of View, Trilogy, Vol. 3" is a magnificent ceremony to the spirits that have long been out of our consciousness but ever so apparent to Tina as she has chosen the road less traveled but so beautifully paved by her love.

Dr. Pat Baccili
Host, The Dr. Pat Show –
Talk Radio to Thrive By!
Founder, Transformation Talk Radio and TransformationRadio.FM

Mission Statement

The purpose of this book is to offer you a different view of what it is like to leave your body at death.

The hope of this book is that you will cease your fear of souls who have left their physical bodies and begin to understand their situation.

The opportunity of this book is the opening of your compassionate heart to those who need help crossing over.

Send them your prayers.

Send these souls your love.

Request Angels of Transition as you say **The Crossing Over Prayer©** to assist them in crossing into the light, no matter their method of death, no matter what this person may have been like in life, and no matter whether or not you loved them or even knew them.

Service to the dead is one of the most compassionate and important acts of kindness, a living person can ever do. <u>No ghost is at peace until he or she finally crosses over into the light.</u> Your service to them means the difference between continual feelings of fear and abandonment, cold and pain versus the joy, and the hopeful delight of crossing into heaven.

Table of Contents

Works by Tina Erwin _____ I
Acknowledgments _____ V
Dedication _____ VII
Preface _____ XI
Testimonials _____ XIII
Foreword _____ XVII
Mission Statement _____ XXV
An Introduction to Understanding Evil and Haunting _____ 1
Retrieving Your Own Soul _____ 3
The Greatest Gift _____ 20
The Manteo Colony _____ 37
The Acting Couch _____ 50
That Terrible Feeling _____ 70
A Stranger in the Shadow Lands _____ 84
The Dental Chair _____ 110
The Lieutenant's Roommate _____ 125

A Hole in Time	140
Echoes of the Inquisition	151
A Rainy Night of Tears	166
A Soldier's Heart	186
Can You Help My Daughter?	201
The Aviation Museum	212
The Twins	227
The House of the Dark Arts	245
The Wrong Side of the Tracks	276
The Pony Express	293
Terror Through Time	304
The Wall Between Time	317
Darling Charlotte	337
When Evil Haunts the Living and the Dead	350
My Own Spiritual Service	389
Prayers for Sending Ghosts to the Heaven World	395
Glossary	407
About the Author	424
BONUS MATERIAL: I Get Questions	426

An Introduction to Understanding Evil and Haunting

We have all had this conversation in some form about a place or event, and it goes something like this.

"I heard that that house at the end of the block is haunted!"

The statement is said in hushed, whispered tones, as if somehow saying it out loud will cause an eerie, diaphanous ghost to materialize right in front of the person. Maybe those hushed words are done because having knowledge about a haunted house is not something people want others to know about themselves. Perhaps the initiator of the conversation is not quite sure that he will be believed and the fewer people that hear that he believes in ghosts, well, you get the idea.

Introduction to Understanding Evil and Haunting

You may also hear a friend tell you that someone, and this could be a relative, or even a stranger, comes to them night after night in an endlessly recurring dream. The living person does not know whether or not to be terrified, disturbed, or excited. Should she simply ignore it? The problem is that if you are being haunted, it's pretty tough to ignore it.

Maybe this has happened to you, you go into a store, or home, or park, or building of any sort and in one particular spot, you feel 'all creeped out' and there is no explaining why. You notice that you avoid that location as much as you can.

Most people go about their day-to-day lives with a basic understanding of the term 'haunted,' thinking it has one simple meaning. But there are all types of hauntings and they can happen for a variety of reasons, as the stories in this book will chillingly show you. As you begin the stories, take an opportunity to review the many different ways a mortal person or location can be haunted that are listed at the end of this book.

Retrieving Your Own Soul

What is it like to have a shocking psychic experience?

What if you have no idea that you are even having a supernatural event?

How do you convey to someone else that your path into the darkness of the supernatural has left you terrified and shaken?

What is it like for your husband to watch you go through a powerful spiritual experience?

I guess looking back, I was lucky to have married the man I did because when my blood ran cold, when I felt like my soul was being destroyed, he was there to save me.

The First Married Naval Officers

I was twenty-three years old, married less than a year to the love my life, Troy Erwin, when he experienced the first psychic episode with me. We were both Naval Officers, stationed at

Submarine Base New London, in Groton, Connecticut. He was a handsome Lieutenant Junior Grade assigned to an old diesel submarine, USS Greenfish (SS 351) assigned as Assistant Weapons Officer. I was an Ensign working at the Supervisor of Shipbuilding, Conversion and Repair, Electric Boat Division where they were building 688 class nuclear submarines. I managed communications and classified material for all new construction submarines.

    I joined the Navy in 1972, graduated from Officer Candidate School in Newport, Rhode Island in February of 1973. In the dark ages of the Navy, which was only 1972, if a woman was married, she was automatically required to leave the Navy. If she became pregnant (if she was not married) and wanted to keep her baby, she was also instantly discharged from the Navy. The Navy did not take women seriously as Naval Officers so the laws regarding having children and being married were different for women than they were for men.

    However, within months of my being commissioned an Ensign in the US Navy, many of those archaic laws changed. So, when I arrived at my first duty station, met my husband the very first day there and then later that same year eloped with him, we found that we were breaking all types of stereotypes and preconceptions that people had about female Naval Officers. Together, he and I were opening doors and breaking new ground. It was an exciting time full of promise and change.

People called us Mr. and Mrs. Navy. In 1974, when this terrifying event happened, we were one of the very first Officer couples in the Navy. That alone was a groundbreaking situation because people weren't quite sure how to relate to us. People may have thought that we were unusual but no one had any idea what an amazing life we were about to have for at least fifty years.

Honey Yellow Mums

The first psychic event began on one of those precious fall days in New England where the air is crisp, but not cold, the sky is a clear blue and the leaves have turned all the brilliant shades of crimson, orange, and gold. I was planting honey yellow chrysanthemums in front of our apartment on the Submarine Base in New London, late one October afternoon. Troy was outside keeping me company. I was having a gloriously happy moment when all seemed right with the world.

The world can change so quickly and, only moments later, a very odd feeling came over me. It was like one of those cartoons, where a dark cloud parks itself over the character. It does not come over anyone else and in this case, that dark cloud surely did not come over Troy. He continued to feel fine, but I was not fine. I began to feel a tremendous sense of foreboding, as if something terrible was about to happen, or had in fact, already taken place and I was about to learn of it. What made this so bizarre is that one moment I was feeling wonderful and then a moment later it was like some eerie, chilling, evil fog slowly, deliberately began to seep into my heart. Words do not begin to describe how unnerving it was. It was like being wrapped in an emotionally suffocating darkness. Someone puts it over your face and while you can see through it, no matter what you do, you cannot remove it – or so you think.

"What's wrong? You look like you've seen a ghost. Are you okay?" Troy asked me this as he watched my happy expression turn fearful.

"No," I replied, "No, I'm not okay. I have this terrible feeling that something awful has happened or is going to happen to someone, maybe someone I know. I can't figure out what's going on. I can feel it but it's not clear. This vague awful feeling is getting stronger with every minute that passes."

Men solve problems, it's what they do: feel bad, take a pill. Troy is a man of action, so his reaction was typically logical.

"What should we do? How do we fix this?"

We had only known each other about 18 months at this point and he had been at sea most of that time. He did not really know me very well yet, much less have had any previous psychic experiences with me. This was our first sojourn into the supernatural.

"It's getting stronger and stronger. Oh God! Someone's died I just know it! We have to find out if it's a family member! I'm going to call my mom to see if everyone's all right because I'm convinced that someone has just died."

I put down the plants and ran into the house as Troy stared after me, dumbfounded.

The Awkward Conversation

"Hey, honey, before you call your mom and get everyone really upset, how are you going to explain this? Whatever 'this' is that's happening? Can you be a bit more specific? I'm not sure I understand it."

Troy asked me this question in a calm, matter-of-fact manner. How do you explain psychic phenomena to a left-brained engineer type of Naval Officer, or to your family?

I blinked. I had no idea. I was so upset that I just wanted this engulfing feeling to leave me; I was desperate to rip it out of me. This toxic energy was penetrating into every cell of my being. A growing sense of panic consumed me.

"I – I don't know exactly, but I'll be careful, I just need to do something right now. I have to know!"

"Okay, go ahead, but be careful." Troy seemed utterly bewildered as he stood by and watched the entire scene unfold.

So, I called my mother. I knew she would know if anything had happened to any family member.

"Hi Mom, just calling to check in to see how you all are doing. How is everyone?" I tried to control the gnawing panic I was feeling.

"Honey, everyone here's just fine, your sister's doing homework, I'm making supper, you know, same old thing. Why do you ask?"

"Sorry to bother you but I've had this odd feeling come over me and I thought I would call to check and see if you're all okay. I don't know, maybe it's some type of premonition. Hard to explain, but glad everyone's fine – even Grandma? How are the boys?"

"Yes, I just spoke to her, she's fine. Your brothers are both fine. I hope you figure it out. Not sure how to help you or even if I can. Did something happen to you?"

"No, well yes, I don't know. I have this sense of foreboding and I'm trying to eliminate family members from the pool of people who might be hurt in some way."

"I wish I could help. Let me know if there is any way I can help. I'll talk to you soon. Good night, honey."

Everyone was fine. When you have a psychic feeling like this you search the logic you know because you have no other way to approach a challenge like this. The process of elimination is all you have. Troy tried to be helpful, but he didn't know what to do with me. I kept trying to shrug off this feeling, but nothing removed it. By this time about an hour had passed and I was not getting any better, so Troy made what he thought was a helpful suggestion.

"You know, maybe if you do ordinary things, like make supper and change the subject, focus on doing what we were going to do, that maybe this feeling will go away."

Make supper? Are you kidding me? How can he even think of food at a time like this? Oh my God! I feel like I'm dying inside and it's time to make supper? Really?

But I had no better answer. So, I went in the kitchen and started to put food together while I was trying to control the panic that made me want to scream and jump out of my skin.

Who Was That?

"Alright. I'll see what I – I can put together for us to eat, but my heart isn't in it."

While I'm cooking, I feel a terrible shudder run down my spine.

"Oh my God, Tina, what's happened to you?"

And a new voice came out of me and answered him. I had never heard this voice before and neither had Troy.

"I don't know what you mean."

"Tina, you don't look like you. The face of a totally different person seemed, for a brief moment, to take over your face. This voice, how you answered me, isn't you. Oh my god, now I get it, something terrible is happening. How do I help you?"

I struggled to take control of my sense of self: I was fighting to stay in my own body.

"What did you see, can you be more specific?" I recognized that voice as my own voice, so I was still in some level of control.

"I saw the face of another woman, not the woman I married, cross your face. It was brief but unmistakable. Tina, what's going on here?"

"I – I have no idea. Let's try and eat supper." Maybe I said that, or maybe whoever was 'here' said those words. I felt that I was holding on, and yet slowly losing my grip. I felt myself slipping away. . .

Somehow, we managed to get through supper, but neither of us ate much. I could sense that Troy was feeling as desperate as I was and was frantically thinking how he could help me.

"I know, why don't we call a Navy chaplain and ask if he can help us. I'll look one up."

"Okay," I replied flatly. I was beginning to shiver almost uncontrollably, like I was standing in the arctic with no clothes on.

I shall never forget the conversation with that Catholic Navy Chaplain. Troy and I both explained this weird feeling I was having, that it had never happened before and could he please help us. This Chaplain became instantly irritated with us, and then proceeded to accuse us of having watched the Exorcist [which to this day I have never seen]. In mid-sentence, he hung up on us. I have long pondered what that man heard from us. Did we scare him? Did we challenge him? We will never know.

The Cold of Death

"Troy, what do we do now? Each passing moment brings more and more fear. I'm relentlessly cold deep inside my body as if death is creeping in. And - and a new phenomenon is beginning to come over me. I'm terrified by even the thought of looking into a mirror. I can't tell you what I think I'll see, but I can't look into a mirror. Please don't leave me! I – I can't have you out of my sight. I'm not sure what will happen, but you are my link to reality right now."

"Honey, I'm not leaving you. I'm right here. I bet you don't want to look into a mirror because you're afraid you'll 'see her,' that 'other' woman who crossed your face. What do you think is happening? I don't know how to help you but I'm here for you. Tell me what you know."

Troy returned to his engineer focused mind, trying to separate feeling from fact.

"Troy, I know that I'm afraid. I'm so terrified that I can't convey what this feels like. I have never known this kind of fear. It's as if, -- if I let you out of my sight, that maybe I'll die. Maybe I'm afraid to be alone with her. You know?"

"Oh my God, there, I can see her face on your face – again, you're right, something terrible is happening. We have to do something immediately. But what is it that we need to do? This is crazy."

When he explained this second incidence of the other woman's face crossing mine, it finally began to dawn on me just exactly, what was happening. I finally got it. I took a deep breath and jumped into the deep end of the pool of disbelief and told him.

"Troy, I think that this woman is trying to take over my body. She's trying to possess me!!"

We are not religious people. We had never considered ourselves especially 'spiritual' either, and yet this very 'spiritual' experience was happening to us. Troy, ever the engineer, logically deduced that if he did in fact have a ghost trying to possess his new wife, then somehow, he had to get the ghost to leave.

"How do we get rid of her? I'd rip her out of your body if I could but how do you pull a ghost out of a person's body?" He paused.

"We just have to get her to leave. I only want to be married to you and I don't want anyone else. Give me a minute. A plan is emerging."

It's Not My Time!

As he put his ideas together, I also began to have an entirely new realization of who this woman was and why she picked me.

"Oh my God, Troy I know what happened to her. I get it now. Somehow, I can 'see' her. She's about my age, 23, who looks or looked somewhat like me. She died in some type of auto accident nearby and was furious that she was dead. She had a life to live, people to see, people who loved her. She had a relationship. She is such a powerful personality that she intended to deny death, to live on and if that meant that she had to possess someone else's body to do that, then so be it.

"She has absolutely no intention of leaving me. She is so determined! Whatever your plan is, we need to do it quickly; I'm struggling every minute to hold on to my soul! She wants me to die in her place so that she can use my body to continue her life. But she's the one who's dead."

I realized I was speaking more to myself than even to Troy as I continued.

"I know she's dead. It isn't my fault that she died, that she's rejecting the idea of death. She hasn't come face to face with the fact that she has to grieve her passing and then cross over. She thinks no one will notice the difference between us. I must look very much like her."

As I am describing her to Troy, I can feel her misguided belief that she will actually be triumphant in taking over my body.

"Troy, she doesn't want our help, she wants my body! Whatever plan you have, now would be a very good time to start it. I'm so cold! I feel like I'm dying inside. Do something! I can hear her screaming that it's not her time, over and over and over. She's so angry!"

"Let me run upstairs and see if I can find the Bible I was given when I was commissioned."

"I'll come with you. I don't want to be left alone for even a second."

We both rummaged around upstairs and on the one tiny bookshelf we had, we found that Bible. As soon as I saw it, I began to have that precious glimmer of hope. We returned downstairs and Troy turned to me as he got settled on the sofa.

"I found it, I found what I was looking for. Let's recite the Twenty-Third Psalm. Come here, honey, I'm going to start reciting this psalm. It's all I know how to do."

I remember feeling utterly vulnerable and afraid, so Troy gathered me up in his lap. He then put his big, strong, loving arms around me, opened the Bible and began to slowly recite the Twenty-Third Psalm over, and over, and over again in his deep, reassuring voice:

"The Lord is my Shepard; I shall not want.

He maketh me to lie down in green pastures.

He leadeth me beside the still waters.

He restoreth my soul:

He leadeth me in the paths of righteousness for His name's sake.

Yea, though I walk through the valley of the shadow of death,

I will fear no evil: for thou art with me.

Thy rod and thy staff, they comfort me.

Thou preparest a table before me in the presence of mine enemies.

Thou annointest my head with oil; My cup runneth over.

Surely goodness and mercy shall follow me all the days of my life, and I will dwell in the House of the Lord forever."

Crossing Over

Troy was so patient with me and, ironically, with this ghost woman. He wasn't angry with her. He wasn't judging her. I remember feeling a deep sense of gratitude for my new husband as I came face to face with his intense compassion for a woman he did not know. He patiently read the 23rd Psalm again and again. And it worked: she began to slowly, gently, almost reluctantly, release me.

There is no way to describe what it feels like to have a ghost leave your body. All I can say is that it's like someone who is gripping you very tightly from the inside, slowly letting go, relaxing, and finally being at peace. I felt strongly that she had crossed over into the Heaven World. I was so sorry she died, but I had no intention of allowing her to take over my life. She had to move on, and so she did. I never knew her name. What I did know was that the attempted possession by one ghostly soul of another living person was a reality, and one that I never wanted to experience again.

Finally, we knew were alone again with each other.

I stopped shivering.

Mirrors no longer held untold terrors.

Troy could safely be out of my sight and I would not freak out.

There was a profound quiet that settled on our tiny home. When we went to sleep, safe in each other's arms that night, we were exhausted from the experience. As I was drifting off to sleep, I said a silent prayer of gratitude for having such an amazing husband and the spiritual tools to help this soul to cross over, into what I hoped, would be heaven.

And that was the positive side of this event. I could not help but wonder why she picked me, other than we looked similar. I have spent a lifetime trying to understand. I also asked myself what I would have done, if he had been at sea and I had had to face this alone, because I also had the strong feeling that this would not be the last time, I would encounter the supernatural.

Epilogue

And it was not the last time. More and more psychic events began to happen to me, to both of us. I am not living alone with this ability. Troy is along for the ride, for better or worse, bless his heart.

I already knew I had an affinity for ghosts. What I did not know was what other abilities were coming, and come they did.

I learned that I could see the future, could know when various events were going to happen with unnerving accuracy – but not everything, just particular events.

The fragile beginnings of being able to remote view began to manifest when we were stationed in Italy, in simple ways like knowing what traffic was coming when I could not possibly be able to see it. Sometimes Troy was so unnerved he had to work hard to wrap his brain around the abilities that seemed to manifest every day.

Psychic ability aside, I still had to focus on being a Naval Officer and enjoy living a whole life. If this attempted possession had taught me anything, I learned how terribly precious life is and how important it is to live every day to the fullest.

In my years of studying the phenomena of possession I have come to understand that for some reason I was in resonance with her, meaning that our frequencies, things about us, our ages, our thoughts, must have been extremely close. This was why she felt she could take over my life. However, I was not about to let that happen. This also taught me that I have more power in any supernatural situation than I may have at first realized. I can say no. I can move them on and I can decide for myself that my life is my own.

I eventually figured out that my fear of mirrors was based on an – at that time – unrecognized understanding that mirrors are gateways between the realms, doorways between dimensions. Of course, I was terrified that I would see her face. Perhaps I felt if I gazed into that looking glass, I would clearly see her and then something even more terrible would happen. I subconsciously knew that if I avoided mirrors that I might protect myself from something even more sinister: the other beings that live in that mystical 4th dimensional realm. Once that experience was over, my fear of mirrors ceased.

As I pondered this whole event, the most critical element of this experience was learning that no soul is ever going to be at peace until he or she walks through the valley of the shadow of death and crosses into the Heaven World. What I did not realize at that time was that the many missions of my military career were but a training ground to my ultimate life mission: helping the dead to cross into the Heaven World and sharing this work with other people intent on spiritual service. The years of study, especially understanding the good and evil in the world as the Navy opened up many doors of opportunity, enabled me to gain insight into the universal spiritual truths.

Learning how life after death works, valuing the experience of attempted possession enabled me to find compassion for this soul and for others who find that death comes too quickly and that the life you are living is profoundly precious.

ing" Ghost Stories from the Ghosts' Point of View Vol 3

The Greatest Gift

Missile Submarines

It was the first week of December 1974, Christmas time. A bitter cold wind whipped around our modest house on the Submarine Base, in New London, Connecticut. We had a tiny, decorated Christmas tree in our sparsely furnished living room. It was covered with the vintage, hand painted glass ornaments we bought at a yard sale. Gazing at them I grew wistful: I wanted to be happy but I was already grieving that I would be taking them down so soon. We had rushed to put up our tree early because Troy would not actually be home with me for Christmas morning. Troy was stationed aboard the ballistic missile submarine, USS Benjamin Franklin (SSBN 640 Gold) in Rota, Spain. This type of submarine had two crews so that the submarine would always be continuously at sea except for that brief week where the two crews changed out. Troy's ballistic missile submarine crew was leaving to rejoin his ship, the week before Christmas. But way back then, that exact time and date, was a closely guarded secret.

Anything to do with missile submarines was a secret. To me, though, the Navy did not make much sense in how they kept some of their submarine secrets, because what was not a secret was his 'set-your-watch-by-it,' unrelenting 90 days at home 105 days at sea schedule. At the end of the 90 days at home, he would fly back to Spain with the rest of the 140 men who manned the Gold crew and take back the ship from the Blue crew who had just returned from sea. The two crews spent about 5 days in 'turnover' and then the Blue crew got to come home, that year, for Christmas.

When your husband is on a 'two-crew' submarine, you have the questionably beneficial ability to look into the future and know for sure what date you will be happy (he is on his way back!), sad (he just left), miserable (it's only halfway through the patrol – ugh) and hopeful (only 10 days and he will be back!).

Nothing, absolutely nothing interfered with this schedule. So, you have to plan any normal life events like birthdays and holidays way before. We had planned to have our Christmas about three days before he left. I should have been excited about celebrating our second Christmas together but something was nagging at me.

That Sickening, Nagging Feeling

I was glad I got home from work early. I watched the snowfall outside the big windows in our living room as I was wrapping presents. Troy wasn't home from the office yet, supper was on the stove, and our two Siamese cats, Sam, and Mindy, were cuddled close to me. The moment should have felt warm and cozy, but the endless grey skies and the cold outside chilled me. I should have been happy. We were together, things were going really well but I kept having this weird feeling that things were not okay.

What do you do with a feeling that something terrible is coming? This sense haunts you day and night, nagging at the corners of your mind like some overbearing shadow that you cannot escape. It follows you everywhere, and no matter what you do, you cannot seem to shake it . . . and it starts at night, coming to you in a faint alarming dream.

You cannot wave away a recurring dream, a frightening nightmare that keeps coming at you like a dark, terrifying wisp, shaking you awake in a cold sweat. The energy of that dream is unlike anything you have ever known. Normal dreams slip out of the threadbare reaches of your mind and are gone with barely a whisper. Maybe you remember them, maybe you don't, it doesn't matter.

This was different. This 'dream' (which was all I called it because I had no idea what it really was), kept pestering me to do something about it, to take action. But what action was I supposed to take?

How could this nightmare possibly be true?

Be Logical. Put the Pieces Together

I reminded myself that I was an Ensign in the United States Navy, a very logical, down to earth person. Maybe if I analyzed the situation, I could figure it out. So, I began to put the pieces together.

Over the past two weeks, this unnerving vision kept coming to me. It seemed like the same nightmare the first couple of nights the dream came, mostly forgotten when I awoke. But by the third night, the dream did not leave me in the morning. I began to analyze it, logically trying to be detached from it. I recounted in my mind what I had seen.

I felt like I was hovering above an intersection. I watched: as if in slow motion, I see a car stopped at a stoplight. I can see the stoplight turn green. The driver hesitates. Then the car begins to move through the intersection and suddenly, in an instant explosion of metal, glass and sound another car runs a red light and crashes into the first car. All the surrounding cars stop. People start to scream and run to the crash scene.

Then I wake up.

I have the first of the puzzle pieces: A potentially deadly car crash is going to happen. I'm now convinced of that. Part of me was frantic to know and part of me dreaded to know:

Who is the driver of the first car?

Who is the driver of the car that runs the light?

I can feel that someone dies at this crash site: but who is it?

Am I the driver of either car? Am I injured?

Is it someone I know in either car?

What do I do about this?

Am I the one killed or am I the one who runs the light?

Am I involved at all?

When does this happen now?

Is this event happening here in New London, or does it happen way in the future, in some other location?

Does this happen to a family member or a friend?

Is this one of my co-workers?

Who causes the crash?

Why is this being shown to me?

I pondered these questions now day and night.

Who could I tell? This was a sickening, lonely secret to keep, and I realized that I had to hold on to this secret at least for a while longer.

Please, I Don't Want to Know This

The next set of dreams, offer more details: it's just becoming dusk, and pouring rain. The same accident happens again. I watch again to see if the scene changes any further: as if in slow motion I see a man in a green sports car stopped at a stoplight. I can see the stoplight turn green. The driver hesitates a bit more than would be normal and then enters the intersection. Maybe he was putting his car in gear? The green car has a green light, but another car doesn't notice that the light has changed, blows through the intersection, and collides at full, un-braked speed, into the driver's side of the green car, instantly crushing the driver. I'm sure the driver dies. I can feel it in a gut-wrenching sense of profound grief. I'm unable to see the driver who ran the stoplight. All the other cars stop. People start to scream and run to the green car.

I cannot help but wonder if the driver of the green car had not hesitated, had gone through the intersection as soon as the light changed, would the outcome be different? Why did he hesitate?

More puzzle pieces come. The event happens at dusk in the pouring rain. A man driving a green sports car is going to die. The other driver is driving a large white sedan. I can feel that that driver is a woman, someone not paying attention. Is she drunk? I don't know.

I dreaded falling asleep the next night as I slipped back into that dream. But there I was again.

I could hear his thoughts as he sees his body crushed in the car.

"Damn. I should have seen her coming. But I just don't feel well and I was thinking about my Christmas gifts in the back seat. Am I dead? What happened to me? I might have noticed the other car coming but I was so sick, I could barely drive. I'm such a careful driver, I should have seen her coming but the rain, the cold, it's so cold. My wife, my poor wife; I love her so much... and my car, I so loved my 'Z'."

He begins to cry.

I felt as if my head and chest were going to explode. My heart was pounding like a relentless hammer. I broke into a cold sweat as my body reacted to this terrible knowing. Waves of crushing grief sweep me and I wanted to scream out in horror! My husband has a green 240Z! But he isn't ill. He's fine. Is this someone else? There are lots of submariners here in New London with 240Zs. Troy is not the only one. But I don't know any of the other men, only Troy. Oh My God, it's Troy who's going to die! And I could feel that this was going to happen soon. But what was 'soon' in a dream? How much do I trust this feeling of time in a dream? But this was not a dream. I knew with a sickening certainty that this was a premonition and that it was definitely going to happen.

If Only This Were Just a Bad Dream

I woke up shaking and crying from this horrible premonition. My husband was lying beside me and my crying awakened him.

"Honey, did you have a bad dream? Was it a nightmare? Here, let me cuddle you. You're safe. It's all okay, you're fine." He tells me these reassuring things as he wraps his loving arms around me, cradling me and kissing my hair.

"Yes, it – it was a nightmare. I'm fine." I murmured. The depth of his love at once warms me to my core and a wave of potential grief almost bursts from my heart. I feel myself silently screaming: "I love him so much; he is the man of my dreams. I can't lose him! I adore him. I love my life with him. This can't happen! Oh God, please, don't let this happen."

I can feel his breathing deepen as he falls back to sleep.

I cannot tell him the truth.

But I'm not fine.

Some 'one,' some 'thing,' some 'force' is trying to warn me that I am about to become a widow, that the love of my life is going to die unless I do something to stop it. Our world, our future, hopes, dreams, plans are all about to be destroyed.

But the questions kept coming in a torrent of shock and bewilderment:

Am I supposed to do something about this?

Is this a future that is supposed to happen?

Why show me if I cannot stop it?

Can I stop it?

Is it possible to change the future?

That is the real question here, isn't it? If you can see a potential future, if you are allowed to see this view, can you change it?

I studied the scenario over and over in my head all that night deciding that if there was any chance to stop Troy's death that I was going to try. I begin to pray, asking God to show me the way, guide me so that I could change this probable/potential future, so that I could save the love of my life. Bad things happen to good people, but what if you can stop them?

This premonition, this feeling, this shadow future never left me alone, never gave me a moment of freedom. It relentlessly dogged my nights and my days.

Maybe I Won't Be a Widow Today

I was about to make his favorite buttery scrambled eggs. It was a usual Tuesday morning. Troy studied the snow outside the living room windows as I was packing our lunches.

"The snow outside is only a light dusting, not too big a problem. I'm going to scrape the windshield of the 'Z' and I'll do your windshield too. I'll come back in for breakfast."

"Sure, that will be great, Troy." I watched him out the kitchen window as he made his way carefully to the cars. He's not sick. He's fine. I – I don't think the crash is today. Maybe I won't be a widow today. What a horrible thing to say. My brain rejected the concept.

The next several days were the same. We watched the endless leaden grey skies of New London for snow flurries. Night after night I experienced the same premonition but now, I can clearly see my husband dead at the crash scene. Seeing his ghost standing by the car grieving the end of his life is almost more than I can bear. The thought that the dead can see themselves, that they can see their body at a crash scene is totally devastating for me. I had no idea.

Somehow, I have to stop this from happening, but how? When? How will I know what to do?

Finally, it's Friday morning and Troy sits down to breakfast with me.

"Don't make plans for Saturday because I'm going Christmas shopping for you." He says this brightly, as if he is thrilled that he is going to do this.

"I think I know what I'm going to get you – you're going to love it."

"Troy, I don't need anything for Christmas. You don't have to do that. Don't go shopping, or at least take me with you." This chills me to the bone because one of the elements of the premonition are the gifts in the back seat.

"Don't be silly, I'm going shopping tomorrow and that's final. We'll have supper together tomorrow night. It'll be great." He flashed his bright smile at me, grabbed his hat and then dashed out to his car.

"Sure honey." But there was no happiness in my answer. I was filled with more dread. But wait, I reminded myself: he isn't sick. He doesn't feel bad. Maybe it is not tomorrow.

Should I have told him my dream? Would he have believed me? At what point do I tell him what I think is going to happen? If I tell him, will I create that reality or stop the event from ever happening? These persistent questions haunted me day and night, a perpetual distraction from my day-to-day moments.

The Insanity of Navy Logic

I went on to work, driving up River Road to Electric Boat division with a sure sense of dread. Troy called me actually a couple of times during the day to tease me about what he was getting me for Christmas. Oh my God, I love this man! My pleas for him not to go shopping on Saturday went unheeded. He cheerfully informed me that he was going shopping in the morning.

And he sounded like the strongest, healthiest guy I know. Maybe what I'm seeing is going to happen next year and not happen now. Maybe the event is going to happen in a year I cannot see. How do you know how to make sense out of the present reality and balance it with a premonition that is haunting you day and night?

Premonitions are never (I was to learn) time specific. How do you go through your life with this type of psychic ability? What a torture! What naive person ever thought that this kind of psychic ability was a gift? The gift of seeing the future sounds great but the reality is frustration, heartbreak, and a sense of gruesome, gnawing dread.

Because it was Friday afternoon, I left work at 4:30, about a half hour early, to be home when Troy came home. As I drove back down that windy path that was River Road, I pondered if he would come down with a cold or get the flu.

By the time I reached our little place, it was dusk and it had started to rain. I watched the sky nervously. Troy would be headed home soon. But it is not tonight, I told myself. I can feel that.

Finally, it was well after six when I heard the unmistakable whine of his dark, jade green 240Z as it came down the road and parked in front of the house. I heard him turn off the engine and I waited to hear him slam the car door and the opening of our front door. But time passed and I did not hear anything. I looked out the front window. He was just sitting in the car, holding on to the steering wheel. As I was about to go and help him out of the car, he finally opened his car door very slowly. He closed it, almost as if he was in pain, and then as he made his way up the steps, he walked as if he was carrying a staggering weight. The shadowy dusk, and his officer's hat, hid his face from me. I wondered if something had happened. This was not the same guy who cheerfully told me he would see me soon at home, at 3pm when I last spoke to him. What happened in the last three hours?

I met him at the front door. He looked cold and feverish. He immediately put his arm around me and neither of us said a word as I helped him upstairs and into bed. He looked like death as he lay down.

We did not speak. I took his shoes off, and then helped him take off the rest of his clothes and into something that made him feel warm and cozy.

"Troy, are you going to throw up?" He turned his ashen face toward me and said "No."

"What happened to you honey? You were fine at three o'clock."

"The jerk corpsman decided to 'shoot' the crew and gave all of us all of our immunizations at once this afternoon so we would have the weekend to 'get over them' before we head back to sea. Oh my God, I'm sick. My arm is on fire. My head hurts. This sucks. I don't know how I drove the short distance home from the office."

I hated the Navy for this. I hated that they never considered the toxic load of so many vaccines given at once to a person's immune system.

"How many did you receive? What were they?" Not that it mattered. They were all toxic.

"Typhoid, cholera, diphtheria, something else, I can't be sure. There was no getting out of it."

I knew that screaming in rage at the insanity of Navy Medicine was worthless. All I could do was deal with my sick husband.

Saturday Morning

Troy was still sleeping hard when I woke up to the sound of the pouring rain. I went downstairs and began to put breakfast together. I was not sure if he wanted to eat. Finally, an hour later he made his way downstairs, fully dressed, and shaved.

"Why are you dressed? You need to be in bed."

"No, no, I - I told you I'm going Christmas shopping for you and I'm better this morning, still a bit foggy but I don't think I have a fever and I'll be okay. I'm going to do this." His insistence had no real fervor to it.

"Let's have some tea and eat a little something. I need to tell you about these dreams I've been having."

"Well, alright. But you know I need to get started with my shopping." He made this statement loyally, but I could tell he was really weak.

I took a deep breath. It was time to change the future, to tell him what was going to happen to him, to us, to our lives. I felt clear and sure for the first time in days. I now knew that I could change the future and this was the moment.

"Do you remember all those nightmares I've been experiencing?" He nodded.

"Well, it's taken me several days, but I have finally put the pieces together. I was not having a nightmare but a premonition of your –

of your death. I know. It's crazy. I don't expect you to believe me, but I've watched two of the three elements of the dream come true and now, I know for sure what's going to happen.

"In the dream, I kept seeing a green sports car and then I realized it was you. It happens in the late evening, at dusk and it's pouring rain. You would be finishing Christmas shopping and a woman in a white car is going to run a stoplight and – and kill you. I saw you die night after night in this premonition. You were dead, and you were standing by your car, looking at the wrecked Z with presents in the back seat.

"Troy, you die in that crash because you didn't notice someone was going to run a stop light. It happens today, this afternoon honey. You can't leave the house today."

He stared at me and blinked his big blue eyes.

"You're sure about this?"

"Well, three of the four elements of the premonition have come true: you were going Christmas shopping for me in the 'Z', you were ill at the time and it is pouring rain. Do we need to find out for sure if the event really happens?"

"But this was the last weekend for me to shop. It's been crazy busy before now. I don't have anything for you for Christmas, nothing to open. I feel terrible. I should have planned better, but I set aside this time."

"You are my Christmas present, sitting right here, in this moment, looking at me with that handsome face and those wonderful blue eyes. You're all I need; knowing you are safe that you aren't going to die is the greatest gift of all. I know, it sounds cliché but it's true. Now, back to bed."

He gave me a long lingering hug, as if there was part of him that was grateful. There was no need for any further words to be exchanged. The future had been changed. We both knew it. Then he went upstairs to bed and slept for the rest of the day. I made Christmas cookies for him to take to sea. The house smelled wonderful when he woke up for supper. He was better on Sunday but he still remained home and rested. It was only then that I finally felt the warmth of Christmas surround me.

Epilogue

The dreams stopped.

Troy went to sea the following Thursday. He did not have a single gift for me and I was delighted.

I flew home to my family in North Carolina the next day, a very happy submariner's wife. I decided after that to simply purchase some things that I liked and have them handy if this type of occasion ever happened again. Then I could just put 'Love, Troy' on it. It has worked for 50 years.

Premonitions can happen to anyone at any time in their life. Sometimes you are going to be able to do something about it and sometimes there is nothing you can do.

Whatever is going to happen will happen. What this terrifying situation taught me is that there are times where karma offers us a choice in how we will spend our future. Will we pay attention to what is shown to us? Will we believe that what we are seeing can actually happen and will we take the initiative to stop that event from taking place if it is possible?

This was not my last premonition. Many, many more followed after that. Some terrible things I was able to prevent, some, I knew with a heavy certainty nothing I would ever do would stop what was going to happen. I had many that involved Troy that changed his life. He could never fully fathom this particular psychic ability but he developed a deep respect for it and he always listened to me when I warned him.

What was/is this source, this miracle that allowed me to see this potential future? One of the biggest challenges in those moments of trying to figure out what to do with that premonition was steeling myself against the towering grief and guilt I knew I would feel if I was wrong about when to step in and stop his actions. That reality of grief, that heart shattering feeling never fully left me. My love for him fills my soul. Even today, when he walks in the room, my heart lights up. I got to stop his death. That fact humbles me. As emotionally challenging as this psychic ability is, I will always be grateful that I could use it to save my husband's life. This opportunity was truly the greatest gift of all.

The Manteo Colony

Is it possible that weather could indicate a ghostly connection if a particular individual is especially psychic?

Can rainstorms connect you to the outpouring of sadness of people long dead?

Technically, you would think this could not possibly be, but in the realm of the dead, or the 4th dimension, virtually anything is possible. If this seems to defy logic, then perhaps the symbolism of the power of the rain may be a more meaningful concept. Rainstorms can be just that: a rainstorm after a hot, sticky day in the South. But for some people, that rain, the emotion of a storm takes on a much deeper meaning, a greater symbolism.

Consider that if compassion and empathy for the lives of other people lives within you, that you might feel the deluge of tears from these souls suspended in the past.

Sometimes your resonance with a particular location can place you there for a far greater reason than you would have ever imagined.

And sometimes, it takes the right person to be in the right place at the exact right time to experience the synchronicity of the moment, the weather, and the dead.

The Lost Colony

It was the memory of a recent warm August night that was troubling my client, Angela. She called to tell me about her lovely trip to the Outer Banks of North Carolina. She should have been excited to tell me about her vacation but her voice was tentative as if something else was bothering her.

"Hey, Tina, I think I need your help with something. I'm not feeling so hot right now. I think I may have brought some 'visitors' back with me and I need to deal with this. I feel like there's someone here."

"Well, why don't you take a minute and tell me how your trip was to the Outer Banks? Did you guys have fun?"

"We had a great time, and we did something that I had always wanted to do, which was to see the outdoor play, The Lost Colony at Manteo. But a huge thunderstorm hit the coast, and it poured halfway through the presentation, yet they told us to stay and watch it in the rain. I guess they do that if the rain isn't too bad, but the rain came down so hard that the show producers finally canceled it twenty minutes later. By then, we had already gotten soaking wet. I guess they felt bad that we were all so drenched, so the show company invited us to come back the next night. Tuesday night was a nice warm summer evening so we went back and saw the last half of the show.

"So then Wednesday morning we went swimming at the beach but there was another thunderstorm and again, so much rain that we couldn't go in the water. Once the rain ceased, we did get to walk along the beach. I just love North Carolina beaches. Then we drove back home.

"I thought the drive back would be great, but I began to feel very tired and groggy. When we got home, all of us were so wiped out it was all we could do to unload the car and then sit and watch TV the rest of the day. We all slept well that night into Thursday.

"Thursday morning my husband, my daughter and I all had good energy and Cranston (her husband) went off to work. But Thursday afternoon I had a lot of fatigue and a headache that seems to be centered in my forehead. I tried all my usual remedies, but nothing seemed to help. As the afternoon progressed the headache got worse and I decided to take a shower because sometimes that helps me with my headaches. My daughter Melissa told me to hurry up because I could see that there was a big thunderstorm coming and it is not good to be in the shower when there is lightning. When I got out of the shower, I still felt bad, even worse. So, I'm calling you and hoping you can help me to feel better. But . . ."

Angela started to sob, not just a bit of weeping, but her entire body seemed to be wracked by profound, gut-wrenching, sobs, the kind that come so hard and so fast that you do not think you can even breathe.

"It's okay, just tell me what you're feeling. We're going to figure it out."

I suspected I knew what this was, but it would take time for all the information to come pouring out. Now I understood all the references to thunderstorms. It was as if there was a thunderstorm inside of her. Hysterical crying was making it difficult for her to speak.

"I'm so sad!" She wailed through her sobs, "I feel this terrible heaviness on my chest that I can't explain!"

"Angela, close your eyes, focus, and relax. I can sense that these emotions are probably not your own. I don't think we're alone in this conversation."

My connection with Angela is so deep that I had a very strong sense of what was happening to her. I could feel that there were several dozen women with her as she was talking to me. It would seem that an entire group of ghosts followed her home from the Outer Banks. Then she began to speak in the first person, but it was not Angela, it was another woman speaking through Angela and sobbing uncontrollably. Grief poured from her in heavy sobs, so strong and powerful they scarcely let air reach her lungs.

In my mind's eye I could see her, even over the phone, even 3,000 miles away: my client, had become an unwilling medium for an entire tragic group of ghosts from the Lost Colony of settlers who disappeared in 1587. The first ghost began to speak through my client, amidst choking sobs.

"I don't understand it, how come my baby died? Our babies die but the Indians' babies survive? How can it be that Christian babies die when the 'heathens' live well and healthy? Their 'savage' babies live and our Christian babies die? Why has God forsaken us? My baby died! My baby died!"

Angela began to describe what she felt as a 'medium' for this soul.

"My feeling is that these babies died because the mothers had little or no nourishment at the time and the women's breast milk dried up and there was no sustenance for the baby. I can feel her anger! I can feel the heat of her rage emanating through my body. It's like my own body is on fire, there are many other ghostly women talking and using this moment to get emotion out that has been building for hundreds of years. I'm not sure whether I'm talking or 'she's' talking."

Instantly, another 'voice' begins to speak.

"I never wanted to come to this 'new country' and start a colony. Some colonists came because they were fleeing religious persecution, or potentially, beheading, but we were different. We didn't have a choice, they expected us to come and start families here or face debtor's prison. We had no idea what we could eat when we got here. We didn't understand the land, the horrible insects, and plants that made us itch. Some of the food and seeds that we brought with us went bad and we had to throw them into the sea. We had no seed to plant crops when we got here. I was afraid we were going to starve.

"I was pregnant during the voyage and I lost so much weight between morning sickness and seasickness. I was so sick all the time that I considered jumping overboard. I couldn't even stand up I was so sick all the time. I had nothing left to vomit and still my body tried to throw up. Finally, my baby came way too early and died."

Another woman's voice slips into the conversation.

"My name is Elizabeth. I'm so homesick all I want to do is to go back to England. I know we had problems there being Protestant, but at least we could find something to eat. There is no food here in this brutal New World. There is never enough to keep us strong enough so that we can nourish our babies. Even after our babies are born, our milk dries up and then our wee ones die. Do you know what it's like to watch your baby or someone else's baby die of starvation? It changes you: it makes you afraid, afraid to 'be' with your husband because you don't want to have a baby here. It's so hard! I want my husband's child but I can't bear to watch another child die like this or freeze to death because we cannot keep our home warm enough.

"I don't understand the Indians, why are some friendly and some are killing us? Yet what little food we have is from the Indians. I'm cold and confused all the time – and hungry, we are always hungry."

"I am so afraid of dying."

"Angela, there seem to be several women surrounding you, all of them look haggard, fearful, defeated, and gaunt. My feeling is that they are all from the 1600s when thousands of English settlers came here looking for a new life."

"I know. I can feel them too. In my mind's eye I keep seeing a young girl maybe 14 or 15 hiding behind a tree. Oh my God, I can see that there's an Indian attack going on, and this young girl's talking to me, pleading with me to help her. She is pleading with me."

"Please, do something! I'm so afraid of dying. I know I'm going to die but I'm afraid it will hurt! I want to go home; I want to go home! Where's my mama!!! Mama!"

"Tina, she keeps crying; she keeps seeing the face of this one particular Indian. His face has smooth brown skin, with a white circle surrounding a dark circle around his brown eyes. Oh my God, he killed her! He hacked her to death! This young girl is reliving her death over and over again. It's shocking, even in death the energy of her fear has not left her. We have to help her! I can feel her horror. Can you help this girl? Can you move this Indian on, make him cross over too?"

Angela is unable to separate herself from the energy of the emotion of so many grieving ghosts still suffering the trauma of their excruciating deaths. I stepped in to assist her and all the souls before her. Many women from several early colonial stacks of time are presenting themselves to Angela.

"There's an angel just there, wrapping this young girl in a healing blanket and escorting her from behind that tree. However, I cannot move the Indian on, because all you are seeing is her memory, an image of the girl's death. The Indian himself is not among the ghosts that I can see and sense, since he didn't die that day and is not presenting himself as needing assistance in crossing over. Now that the young girl sees the angel, feels the warmth of being wrapped in grace, she will be able to transition to the Heaven World."

But the Worst Was Yet to Come...

"Angela, are you feeling any better? Is she the last one or is there someone else? I feel like I have missed someone. What do you see?"

"I can see a young woman hanging by the neck in an oak tree by the beach. Oh my God, it's such a horrible image, but I'm confused. I didn't think Indians hung people."

"She needs to tell us her story. I think she's the last one with you. As hard as this one is probably going to be, you have to let her tell you what happened to her."

"I'm – I'm glad to help. I'm listening. Just a minute, I hear her now. What is your name?"

"My name? What does my name matter? I am worthless, a murderer! I tried to tell them, I tried to get them to understand but they . . . they didn't want to hear me. There was no food for us. My beautiful baby was crying and crying and my milk dried up. I kept feeling my little boy's horrible pain in his stomach as he slowly starved to death. Hour after hour he cried in agony. I couldn't stand it. I did it. I killed my baby rather than letting my sweet little boy waste away. Surely a quick death was better than the agony of starvation? I couldn't bear to hear his endless tortured cries night after night, day in and day out. In God's name, there is no worse torture. But the other mothers called me a murderer. What was more Christian: death by slow starvation or a quick, merciful death? I felt a quick death was the most compassionate death I could provide for my child. I could no longer bear his agony.

"I guess they believed I was very bad because they hung me the next day. There was no trial, just a swift death. These people had been my friends. That part hurt so much. Maybe it was better for me to die. It was horrible in the settlement. There was no way to survive this. There was no food. What paltry little food we had, came from the Indians, and then they turned on us. If the Indians didn't kill us, then the torture of starvation and cold got to us. Maybe they did me a favor. Maybe I deserved this. I should never have come. God has punished me for my sins."

"Tina, you have to cross her over because I can't bear it, her grief, her guilt. I had no idea it was so hard for them."

"All mothers know the pain of listening to a hungry infant. Without mother's milk, there was nothing else to feed a baby, and watching your child die was unimaginable agony. Angela, I have provided this woman and all the other mothers and children with angelic help, healing, and blessings. In the end, her heart was always with her child. Perhaps, they can now begin to heal."

"Thank you, thank you for helping them. I so wanted to hug them, to help them with their pain. I haven't cried like that in a very long time. You know, you understand."

Epilogue

Some ghosts exist because something horrendous happened to that soul or that group of souls. This is also called group karma. An event or series of events occurred that were so traumatic that these people did not move into the Heaven World once death ended their story. The lingering energy of the method or circumstances of their death translates into predecessor energy, which can linger for hundreds of years. It cannot be processed at the moment of death and it cannot be processed after death without spiritual help. Sometimes the towering power of a soul's grief requires that someone else act as his or her voice.

My client had picked up a group of ghosts and she was able to feel the energy of their sadness. That often happens with people who have psychic ability. Sensing the sadness of a ghost is not the same as being possessed by a ghost. Possession is a situation where the ghost tries to take over the person's body. This was not the case here. These desperate women wanted someone to hear their story so that they could finally find peace.

Perhaps this situation begs the question of why my client was in resonance with women who had lost children. Several years ago, my client's five-year old little son died very suddenly of pneumonia. Her grief and that of her husband and remaining daughter was like an endless tidal wave of sadness that took time to heal. I imagined that listening to these women talk about their lost children brought Angela's grief surging to the surface again. When you lose a child, you continually heal it to the degree necessary so that you can go on with each day. But there is a part of you that never loses that longing for the one you lost, never forgets that part of you that is forever missing. This meant that Angela was in resonance with the grief of these women.

When your child dies, the torture of your grief is something that haunts you even in death. There is no way to convey that feeling. My client's heart-shattering sobs were the same ones she shed when her own son died. She knew, in an intimate way, how these women felt. Her desire to assist them was so sincere, so pure that she unconsciously allowed them to come into her body. That would explain her fatigue, her sadness, and her feeling of a dark cloud covering her. The pouring rain and thunderstorms that seemed to surround her felt to me as if these were the tears of the dead welling up and washing over her as these lonely ghosts asked for help.

This description of what life was like for some members of the lost colony of Manteo, is so heartbreaking that it reminds us just how much we owe those brave souls who took on the New World and felt as if they failed on every level. Not everyone triumphed. Not all colonists survived, and not all children made it out of babyhood.

May God bless and keep all of those valiant souls who paved the way for the lives we currently lead. And may God bless my client for her service to these mothers.

Ghost Stories from the Ghosts' Point of View Vol 3

The Acting Couch

Hollywood is frequented by untold numbers of emotionally empty, desperate souls seeking the limelight. Yet the light they seek can never be found in the studios, production back lots, stage spotlights, movie theaters or television studios they endlessly haunt. There are thousands of ghosts patrolling the sidewalks of embedded stars, moving in and out of seedy bars that line Sunset and Vine, seeking that last desperate sip of whiskey or that last hope of fame. Other ghosts are stuck in the decades-old homes that elegantly grace Hollywood, Beverly Hills, Los Feliz, and the Hollywood Hills. They also fill the less glamorous condos, bungalows and apartments throughout Hollywood and the greater Los Angeles area.

Foreshadowing the Darkness

The cinematic ghosts of Hollywood who have so colorfully lit up the silver screen do not hold a candle to the apparitions who constantly frequent the homes of the living, looking for help, or recognition. However, there are other ghosts, those unexpected souls who have no idea that they live in an empty city of dreams, and although they may be trapped in a different dimension, they still want their most basic dream to come true.

Perhaps my level of insight made me rather wistful as I agreed to help my new clients who live not too far from Hollywood Boulevard.

"Hi Tina, Conrad and I got this newly renovated condo and we need you to look at it. Since we moved in, things have not been the same between us. We love each other, but we fight all the time. Both of us feel 'off', you know? Like something is terribly out of balance and we just can't make it right. Oh, and we feel sad. Sometimes we feel nauseated with stomach pains for no reason and then suddenly the pain is gone. This condo is so weird. Conrad has agreed with your remote viewing it. He feels all this peculiar stuff too."

"Sure, Julie, I'll be glad to look around and see what I can do. Is there anything else you want to share and at the same time, not give me too much detail? I don't want to 'find it' because you already told me it was there."

"Well, we seem to be having a constant problem with that nagging sense that there is someone there. That shadow out of the corner of your eye never seems to be gone."

"Thanks, time to get to work."

Even before I began, I also felt a sickening and oppressive sense of sadness that seemed to cloud the edges of my moments right before I began the remote view. I could feel – something. Something unseen but not unfelt, something that needed resolution and an unusual level of compassion.

"Are you an agent?"

I had no sooner started working on this condo when I saw her standing there, complaining to no one in particular about how unhappy she was with her life. She seemed to notice me immediately.

"Have you come to help me get a part? Are you an agent? How did you hear about me? I guess you already know that my name is Belle Lawrence."

"It's nice to meet you, Belle." She may have never had an acting part, may never have had her name known by anyone other than her landlord, but her presence could still be easily felt even 75 years after she left that space.

She was old, perhaps in her late sixties when she presented herself to me but that actress aspect never left her personality. Her dream kept her in this apartment.

"Um, I'm not exactly the kind of agent you're thinking of, but I can help you. I do represent someone pretty high up. Is Belle your real name?"

"No, I made up that name so that it would look good up on that there big screen in them movie houses. I wanted my family to see that I did come to some good. My daddy said I would always come to no good but that ain't true. I – I could have made it. I know it."

I could hear her, almost as if she turned away from me and began talking to herself again, as if she was still pacing the floor of (what would have then been) her apartment.

"Can you tell me what happened to you in this apartment? Did you ever get any acting parts?"

"Help me please! I don't understand! How come there was always a couch in the producer's office? How come my acting ability, pretty face and body weren't enough for that producer or director to know that I could act the part, do the job, hit my marks, know my lines? All I wanted to do was to be in them silent pictures! I wanted my family back home to see me up on the big screen in that movie house and know that I made it!"

"I know, Belle. I can only imagine how hard you tried. Tell me what happened to you. Please."

"I tried to tell my family, a whole bunch of times, especially after. You know . . . after."

"No, I'm sorry, I don't know what you mean. I've got plenty of time. Tell me what you mean when you say the 'after' time. Perhaps you had better start at the beginning, when you decided to come to Hollywood and be famous."

Stars in My Eyes

"My papa always said I had stars in my eyes and that was how come I never could see clearly. Papa said I would come to no good. I don't know why he always treated me so bad but he told me that over and over, you know, that I was 'no good.' But I didn't believe it. Mama said I was such a pretty young thing and so smart. How could Papa see me so different like; I reckon he didn't really see me at all.

"Mama said it was probably because he done wanted a boy and I was just another useless girl. It weren't my fault I was a girl. I guess when you ain't wanted, when you ain't worth nothin', you gotta' go prove you're 'somebody.'

"I loved them picture shows. Them beautiful ladies looked like they was havin' so much fun. They looked happy and I ain't never really been happy. So, I saved up all my egg money and set out for Los Angeles from my tiny town in Iowa. I just knew there was more to life than farmin' an raisin' livestock.

"I got me a one-way bus ticket to LA – that's what I called it, - to Los Angeles so I could be in them picture shows on that there big screen. Then lots of folks would love me and finally I'd be somebody and Papa and Momma would be proud of me. Then he'd be darn proud that I was a girl, now, not a useless girl."

The defiance in her tone, showed her stubborn resolve to make something of herself.

"And Belle, what happened when you got here? What year was it? What was it like for you at that time?"

Belle looked at me and then looked around her apartment as if it still looked like it did then. She sat down on what would have been the only chair she had in the room back then. Then she looked up at me with such anguish. Very probably her lament was the same for thousands of other young ingénues who believed that they could become the next Mary Pickford or Greta Garbo. The years before the Depression were so hard and it was especially difficult for single women to make a living. Hollywood must have looked so easy, so inviting. All you have to do is memorize your lines, learn your marks and you can become a star! There was not even that much acting to do with silent pictures.

If only it were all that simple...

"I 'member gettin' off of that bus and feelin' the pure glory of that warm California sun. It was April 1925. My dream had come true. I was here. I had started! I did what I said I'd do! But I had no place to live so I found me a boardin' house to stay in and then I quickly got me a job waitin' tables. I had heard that if you waited tables, that maybe a big-time producer or director would see you and you could be 'discovered.' That was my dream.

"There were other young women there, livin' at that boardin' house and one of them asked me if I could 'act.' I said yes even though I couldn't really act. She said I was lucky because she went on a casting call and was told that she couldn't act and she didn't get the part. So, I got me another job to pay for actin' lessons. I couldn't afford many but I figured they were silent pictures and I had watched so many of them pretty girls just mouthin' their lines. After a couple of weeks, I felt like I could handle it, so I kept the second job and then got a real tiny cheap apartment. I worked my jobs so that I could go on all the casting calls and I'd be okay."

"Did you get many casting calls? How did you find out about them?"

"Them studios posted the jobs they had for extra folks and even real actresses on a bulletin board outside of the entrance of the studios. I studied those posts every day. I went on every casting call. It was all so excitin' I guess until - until it wasn't, well I just wasn't prepared for it that's all."

"What weren't you prepared for Belle?"

"I – I wasn't prepared for all them producers or directors, or whatever they was called. I didn't know. Nobody warned me. I didn't know what to do."

The Lamb in the Lion's Lair

Her face contorted into a pout. Something happened to her. I had a sick feeling I knew what it was.

"I remember that on one castin' call, this here producer said that he liked my face and he called me over. He said that I might be right for the character I was reading for even though nobody was ever gonna hear my voice.

"I was so excited, I couldn't breathe, you know? Finally, someone saw me. I was <u>somebody</u>! I couldn't believe it. That there director said that there was a love scene in the movie and he wanted to see if I could act. He told me to come back later that day so I could rehearse with him."

"And did you go back and rehearse with him?"

"Yeah, I did. I put on the only real pretty dress I had. Another actress did my hair and put a little makeup on me, so you know, so that I would look professional-like and I was there, right on time, ready to rehearse. And he was there, working on scripts or somethin' and he had me wait for a while before he called me in. He told his secretary she could leave. She looked at me real funny, not friendly like at all. I couldn't understand why. I felt a little uncomfortable bein' there alone with him. But I wanted that part so my papa would be proud of me."

"What happened?"

"He finally called me in and I stood there for a few minutes 'til he looked up at me. Then he told me to turn around real slow-like. He said he wanted to see 'how I moved.' So, I did that.

"Then he handed me a script page and asked me to read it out loud to him. I was confused 'cause I thought all I had to do was mouth the lines, but he said that real soon, sound was coming to the movies and actresses would have to talk out loud and he wanted to hear how I sounded. He said he wanted to see if I was everything the part required.

"I remember he nodded his head at all the stuff I did and he said I was doin' a great job. Then he handed me another script page and it was a love scene. I had been standin' all this time. He says that he'll 'run lines' with me if I just sit on the little couch he has right here.

"So, I did. I sat on the couch and then he sat next to me. The scene called for a kiss. I remember those movin' pictures and people just barely kissed so I figured that was all he wanted.

"But it wasn't all he wanted. He pulled me toward him and I resisted. He said movies were changin' and that love scenes were becomin' more and more visible, especially with 'talkies' as he called them. He had to see how I would react in a real love scene with a real man. He pulled me to him, this time real slow and I – I let him do this. And he then began to put his arms around me. I felt myself pull away from him, 'cause somethin' felt wrong about this.

"He was a short, fat, ugly man. His breath smelt like cigars an' coffee and his black hair was all greasy. He told me I had to 'run my fingers through his hair' 'cause that's what the scene would call for. I was gettin' more and more nervous like, you know?

"But I did what he asked. Then he said I had to really kiss him, not fake it, but really give him a kiss – on his lips. Well, I ain't never kissed a boy even back home, so I give him a peck on his fat cheek. He laughed out loud. I felt real stupid and I was gettin' a scared feelin' in my stomach.

"He took his time and he pulled me to him and he made me do this over and over till I got it right. Then he made me kiss him over and over and he made the kissin' part more forceful like. He was a strong man. I reckon he done kissed me maybe 10 times and he made me start over and over where he pulled me to him and he kissed me.

"Then there was the final time that he pulled me to him and he kissed me real hard that time, harder than before. I tried to pull away, but he was so fast, he turned me around and laid me down on his big brown couch and he said he wanted to look at me lyin' there. Then before I knew it, he took his pants down. I ain't never seen man parts like that before and then . . . he took terrible advantage of me.

"I believed that your 'first time' was supposed to be special, not violent like this, not make me want to vomit.

"I didn't think it would ever be over. He smelled of BO. I started to cry when he was doin' this to me. And then I – I couldn't stop cryin'. He got mad at me and yelled at me to shut up.

"Then he screamed at me to get out, that I was a terrible actress and I wasn't right for his part. I remember thinkin' that all I had to do to be an actress was mouth my lines . . . ."

If only that was all you had to do. What this young woman never quite realized sitting on the farm in her flat Midwestern state, was that you also had to navigate through the male-dominated politics of the studio system. You especially had to gauge how to handle yourself in the offices of the barely concealed rapists that would describe many a Hollywood producer and director. These men routinely took reckless and disgusting advantage of these hopeful young women.

Denial

"Belle, how did you recover from that rape? Did you report him, tell the police, or tell anyone?" I already knew the answer, but I had to ask her, had to help her get her story out.

"No, no, I didn't tell nobody. I felt like I didn't know who I was, that the 'Belle' who walked into that office died in there, and another girl walked out. I went home and took a bath and I cried for a long time. I didn't go on auditions for a week and then I got up my courage and tried again. I told myself that it would be different in the future. I understood how things worked now."

"Were things different for you Belle? Did you finally get parts?"

"No, it wasn't parts I got. It took me a while to realize, that what I got, was pregnant. I didn't think you could get pregnant the very first time you had sex. I guess I was denyin' it at first. I was pretenden' I was just gettin' fat. I wore big clothes to hide my belly. I didn't know many people, didn't have many friends, certainly not friends I could ask for help. I was one of them girls who got 'in trouble.' I was so ashamed."

'In trouble' was that cruel label used to describe a girl pregnant outside of wedlock.

"I lost my figure real fast. I knew there was such a thing as gettin' rid of the baby, but I didn't know who I was gonna' ask. I had no money to pay anyway. What was I gonna' do?

"My two jobs barely paid for my apartment and the little bit of food I allowed myself. I still wanted to go for auditions but as the weeks and months passed, my belly began to show, and I had to stop going to the studios. I counted myself lucky to still have my waitressin' jobs.

"Then the baby came and labor was hard. I was so alone. I took a cab to the hospital and had the baby. I left as soon as I could. When they handed me this pink, wigglin' little girl, my heart sank 'stead of bein' filled with delight. I named her Sarah Jane but I don't know why I picked that name – maybe after Sarah Bernhardt?

"I didn't know how to nurse no baby. There was no crib, or baby clothes. This wasn't ever going to work. The baby cried and cried. I couldn't stand the cryin'. I bought rat poison and fed it to the baby until she died – which wasn't very long.

"I killed my baby. I told myself I would have been a terrible mother anyway. I had always been a good Christian girl and now - now I had killed my baby. I didn't know myself anymore.

"I worked real hard to get that pregnancy weight off my body so I would look good in clothes again. I went to more auditions. I was gettin' better and better at this acting stuff, learnin' lines, and understandin' what the studios wanted.

"But always there was the sex part with the director, producer, or casting director. I began to wonder who I was. I never did figure out how to meet with these men and not get taken advantage of, you know, in that private way.

"You ain't gonna believe this, but I got pregnant three more times. I had a baby every year for four years. I named them JoJo, Frank, and Baby Mae. And I poisoned each of them right after they was born 'cause I couldn't ever go back home to the Midwest with them. My family would never have accepted me with four bastard kids from four different fathers. The scandal! Oh, my mamma and papa would have disowned me. I'd a been an outcast in my own small town. My 'children' weren't never gonna' be accepted. Everyone would have called them bastards.

"I didn't want to go home a failure; still "good for nothin'" as my papa believed. I reckon that givin' up and denyin' my dream was not something I could face at least the first three times. Sometimes I felt horrible for what I did. Sometimes I simply didn't feel nothin' at all when I thought about how I murdered my own kids. It was almost as if sometimes I guess I was plumb separated from that murderous woman I had become – almost.

"I disposed of their little bodies by wrapping them in old newspaper and puttin' them in a trashcan down the street. I'd slip out in the middle of the night so that no one could see me, could see how horrible a mother I was."

Getting Away with Murder

"After killin' the 4th child, Baby Mae, somethin' inside of me died with her. I gave up on my dream, my bein' an actress. I took the last of my waitressen' money and bought a ticket home. I cried that whole bus trip back to Iowa. I didn't know who I was anymore. I sure weren't no Belle Lawrence: actress. I went back to bein' Becky Sue Jones.

"Becky Sue or – uh - Belle, what did you decide to tell your family on that long ride home?"

I imagined that trip was her final descent into downheartedness: dreams shattered, body violated, sense of self, destroyed.

"How was I gonna' face my family, especially after I had told them about all of my auditions? They was so excited for me. What could I say? I knew I would face the shame of havin' failed at makin' my Hollywood dream come true, but I plum didn't have it in me to face another producer and his damned couch. I couldn't bear to have another baby and kill another little body.

"I thought long and hard about what to tell my mamma and papa but when I got there, I walked in the house and said I was home for good. I reckon there was somethin' about the way I said it that they didn't ask me no more questions. No one ever mentioned Hollywood again.

Life After Hollywood

"Becky Sue, how did you live the rest of your life?"

"I never got married. I couldn't bear to be with another man, no matter how kind. I didn't deserve to be happy. I spent the rest of my life takin' care of my parents and the farm. Hard to believe that them four short years destroyed my life. <u>I am a failure</u>: God's gonna' punish me because I got away with murder. No one ever found out it was me who killed them babies.

"One day my breasts got real sore, not the way your breasts get achy when you're pregnant but a terrible kind of pain. But I waited and waited until these horrible oozing sores were all over my breasts. The doctor said I had breast cancer. I passed away before my momma died."

"Becky Sue, can you tell me why you named each of your babies? Wouldn't it have been easier if you hadn't named them?"

"Do you think I wanted to give a name to them babies I killed? I had to give the nurse a name for their birth certificates. She kept askin' me what I was plannin' on callin' them. I had no choice. I still remember their names. They haunt me even now that I'm dead."

Maybe her cancer was the metaphoric relentless nagging of her conscience sickening her to the point of death. Breast cancer can represent a deep emotional sickness, guilt, or shame made manifest by an unwanted growth of some type of tumor.

"So, Becky Sue, if you died in Iowa, why are you still here in this apartment in Hollywood, California?"

"I - I reckon that I didn't feel welcome at home. Once I died and left my rottin' body, I didn't feel comfortable watchin' my parents grieve me. I didn't rightly deserve anyone's tears. Next I know, I'm back in this here apartment rememberin' those horrible four years. Those dirty, cruel years that destroyed my whole life. I weren't never the same after that."

"When you found yourself back here, did you notice any other ghosts?"

"No, I'm here alone. Ain't nobody here with me."

But Becky Sue wasn't the only ghost that I could see there, although for now, she didn't need to know that. Her physical and emotional suffering shut her out from all other souls, living and dead.

I quietly brought in an Angel of Transition to escort her to the Heaven World. I wasn't quite prepared for her reaction when she saw this gorgeous being.

"Hey, is that an angel standin' there?"

"Yes, this angel is for you, to guide you to the Heaven World. Go ahead and take the shawl she's offering you."

"No ma'am. I don't be deservin' of any pretty angel or that – that there golden shawl. No, I murdered my babies, all four of them. Ain't no good ever comin' to me. No way. I read the bible; I know I'm goin' to hell."

"My dear, God welcomes all his children home, even you. And it doesn't matter what you think you deserve; this angel is taking you across that Light Bridge. It's all right now. There is help and hope for you." I said this as I nodded to the angel to take her home.

She looked up at the angel and tears flowed from her eyes in an unending stream of grief and perhaps the relief that she could finally leave the hell of her shattered dreams and the murderous shadow that haunted her personality. She crossed over without another word.

Conceived in Rape

"Is she gone now?"

I turned to the tiny, tiny voice that asked this question.

"Yes, your mother's gone now. You're safe."

I gazed at the four babies, each laying on the bed with faces contorted in pain, laying there where they died. A horrified shudder ran through me as I looked at them. Immediately, I brought in four angels to pick up and wrap each little body in a blanket of healing light. Because these warming blankets came from the Heaven world, they began to restore each baby's soul and remove the wrenching pain they felt in their tiny stomachs. I could feel them relax as the warmth seeped into the inner reaches of their souls. Then the angels turned beaming smiles toward each tiny face and begin to hum sweetly as they gently rocked each child.

"Why did she do this to us?"

I could not tell which child was which. They all looked almost identical so I addressed them all.

"Could you all see her?"

"Yes, we could but she couldn't see us. We didn't really want her to see us either in case she would try to kill us again. Do you know why we were killed? Is that what being 'unwanted' means – that your mother kills you? When we were inside of her, we could feel that she didn't want us."

"I cannot answer for the cruel actions of your mother. Right now, what I can do is to offer all of your little bodies the healing light of these Divine golden blankets and the gentleness of these angels. Are you all feeling better? Let me assure you, that although your mother may not have wanted you, God loves you and wants you. It's time to return home to the Father."

I gave the angels the nod and they lovingly carried those precious babies into the Light of the Divine.

Epilogue

Becky Sue's four newborns were also haunting the condo since this is where each of them died. Two of them lived only a few days; the last two children died barely a few hours after returning home from the hospital. We will never know the emotional pain and physical trauma these children experienced because they were each so profoundly unloved. Conceived in rape, they were unloved and unwanted from the very moment of conception.

Not wanted: what a terrible energy to give to any child for nine long months. They never knew even a moment of compassion. I cannot comprehend their individual pain or the karma of such a birth. Surely Becky Sue would have known what that felt like since she too had been an unwanted child. However, it is not up to us to judge her.

The murdered babies had no idea what to do after death. They stayed there, crying for decades of mortal time. However, for these babies, there was no time, there was only the moment immediately following their deaths as they slipped out of those bodies. It is knowing that they are now in the Heaven World, that enables me to continue to face these poignant situations.

I also wonder what the karma will be of each of those serial rapist producers who thought nothing of destroying the lives of so many young women. The horrific part of this is that none of these men saw anything wrong with what they did. This also makes me shudder to think of how many other unwanted babies were murdered because of the damage done by these men. Yes, of course, the mothers had free will. They could have made different choices, but then isn't life only about the choices we make in each moment and the echo effect of all of those choices?

I took a deep breath and returned to my work. I systematically cleared the energetic echo of this actress and her dead children from the condo. The walls will no longer be able to talk to any psychic or fill the spaces with the energy of Becky Sue's tragic life and the deaths she caused.

My clients were pleased that their condo was now free of these dead souls and the energy of murder and despair. How simple that sentence yet how powerful that service is to those souls who now reside in the Heaven World.

That Terrible Feeling

"I'm So Bad, I'm so Bad, I'm So Bad, I'm so Bad..."

My close friend Mary called complaining of a headache in the middle of her forehead. She said she felt an uneasy, heaviness surrounding her, and that she just did not feel well. This was very unusual for her because she always enjoys wonderful health.

It was precisely because she is always in such good health that the 'heaviness' did not feel normal. She said it felt as if there was a presence with her, something 'other worldly.' She would have felt self-conscious sharing this with me but by now, we had been friends long enough that telling me she felt like there were multiple ghosts with her was not that unusual. This is an exceptionally psychic lady. She was wondering what this could be and asked if I could help her.

Often, when you have that kind of ghostly spiritual presence, the energy can manifest in physical symptoms of nausea, lethargy, headache, cough, or all four. She only had a headache, but she did not want it to become anything greater. I told her I would take a look.

I remote viewed my friend's house to see what was causing her headache, and in this particular case, she and I were both astonished with what we found. My friend could sense what I thought were only a few ghosts, but what tipped me off was her pounding headache, almost as if it was a group of people and the energy of this group was creating a type of spiritual pressure on her.

"Who Are All These Women?"

The darkness that surrounded Mary's house confronted me in a black, sooty, suffocating cloud of emotional pain. Patiently, I waited for a recognizable scene to unfold.

It looked as if I had stumbled upon an opening to the underworld, an abyss of pain. In these realms, you can see emotion. The evidence of tragedy surrounds a group of souls, and it looks like clouds of dark, thick, almost oily looking black soot clogging the pathways of their hearts. The evidence of profound tragedy can appear smoky, grimy, and dirty or it can seem to be depressed, flat, and gray. Some emotions are rage-filled: red and angry.

Whatever happened, this was truly a hell that they all shared, but I had no idea who 'they' were. All I could surmise was that they were each in deep emotional resonance with each other. As I cleared this black fog, I saw thousands of women in a state of severe depression, women who hated themselves. They were surrounded by gray to black dusty swirls, and flashes of angry, red electricity.

Sometimes to help a soul or a group of souls, you have to understand why the specific group in front of you has been presented to you. Not all souls require the same type of assistance. Some want you to listen to their story. But others want forgiveness, which is not up to me to provide. Forgiveness has to come from within a person. But if a woman feels that what she has done cannot be forgiven, she will send herself to hell to be punished. My job is to ask for assistance from the Heaven World on behalf of each of them.

Other souls want you to tell them what to do or to help them to understand where they are. The ghosts in this manifestation of hell needed more than just directions, they needed the very essence of compassion, itself. This was a unique group of souls, with similar issues. Some were weeping, others screaming, some were rocking back and forth, muttering to themselves. When a soul is in a terrible state of deep depression or self-hatred, it is necessary to elevate their frequency so that the ghost can begin to make that transition. At least some part of them has to heal enough to make the crossover. Usually, an angel performs this healing in mere minutes.

As the Angels of Transition began to assemble, I watched the women recoil in horror as the angels moved towards them. The presence of these Divine beings was more torture than assistance: obviously, I was missing something huge.

"I Wanted to Keep Her, I Wanted to Hold Her."

I realized I needed to hear them, so I began to approach several women and asked them to share their stories.

The first woman I encountered was sitting in dirty, bloody clothes. Her hands were bloody too, although it seemed that her hands were symbolically bloody as if they represented the energy of her action more than the fluid itself. She would not tell me her name. I repeatedly assured her that I would not judge her; I was genuinely here to help her without any prejudice whatsoever.

The energy of the angel standing by her, glowing warmly in this chilling place, was the only hopeful element present. Perhaps it was that angel's presence that gave her enough courage to begin to open up with her story.

"I'm so bad, I'm so bad, I'm so bad." This was all she would say at first as she sat there in her red stained clothes. Her arms were wrapped around her thin, stocking covered legs, as she rocked back and forth, back, and forth. She behaved almost as if she were in some type of catatonic trance.

"Whatever has happened, let us help. Remember if you were not worthy of help, then I simply couldn't be there." After a few minutes she began to slowly speak, almost as if she was choking on each tortuous word.

"I don't – exactly - know - how it - it happened. One day," She sighed heavily here, "I realized I was pregnant and I knew that I was going to be damned forever. The church says that being pregnant out of wedlock is a sin against God. The priest said that I was forever damned to hell. I see that angel, but the priest says that God cannot love or ever forgive me. I am a sinner, a sinner! I'm damned! What've I done to my child? What have I done?" She screamed these last two sentences in a piercing agony of emotion.

What a terrible sentence her church had imposed upon her! I could not tell exactly what era of time she was from, but from the look of her clothes, I guessed she had lived sometime about 150 – 200 years ago. I encouraged her to continue.

"Tell me, what happened to your baby? Did you get to keep your child?"

Again, she rocked and cried for a while before she could continue speaking. I asked the angel to place a blanket on her shoulders.

That Terrible Feeling

"I wanted to keep her! I did! I wanted to hold her, at least once, to feel her sweet skin against my face. I wanted to kiss her pretty little fingers. I longed to rock her and comfort her when she cried. I didn't care that God had damned me. I wanted her so much; I loved my little girl. She had such a sweet face..." she begins screaming. "Why? Why? Why did it have to be this way? Why is life so cruel? Oh, I can't breathe, I'm suffocating! I feel like I'm dying again and again. How many times can one person experience the feelings of a crushed heart?"

I let her regain her ability to speak knowing that sharing her story was healing in its own way. Sometimes you have to get the darkness out.

"The priest in the village said that I could not keep my child because it was a crime against God. So immediately after she was born, the midwife showed her to me and took my baby from me. I never saw her again. Pretty soon, a barren woman in a nearby village 'had a baby.' I knew that was my baby. I think God made this woman barren because she should never have had children. She was cruel to my little girl. My child had a terrible life with her. I heard the gossip about her and my baby. It was all my fault. I should have found a way to care for her. I should never have let them take her from me, but I was only fourteen and my father didn't want another child. My father didn't want our child around reminding him of what he did to me."

And the Stories Kept Coming

About this time, another woman spoke up.

"They done took my little baby boy from me and give him up to an orphanage. My family don't want me shamein' um with no bastard child runnin' around. After daddy found out I was pregnant he done beat me so hard. He called me a slut an' a whore but my brother done this to me! How was I gonna' tell my daddy? I weren't allowed to visit my son in the orphanage either or my daddy woulda' whoop me even harder. I cried every day forever. I never got to see him again."

A new voice penetrated the darkness. The courage of the other women must have empowered her to tell us her painful story.

"When the priest found out I was pregnant, he kept me out of sight in the convent when I began to show. I had a big belly. Once my adorable baby boy was born, I overheard the priest tell the Mother Superior to take my son outside, kill him and bury him. How can a priest who got me pregnant order someone else to kill his own baby? The priest said that God wanted the baby dead to punish me for my sin of being a woman. I wish they had killed me too."

More and more women began to tell us their stories. I could hear their cries. Their tortuous guilt and self-hatred generated the sooty, rage-filled clouds that surrounded each woman.

That Terrible Feeling

"Despite the women's movement, the freedom we thought we had in the sixties, once I got pregnant, well, that 'freedom' went out the window. My boyfriend told me that he wouldn't marry me if I had our baby and he insisted that I get an abortion. He said that when we were married, and had more money, that we could have a baby. He said it was just a bunch of cells anyway.

"The day of the abortion, he went to the clinic with me and helped me through the 'procedure.' He was totally elated when the 'procedure' was over. He told me that now we could plan our wedding. I threw up. I had murdered my baby and he was relieved. We broke up and I never saw him again. I have considered myself a murderer all of my life. I don't deserve any angel you send to me."

"Well, if I had been able to have an abortion, at least I wouldn't have had to watch as my child was given to someone who didn't love her."

And another woman spoke up.

"I was twelve when the stranger abducted and raped me. I didn't know what sex was but I got pregnant anyway. I didn't want that nasty life in my body – the child of a rapist! I was glad that my parents helped me to have an abortion. But the rest of my life I felt so confused. After all of that, I never even wanted to be with a man or even think about having children."

A younger blonde woman added story.

"I was raped at 22 by a black man and I had his baby. I tried to raise the child. I did. I did everything I could think of to try to love this little boy, but no matter what I did, when I looked at him, I saw the man who raped me. Finally, when he was three, I gave him up for adoption to a bi-racial couple that wanted him very much. I hoped he was happy. I still feel terrible about this. I should have had an abortion rather than having him and giving him up. Which was worse? I'm tortured by what happened to me and to this child."

"My son got his girlfriend pregnant - twice! And he insisted she abort both babies – and she did. He's a doctor! She's a nurse! How can people who are supposedly dedicated to doing no harm do this? They are married and have two kids now. But when I see them, I feel that I can still see the other two children standing there. They haunt me. I should have taken them. I should have talked my son and his wife out of aborting those babies. I deserve to be punished. I know why I'm here."

"I had ten abortions before I finally got married and had my two sons. Hell is where I belong."

"I got pregnant by the Earl himself. I was his chambermaid and one day he just 'took' me. I had his child, which he, of course, denied. But I loved this child. Finally, I had someone in my life to love. The Earl was furious that I kept his bastard child and he banished me from his manor house. He made sure that no one else would ever

That Terrible Feeling

hire me. It took me a long time to find a place where I could live with my child and make a living. Finally, the vicar in a nearby village took pity on me and hired me to be his housekeeper. At least now I had a roof over our heads but life was hard for my son. Everyone called him a bastard. I felt horrible for putting him through that. If I could, looking back on it, I wish I could have had a way of ending the pregnancy rather than put him through a lifetime of torture and finger-pointing."

Quietly, the angels began placing shawls around the trembling shoulders of each woman.

The stories continued from all different time periods, including modern times. I was quietly taking it all in, sending these women love and compassion. When enough of them had finished, they all were finally in a place where I could speak to them.

"I want you all to understand that you are each, very much worthy of God's love, that no one is ever in any position to judge you. It is my sincerest hope that you can all feel the profound compassion overflowing from my heart. I am sending you all my love, and I wish I could hug every single one of you.

"Sometimes we cannot know exactly why something like this happens. This moment, as we are all together, I am offering you the healing of the Light of Compassion, and the Light of Christ Consciousness. I hope that you can heal, that the love you have had for the children in each of your situations was not in vain and did not go unnoticed. Let no one judge you. I am offering you the hope that someday you will be able to cease judgment of yourselves. Perhaps in time, you will be able to forgive yourselves."

The agony of each of their positions was staggering. I wanted to comfort each of them individually, to hug them. But I knew that only the true comfort of the angels and crossing into the Heaven World, would facilitate these women beginning to heal. My job was simply to assist them in their transition – and to hear their stories without judgment or prejudice.

I also explained that once they each crossed over with their angelic escorts, that there would be Divine Beings there who would help them understand the life just lived. <u>Understand the life just lived.</u> What a profound statement. This is one of the most important reasons to cross over, to understand how all the life events played out in your life and how they affected you and what you can learn from them, to make sense of all of your trials and struggles. It's a critical point to embrace.

The angels nodded to me that they were ready to escort these women to the other side when I gave the word.

The scene before me slowly but surely began to brighten as hope began to penetrate the inner soul of each woman. One by one, the warmth of the Divine blankets allowed the women to stop crying, and to begin to stop punishing themselves. The angels compassionately guided each woman into the light until the scene closed and they were all gone.

Epilogue

Mary's headache left once I had finished assisting these souls. I was a witness to the spiritual and emotional burden that women have suffered throughout the ages, with an unwanted pregnancy. Incest and rape were and still are so common. Yet it did not matter to many of these women; they chose or tried to love the life growing inside of them but the circumstances of their lives precluded them from ever feeling truly happy about the birth of any of their children.

Their guilt and grief were so tremendous that it lowered their soul frequency to a point that they could not cross over without help. I felt honored that I was able to assist them. I still have no idea how many women were helped that day. I suspected that it could have been thousands since I could not adequately count the women there. Eventually, with sharing their stories and receiving attention, they were finally able to make that miraculous transition to the Heaven World. I always find hope in the gentleness, the tenderness and relief that the angels bring to each soul.

I found myself impressed by Mary's deep sense of empathy and her dedication to the service of assisting all of these women once I told her what had happened, and what was causing her headache. Mary is a tremendously kind and compassionate person, and she loves children. She experienced numerous miscarriages and lost a child due to a terrible illness. These experiences may have made her especially vulnerable to the plight of other women. They sought her out for help. We may never fully know for sure; her sympathetic effort to help whoever was there was the most important element of her service.

Ghost Stories from the Ghosts' Point of View Vol 3

A Stranger in the Shadow Lands

The Question of Jurisdiction

When a friend of mine called and asked a prickly question: can you honor a request to remove a crowd of ghosts if the petitioner is a 9 year-old child, I knew there had to be more to the story. The spiritual world has very specific laws that cover jurisdiction of the application of psychic assistance. You would think it would be pretty straightforward: someone asks for help to remove ghosts and you just go in and remove those lost souls. That can definitely be true. But it becomes much dicier, when the requester is a child who is suddenly seeing thousands of dead souls. But in this tragic and challenging case, it is far more complicated than that. In this situation, the sticky issue is why this little boy is seeing thousands of ghosts all of a sudden.

Can you help someone else's child without discussing this with the child's parent? No, you cannot. No psychic has the spiritual jurisdiction to help another parent's child without that parent's express permission. Nor can you assume that the parent would agree or try to acquire permission by asking 'Spirit.' No matter how difficult or awkward it is, you must follow spiritual law and ask the living parent's permission to help that person's child or teenager.

Little did my friend, Alexis, and I know that this issue would become more critical as we went deeper into the issue of why this child was seeing so many ghosts. This bizarre mosaic of complicated situations takes a bit of patient explaining.

The Echoing Damage of Words

Sticks and stones may break your bones, but words are deadly, especially in a divorce situation. Maybe parents don't realize how their words program the behavior of their offspring and what the chilling consequences of those words can be. Often, because there is so much acrimony between parents, many harsh words are said to children. If parents knew the towering damage their words to each other as well as to their children could have, perhaps they would behave differently.

The negative assaults angry parents sling against one another and often against their teenagers, projects that parent's anger on an emotionally defenseless child. Consider situations such as:

"I can't stand to even look at your mother." What happens when the child looks exactly like their mother?

Then there is the parent who denies financial obligations to hurt the other parent, such as refusing to pay for eyeglasses or school activities such as band or sports, even though this parent has plenty of money.

"You are just like your father." That mother now is now telling her child, that he or she, on a certain level is hated by that mom.

Parents who refuse to spend time with their children to punish the other parent make their kids feel terrible, rejected, abandoned and guilt ridden.

Parenting is a tremendous responsibility. Parents unwittingly commit verbal and thought violence against their children. This is particularly insidious because the subconscious part of a child absolutely believes the words of a parent - the parent is 'like a god' to a child. When a parent tells a child that he or she is fat, dumb, ugly, and good for nothing, or a bad driver, the parent is always surprised when the child grows up to be just that.

And when that teenager is a new driver, parental projected anger can create the perfect storm. This disaster in the making becomes compounded when one parent tells their young driver that he or she is a terrible, irresponsible driver. So now you have an angry, grieving teenager, who is told that he is an especially terrible driver: the critical elements for tragedy are now set in motion.

And these elements were the basis of why this nine-year-old was fervently requesting help. Confused? Now it is time to go back to the beginnings of how this convoluted story began because understanding how what you say and do affects other people is the point of this entire karmic saga.

One Shattered Family

"Alexis, please tell me more about this child, his psychic ability and what is happening with this divorcing family."

"Our friends, Sherry, and her husband Chuck, have two children: Oliver and Hunter. When their marriage fell apart, their boys felt so lost. Sherry moved to Atlanta, Georgia and Chuck stayed in Savannah. I think they are living far apart because the divorce was so vicious. Now their boys commute back and forth over weekends and holidays between two angry, confrontational parents. It's heartbreaking. These parents deliberately, or maybe they don't mean to, but it seems like they have used their children to punish each other. The divorce left Sherry tired, heartbroken, grief-stricken, and depressed. She could barely make it through the day so often that her boys felt adrift in a sea of vicious words and shattered family dreams.

"Oliver is the nine-year-old, struggling with his growing psychic ability, which is why he is increasingly seeing ghosts. Poor Oliver feels alone, unloved, and inadequate to help his visibly struggling mom. He tries to be cheerful, but it's so hard in that house of heated phone calls and endless emotional and financial frustration.

"Then there's Hunter: seventeen and angry. Neither parent has any time for him. I was worried about Hunter before this event happened. I mean, I watched him ask for help in learning to drive or to become a better driver. But neither parent had time to teach him and yet they would say crushing things to Hunter, like 'Oh my God, you're such a bad driver!' They really believe that their son is a terrible driver. They never patiently helped him to understand how to be responsible. I know Oliver watched this. This is so sad. I know how it happened; I just don't know how to help them."

One worried child and one angry, frustrated teenager driver, with no reason to believe in himself. The stage Alexis described was ripe for disaster.

Thousands of Ghosts

"All of a sudden, Oliver is seeing ghosts all day."

"Alexis, I'm confused. Has Oliver always had psychic ability or is this something new that just developed overnight? I get the feeling that there is an initiating situation here. Bet there's lots more to this story."

I felt there had to be more. You can be a psychic person, but to go from seeing an occasional ghost to seeing thousands of souls means that something major happened.

"Yes, Tina, there are so many facets to this story: it's not just about Oliver or his brother or his parents. I almost don't know where to begin."

"Ok, begin by telling me what happened to Oliver that caused him to see thousands of dead people."

"Oliver has spent the last several days in the hospital because his brother Hunter was in a car accident."

"What happened? I have a feeling that the ghosts are not the only issue here."

"Hunter was in his mom's SUV, doing a bit of joyriding with his friends somewhere in Savannah. There were two cars: Hunter was in the lead and there was another car full of teenagers driving behind him. I know what you're thinking: this must have ended badly. Well, it did. Frankly, I don't have all the details but this is what the police think happened. The other car of teenagers was behind Hunter watching dumbfounded as he inexplicably decided to cross the double yellow line on a blind curve: dead man's curve is actually what they call it. I know, what a cliché, but that's what it's called. Anyway, he had a head-on collision with a Cadillac Escalade. It was a terrible wreck. They had to use the jaws-of-life to get all of them out of Hunter's car."

"How many teenagers were in the car with Hunter and how bad were their injuries, and what happened to the second car following Hunter's car? Oh, and the Cadillac Escalade?"

"All the people in the Escalade walked away without a scratch, although their car was totaled. The car following Hunger's car just pulled over and called 9-1-1. None of them were injured. There was another couple in the back seat of Hunter's car."

"So, Alexis, there were a total of four kids in the wrecked car Hunter was driving?"

"Yes, the couple in the back seat were badly banged up but were treated and released. Then there was Hunter, who was driving. He broke his leg, had a severe concussion, a lacerated spleen, he needed stitches on his head and face and broke his ribs. He spent two days in the hospital and was then released. But while Hunter was still in the hospital, the police read him his rights. Apparently, Hunter's front seat passenger, his girlfriend, Tiffany, is not expected to survive. Hunter could be charged with vehicular manslaughter. She is currently in a 'non-responsive, non-medically induced coma.' It's bad, really bad.

"My friend Sherry is in shock. She calls me every so often with updates. Frankly, all I can do is listen. Sometimes I really don't know what to say."

"I can only imagine."

"Oliver keeps calling my daughter, begging her to ask me to help him remove all the ghosts who keep coming at him in the hospital."

"Why is Oliver still at the hospital every day?"

"Because Sherry keeps going there to try to make it better with Tiffany's parents. Sherry waits to hear any updates, hoping desperately that Tiffany will be fine, that she will go back to being her son's girlfriend. But every day is like the last, no word from the staff (who can't tell her anything anyway). Tiffany's parents don't want to talk to Sherry or Hunter. It's such a nightmare. And all the while, poor Oliver is by his mom's side in that hospital seeing all these ghosts. I don't know what to do to help any of them."

"Is Hunter home alone?"

"Sherry goes between home and the hospital trying to make it all better for everyone and it's never going to be better for anyone."

"Have you had any opportunity to speak to Sherry about helping Oliver?"

"Yes, she knows her child needs this psychic help right now and I think this is bigger than what I can handle. She can't even think clearly. But a few months ago, before this all happened, she gave me carte blanche to help Oliver any time ghosts were in the picture. Does that give us jurisdiction?"

"I would prefer you ask her again, but technically it does. Why not put in another call and at least try again."

"Alright, but are you sensing something else? I'm hearing a heightened level of concern in your voice."

Life in the Shadow Lands

I was picking up something else. I was feeling Hunter's girlfriend, Tiffany, and her distress at finding herself in the world of the 4th dimension.

I have heard some people call it the Shadow Lands and that would be a good name for it. Until you pass through that 4th dimensional portal, you cannot fully know, understand, or appreciate the emotional devastation that comes as a consequence of finding yourself walking, floating, or wandering in this place of sooty darkness. Glimpses of light in the sea of shadows, tiny flecks of hope strewn about, remind you that you may not have to stay in this netherworld forever, this world without time, space, and gravity.

The ever-present sense of being cold haunts you, shadows you like the daunting memories of the last moments before you found yourself in this place. Fear dogs your fluid movements as you move in slow motion yet travel with the speed of thought. The essence that is you screams out: "I don't belong here! How do I get out?" But there is no one to hear this, no one to ask, no one who responds to your worst nightmare and eternal waking reality.

You do not eat or sleep. You are not dead and you are not alive. You 'are.' You exist, but your existence has no meaning, no focus, no direction, no anchoring in the comfort of knowing where you are, who you are or what future you might experience.

Welcome to the Shadow Lands.

But you may not have to stay here if someone helps you out.

You may get to leave if you can find your way back.

Back: how do you define to yourself where you need to get 'back' 'to,' much less where you are now or how you got here? You remember the moment before now and nothing else. Are you still in the same location just a different dimension? How do you leave one dimension and return to the dimension of real life? What is the mechanism to leave this hazy existence?

How do you know if you are dead are just waiting in this place but not a place? Can you get back to the life you know? Is that possible?

However, to find your way back, to get to leave, someone has to guess that you are here, that you need help and then, that person has to know how to help you to find your way home from this 4th dimensional eternity.

What now constitutes home?

Home can be many places. If you are dead, meaning not alive in a viable body, your silver cord forever severed, home can permanently be the 4th dimension unless you ultimately cross over into the Heaven World. If you are not dead, home is that elusive reality back safely in your physical body. Home in this case is the hope that you are back in your body, but you may awake to a new reality.

But what if you have no idea where you are, or more chillingly, whether or not you are alive or dead? Really, how do you know you are dead, if you have no memory of how you got here except for that one staggering moment before this void of existence?

How Do We Help Her?

I returned to Alexis' question: what was I sensing?

"My concern isn't removing the ghosts. My concern is Tiffany. As we are encountering the ghosts, we may also find that Tiffany is among those ghosts and that would be quite a problem. We have very limited ability to help Tiffany."

"But wouldn't you imagine that Tiffany's parents would want us to help her?"

"Help her how? Cross her over, meaning she would die? Assist her in returning to a body that may never function again? If there is no brain function, there is no 'body' to return to, or inhabit. This is tough. Once we begin to work on those hospital ghosts, and then move to the ghosts by dead man's curve, we, more than likely, will see that Tiffany will find us; that she will seek the light we will be providing. And it's not like we can simply call Tiffany's parents and discuss this with them. Calling them with this request at a time like this would be awkward at best. Some people might even call that harassment and think we are crazy.

"Unfortunately, Tiffany's family is reeling from not knowing if their daughter will live or die. Even trying to explain what we think we see, will seem like we are cruel. Our offer will not appear helpful. There is no way we can talk to them."

"What do we do, what can we do if we encounter Tiffany? What does spiritual law say in such cases?"

Free Will Choices

"It's challenging because no matter how much we may want to help, we are still bound by the dictates of spiritual/karmic law. This means that we have to be extremely circumspect in determining if we can help, how we help and how much we help her.

"My feeling is that Tiffany will probably have absolutely no idea what has happened to her, where she is or what she's supposed to do next. Ghosts, we can remove them all day long, no problem because a hospital or a roadway is a public place and those ghosts use their free will to ask for help.

But people in a coma are another story entirely. We cannot interfere with Tiffany's free will."

Alexis seemed genuinely baffled.

"I'm sorry, I don't think I understand why this is so hard. I mean we haven't even started to look for the ghosts. We may not even encounter Tiffany. Why are you so concerned?"

"Because I can already feel her. I can sense her fear; hear her pleas for someone to help her. She is connected to Oliver through Oliver's brother Hunter, so when you follow the aka cords all the way: I'm connected to you and the spiritual circuit is now complete. I can feel her. It would be so much easier if I couldn't sense her unending feelings of panic and abandonment."

"Does she know what happened to her? Can you feel what happened to her?"

Suddenly, as Alexis asks me this, I can instantly see the accident scene, the blind curve, and the surrounding woods. I can now also see why this accident happened here, at this particular site. There were other violent car crashes that took place here. Other people died. I can see those ghosts waiting for help. This stretch of road is in resonance with deadly accidents. I can clearly see why they call it Dead Man's Curve: children holding their blood-soaked blankets looking for their parents, teenagers, with severed limbs, cut throats and glass encrusted faces, men wandering around asking what happened, where are their families, and their cars. There are even family pets endlessly seeking their masters. Chronic accident locations can even mean that the ghosts of the past jump into the cars of the living and then out again further down the road. Removing those ghosts helps the living and the dead.

"Yes, I can see that when the cars collided, Tiffany's soul was knocked out of her body because she was struck by the massive force and violence of the collision. The essence that was/is Tiffany was thrown across the street from where the car came to rest, into the dense woods. She cannot find her way back into her body. There are terrifying things in those woods; they look like Lower Realm Intelligences to me, tormenting the dead and anyone who wanders that stretch of road in the 4th dimension."

"Tina, what can you do then? What should we do?"

Tiptoeing into the Void

"We will ask for Divine guidance. That's our best we option. At the least, we can open a doorway and remove these ghosts, so let's begin. We will deal with the issues that Oliver is facing at the hospital first. We can find what he's seeing and help those souls."

And we did, we removed thousands of ghosts from various stacks of time who were attached to Oliver. The hospital had been there for decades, so there were ghosts from many years back. We opened a Lightbridge to the Heaven World and provided angelic escorts to all of these souls. There were grandparents and teenagers, motorcyclists, and babies. Death comes to people at every age and walk of life in a hospital and no one ever thinks to help them find the light of the Divine to make their way home. (Ghost hunters utterly miss the ghost hunting boat when they look everywhere but hospitals.)

Then using remote viewing, Alexis and I psychically headed to that deadly curve to address the dead lingering there.

Tiffany found us pretty quickly. As soon as she saw us and realized that we could see her, she wept tears of grief and relief. How can they be said in the same sentence: grief and relief? The Lightbridge to the Heaven World is extremely bright, gloriously welcoming, warm, and so loving that it is very difficult to resist, but we had to stop her at the bridge. She was not dead.

"Can you see me? I see you; I see you both, looking bright. Have you come to help me cross that bridge? It's so beautiful! I can feel the light to the Heaven World. When I stand near that light, I'm not cold anymore. Finally, someone I can talk to! It's so weird here. Are you from heaven? Can you help me speak to my parents? You can help me, can't you? I mean I can see all those other people crossing that bridge and I want to go too. At least I think I do. I miss my parents, my brothers and sister, and all my friends. Can you help me to talk to them?"

We could feel her bewilderment. If we could see her, she began to realize, what did that mean for her?

"Am I dead? Is that why you've come for me? Do you know? Can you tell me what happened to me? Can you tell me where I am?"

I listened for guidance, took a deep breath, and began to speak to her in a measured voice: calm, reassuring and helpful.

"Tiffany, you were in a terrible car crash while you were riding with your boyfriend and the other couple. The car you were in had a head-on collision with a Cadillac Escalade. Your friends and Hunter survived and have been treated and released. You have not awakened from the coma you are currently in at the hospital. Your family and friends are so worried about you."

"Wait, so how can I be here, wherever this is and in a coma in the hospital? Nothing makes any sense to me."

"It's difficult for me to explain where you are. We call it the 4th dimension. This is the place where people come when they are in a coma. We realize that you have no idea how you got here. Let me explain. When you are in such a violent accident, sometimes, your soul is flung out of the body and enters the 4th dimensional plain of existence. You, or the 'you' that is your personality, became instantly separated from your mortal, physical body. We call this place where you are now, the Shadow Lands because all you see are shadows. There are other ethereal souls here that you can sort of see, sort of sense but you have no real contact with them. The Shadow Lands or 4th Dimension is a place of where time does not exist. There is no gravity here and unfortunately for you, no future either. Tiffany, I'm so sorry that this happened to you."

Tiffany looked from Alexis to me and shook her head.

"Okay let me get this straight, you're saying that I'm not dead but I'm not really 'alive' either. So, what happens to me next? I'm so confused."

I braced myself because I could instantly feel her anger rising, or was it panic?

"Why can't I talk to my parents? Can't you help me to talk to them? Can you be the go-between, - what do they call it a - a medium and talk to my parents? I've got to tell them I'm okay."

"No, Tiffany, I can't. You know them better than I do and the truth is that in their state of grief, and shock, talking to a medium is not something they can handle right now."

"Look, you have to help me! I'm a straight 'A' student! I have a future! I'm going to college. I have a life to live! I want to fall in love, be married, work, have kids, and see the world. Are you telling me that none of that is now ever going to happen? Tell me the truth: am I dying?"

And then, it was as if she realized that she had no idea who we were, no clue who she was talking to and she demanded to know.

"And who are you, anyway?"

"Tiffany, we understand that you had/have a life to live, people who love you and a future. Perhaps you still have that. Your future is not for us to tell you. And no, you're not dead.

You're in a coma in the hospital. As for us, well, we're psychics who came primarily to help those souls who are definitely dead, to cross over into the light of the Heaven World, which is what you are seeing. We are still alive. We are just a pair of ordinary people, who have the ability to see into the dimension in which you find yourself.

"I would imagine you have been on a rollercoaster of emotion. Maybe it would help if you shared with us a bit more exactly what you're feeling."

She stared at us and we could feel her challenges, her emotions begin to come roiling to the surface.

"What am I feeling? Are you kidding me? I'm beyond terrified! I have no idea where I am. I can't find help. My friends are gone. I keep reliving those final moments over and over. I can see the accident scene unfold. I'm frantic! Hunter's going too fast! We're screaming at him to slow down! Don't pass! I'm screaming and screaming. I'm beside myself. I can't believe that this is happening! And then I'm out of my body by the side of the road. I bounce between reliving the moment of - my God, what do I call this? - the moment my life changed or died, or I don't know what. You say I'm not dead, but God, I don't know how to describe this emotion, this rage, this frantic feeling, this hopelessness. I want to scream! But no one hears me! I had no control! He was so angry and driving faster and faster. As he pulled into the oncoming lane I remember screaming: "Hunter, don't!!!" And then I was standing next to my body. Then it went black and I'm walking in what you call the 'Shadow Lands.'

"I've had no one to talk to and no one to hear me. I don't understand what happened. I guess I'm dead, but not quite? I feel pain and shock and above all, a betrayal of my life. I'm angry at Hunter for doing this to me. I want to be normal. But if I go back, I won't have my same life: I know it has changed forever. I don't want to have to decide. I don't want to be a burden to my family but I don't want them to grieve me either.

"I'm miserable! I cannot face a life of unending physical pain. I don't want a life where I survived but I'm not living. I've been so afraid of what death was that I couldn't face it. I couldn't have imagined that death could be a better choice. In the peace I'm feeling, near that light, I know I can heal.

"What's going to happen to me? What options do I have right now?"

The Agony of the Final Decision

This was the part I most dreaded. When you help people who are already dead, it is a wonderful feeling because you can relieve their situation and help them find the peace of release from this featureless dimension. Helping a person in a coma is very tenuous, very delicate: you don't know how it is going to end because the soul still has free will to decide to live or die.

"Tiffany, we cannot tell you what to do. What we can tell you is that once you walk across that Light Bridge, you will surely have made the decision to end your life. You will no longer be in a coma; you'll be declared dead: your heart will flat-line.

"If you do not cross that Light Bridge, then you are choosing to keep the door open to re-engage in mortal life in some way. You will be offered a pathway to re-enter your mortal body somehow. I don't exactly know how that works, but it will be as if you sort of slip into sleep and wake up in your body in the hospital.

"Re-engage in mortal life? What does that mean? My God, are you saying that I'm brain dead and that I will be forever tied to a body that won't die but can't ever really be alive, dance, think, love, drive a car, feel, . . . be who I have always been?"

She begins to 'cry' as if she were in a mortal body. Crying in this dimension is awkward to describe because there are no physical tears but there is the emotion of crying, the energy of grief. What made this doubly hard for us is that we had no real information on her condition, nor were we entitled to this information.

"Tiffany, all we currently know is that you are in a 'non-responsive, non-medically induced coma.' Could a miracle happen? Absolutely, this is why we're being so vague. You're not dead. Anything can happen. Your future as it stretches before you, is, as yet, unwritten. Remember, you still have the potential to make a full recovery."

"Is there something I can do to help myself?"

"Yes, you still have free will, meaning that you have the ability to make choices. All we are allowed to do is to share with you your options: option one is simply to cross that glowing bridge that will mean that you will definitely die. It's a one-way exit. You will not return from that cross over until you reincarnate again.

"Option two is a bit more complicated. You can request the services and advice of the angel we are providing to you right now. Your conversation with this angel is private. We are not permitted to hear, nor participate. You can discuss with the angel what to do: cross over or stay and re-enter your body and accept whatever type of life/existence that this choice is going to mean. Even the angel cannot tell you what to do. The angel cannot violate your free will either: because although you are in a coma, you are still alive in a mortal body. As hard as this is to say, we cannot advise you further."

"What if I decide that I want you to cross me over right now, get it over with, will you do that? I would be exercising my free will."

"Please don't make that decision right now. We have assigned an angel to you so that you will no longer be alone in the Shadow Lands. Discuss your options with the angel. Your discussion with the angel and your decision will be private; we will not hear it. You can choose to cross over with that angel, but neither he nor we can tell you what to do. It's the blessing and the challenge of being mortal."

"Oh my God, you're going to leave me here, aren't you?! Please don't abandon me! I mean, I love having the angel, but having an angel feels like I'm already dead and that's terrifying."

Tiffany's plea broke my heart. This job is so hard. The discipline required to always follow spiritual law is why I can do this job but there are those days when I fleetingly wish this were someone else's job.

The reason we strictly adhere to spiritual law is because there are always unseen, and unknown karmic law issues. We have no way of knowing what karma is being balanced, why this happened, or the karmic lessons that must be learned not only by Tiffany but her family, Hunter, and his family. The karmic echo of this event will continue for an eternity.

"Tiffany," I told her as gently as I could. "We must take our leave of you now. We wish we could hug you, and make you feel better, but we are limited. At least, the angel will keep you safe and warm, and he will keep you company until you reach your decision. We know that in the end, you will reach the right decision, whatever that turns out to be."

The Tension of Waiting

It was so hard to leave Tiffany there but at least she was no longer alone. Then the really hard part began for us: waiting to see what would happen. We could not look in on her again, touch base or inquire. We had put our toe on the karmic line and that was as far as we could go. I am able to do this job because I do not violate karmic law. There is tremendous karma attached to every event in a person's life, including ones with life and death challenges such as this.

We were able to remove the dead from that location and we helped Oliver by removing the ghosts in the hospital who had been haunting him.

And then our job was done.

Epilogue

We reached the limits of what we are allowed to do for Tiffany. Being in the arms of the angel made her better able to think and decide what course of action to take. I directed the angel to assist her within the confines of spiritual/karmic law and we left. I knew she watched the reunions of the other souls crossing over and the love that they felt with those happy hug-filled greetings. I knew she was tired of the pain and the struggle and fatigue yet she had a solitary decision to make.

Tiffany stayed in a coma for another 48 hours after we left her, and then she woke up. She chose the long, challenging road back to health and healing. Sherry told Alexis that Tiffany is bitter that this happened to her. Neither she nor her family can handle any contact with

Hunter or his family: it's simply too painful. The reality of lives irrevocably changed forever is too fresh and raw.

Tiffany has had to relearn how to walk, talk and study again. Her progress is slow and steady. Perhaps, in time, she will gain perspective on this life-changing event and turn tragedy into wisdom and growth. As I write this, I am reminded how critical it was in those moments with Tiffany to allow her to choose her fate. Karma never wastes energy and it is worth pondering what Tiffany's karma was in this situation. Why did she need that experience of the accident and being in a coma? What can she learn from this event? How will she face her life as each day goes on? Will she embrace the lessons karma is offering or will she live a life of bitterness?

Hunter moved past the initial shock of his actions and fell into the depths of despair at the damage he inflicted on his girlfriend in that one fateful moment of tragically poor judgment. He became so depressed that he was placed on a suicide watch. Although initially, counseling had little effect on him, eventually he was able to work his way out of his abyss. He learned the value of atonement: making life better for others. He came to realize that he could never change what happened to Tiffany but he could do something to help others with their challenges. Hunter began to volunteer in the physical therapy department of the hospital. He is helping other victims of accidents rebuild their lives. This job constantly reminds him of what he did to himself and the others in that car. He knows he cannot change the past but he can make a positive difference in someone else's future.

Hopefully, lessons that Hunter learned are priceless and the only positive in this entire situation is recognizing the value of any experience, no matter how painful. However, karmically Hunter still had free will. He made a conscious decision to cross that double yellow line on Dead Man's Curve. He may spend the rest of his life wondering why he made that decision.

Sherry and Chuck had no idea the crushing power their words would have when they convinced Hunter that he was a terrible driver. Did Hunter unconsciously live up to their negative belief in him? How much did their words and attitude contribute to this accident?

Neither could these parents understand the pure poison they hurled at each other or how that toxic energy damaged their sons. None of us lives in a vacuum: the karmic echo of their actions is going to ripple out for eternity. The emotional damage that they visited upon Hunter had a hideous impact on Tiffany and her family and friends, not to mention on the individuals and the families of the unsuspecting passengers in that Cadillac Escalade. All families involved will live with the aftermath of this couple's words for the rest of their lives, wherever that 'life' may be.

Ghost Stories from the Ghosts' Point of View Vol 3

The Dental Chair

"Tina, I'm so upset I don't know how to come to terms with what happened to me! It happened so fast." I could hear the catch in her voice, as if whatever this trauma was literally took her breath away. She seemed on the verge of a flood of tears.

"Is your family alright, Elena? Is someone hurt? Did you get hurt?"

"No, no, my family's fine and I'm not hurt but I am or I thought I was . . ." She chokes here, as if she cannot get the fateful words out of her throat.

"Tina, something so horrible, so terrifying happened to me today." Then, as if she is censoring herself: "I can't tell anyone. No one will believe me! I can't share this with anyone but you. You'll believe me. Please tell me you'll believe me. I'm empty, almost, you know, as if I were dead inside."

"I'm not the same now."

My long-time client slowly, steadily began to share what had become, a life-changing event. I kept reassuring her that I would believe her, that whatever it was that happened to her was real and that we would somehow find a way to make some sense of it. I needed to give her the time, the emotional reassurance and space to find the pathway to tell me whatever it was that she experienced.

"I'm not the same now. I'm different since this happened."

She told me this flatly, matter-of-factly as if the person she was the seconds before this event took place, was gone and that person would not ever come back.

"I'm afraid all the time. I don't sleep. Sleep is terrifying for me now."

"Take a deep breath, Elena. Let's face this together. We are going to work through this. Have you told your husband or your daughter?"

"Oh my God, no! I couldn't tell my husband. Randy wouldn't believe me. He won't understand. My daughter's going to be a doctor; she's so rooted in science that I know she won't even have the patience to – to hear me."

Then the tears began, as if the emotional isolation left her a stranger in her own family.

The Routine Visit

"I had a referral to this dentist so that he could remove a molar."

"Had you been to this dentist before?"

"No, this was the first time. I didn't know him."

"What happened when you got there?"

"I immediately went into the bathroom – and this was so weird - I called my daughter and told her that I loved her and . . . and that I would see her later, almost – almost as if – I don't know why I called her. I just - just needed her to know that I loved her."

I knew exactly why she called her daughter. Elena was already terrified of what was coming on a subconscious level. She reached out to her grown daughter for reassurance.

"Then you went into the office?"

"Yes, and then the dentist had me sit in his dental chair and then I had to sign a bunch of papers. They were full of legal terms and I didn't understand what they meant. I had to get the bad tooth out so I just signed them. I didn't know what was going to happen. He didn't explain it."

"Alright, what happened next?"

"I thought he was going to give me a shot to numb my tooth but instead he put a mask on my face and then . . ."

"So, you didn't know he was going to give you Nitrous Oxide? You didn't know he was going to use gas to put you to sleep?"

"No, and when the gas started, I didn't go to sleep. I – I think I died right there in that chair! Instantly I was not in my body. I was flying out of my body. I knew I wasn't alive anymore. I was terrified! I kept saying: 'I'm not ready,' 'I'm not ready!' I felt this tornado pulling me, this great wind pulling and pulling me into I didn't know what but I knew I was petrified to go into that wind. I knew somehow, that once I let myself go into that wind, that I would never come back."

Sobbing and shaking, Elena continues.

"The wind was relentless, pulling at my feet, trying to suck me into complete death. I fought that wind! I wasn't ready to go! I kept saying that. 'I'm not ready to go. I have a husband, a daughter and a little son and they need me! I can't leave now! It isn't my time!' I remember screaming this out loud. I screamed in my head because I don't think I said anything out loud. How do I know this? How do I know in my very soul that if I let go of my hold on this world, if I let that tornado pulling at my feet take me away, that I would die? I knew I would never come back. I – I would be dead.

"It felt like I fought that wind for an eternity. It was as if there was no time. I don't know how long I struggled. Tina, I worked so hard to stay here. I could feel that death was coming for me."

"I can't leave them now!"

Elena takes a long deep breath, and then she breathes a deep sigh.

"Everything went black, a black that had no up or down, that had no beginning and no end. I was aware that out of that darkness there was a door and I could see a light underneath that door, just a faint glow. It was as if my family was on the other side of that door and that I couldn't ever go back to them. I couldn't get to them. I began to grieve them. I felt myself screaming: I can't leave them now! They need me! I love them; I want to be with them. I want to live! My son is only four he needs me so much! I want to see my daughter graduate and be a doctor. I love my husband and I want to be with him! This can't be happening to me. I'm not ready to die!!!!

"I felt like I was pleading with someone but I didn't know who. All the time I felt this incredible wind pulling me into the depths of death. I screamed in terror. I felt myself grieving and fighting all at the same time in this darkness, this emptiness that began to suffocate me.

"I was me but not me, alive in my heart but not alive in my body.

"Then – instantly - I became a ghost. I wasn't in the dentist's office anymore. I was outside on Coast Boulevard watching as cars were speeding at me so fast! The cars drove right through me! I was a ghost! I believed I was dead and I was praying at the same time that I wasn't dead, that I could have a second chance."

"Elena, this is incredible. I cannot begin to imagine your terror! Then what happened?"

"Then I heard a voice begin talking, but this voice, this female voice wasn't talking to me. It was as if she was talking to someone else and I had no idea who that was. Who were these people, these beings talking about me and not to me?

"Finally, I could make out what one of them was saying: 'She's not ready.' I knew that this voice was watching and observing me in traffic, fighting the tornado, fighting death with all my heart. I did not recognize the voice. I have never heard this voice before.

"Instantly, after I heard that voice I woke up."

"What the hell happened to her?"

"As I woke up, I heard the dentist say, 'What the hell happened to her?' and he stopped the procedure because when I woke up, I couldn't stop crying. I was sobbing and sobbing. The dentist was really upset. He looked at me and left the room. He said nothing to me, didn't try to comfort me, help me, or talk to me about what happened. I was shaking, crying and unable to fully grasp what happened.

"I died in that dentist chair. I know it. I was a ghost for I don't know how long. I asked the dental assistant how long I was out and she said I was only out for a few minutes, not more than two or three minutes, but to me it felt like an eternity. I don't believe her. I asked her what happened and she said, 'Oh nothing happened, this is routine; you just woke up and the dentist decided not to continue the procedure.' I looked at her and I knew she was lying. Neither she nor the dentist asked me why I was crying or how I was. How can people be so cruel, so heartless?"

"My God, how did you drive home? Did they make sure you were all right to drive before you left?"

"No. I was sobbing as I left the office and no one cared. No one asked me if I was all right to drive. I had to go pick up my son. I had to drive and I don't know how I got there. I couldn't stop crying. Tina, this was so horrible! It was so traumatic. I don't know how to understand this. Please help me. I'm so confused and so depressed."

"How do people prepare for death?"

"How do I go on living after this? I'm terrified to go to sleep. I keep reliving the darkness, the tornado, standing as a ghost, and watching cars drive through my body. I have redone my life insurance policy. I no longer take my life with my family for granted. I love them but I'm fighting the depression of leaving them all someday. I keep grieving my own death and yet I'm living. It's horrible! I can still feel it coming, as if what happened is still lingering with me, as if I can die at any moment: I feel as if the line between living and dying is almost imperceptible.

"How do people prepare for death? I'm afraid, so afraid. Do you see why I can't tell my family what happened to me?"

I privately took a long, deep breath. I completely understood. This is so intimate and personal, so real, profound and life altering that if someone didn't believe her it would be as if her very sanity was being questioned. She cannot bear the thought that she would not be believed. This experience created a fragile, vulnerable element to her personality. All she thought she knew about life and death were forever altered.

"The thought of leaving them, and of how they would live without me, is tearing me apart. I know it can happen. It almost did happen and I cannot come to terms with it. I know for sure there are ghosts now: I was one, even if briefly. And when you say that the dead grieve, oh Tina, I absolutely know that this is true! I immediately began grieving my death and I can't seem to stop doing that. How do I deal with this?"

"Elena, it's true, people don't prepare for death, and have no idea what to do when it happens. Grief overtakes them. Religions don't prepare people for death either, other than the Buddhists. They have a clear understanding, but Western faiths are oddly silent on this event that will eventually embrace us all."

"Is there anything that tells us what to do when we feel ourselves dying?"

"Yes, actually, the 23rd Psalm offers clues about life immediately after death, but you would have to know how to read those signs and symbols. When we have to pass through a darkness of the 4th dimension, this psalm tells us what to do. Think about the passage: 'Yea, though I walk through the valley of the Shadow of Death, I will fear no evil, for thou art with me.' This means that that darkness of the 4th dimension can be felt to be evil, filled with terror. It doesn't have to be, but darkness is inherently fear inducing. This psalm is a reminder to look for the light, ask for God and an angel to escort you as you prepare to enter the house of God.

"However, your situation was so sudden, so unexpected. You did not have one trauma. You had a series of spiritual blows that have shaken you to your foundation. The staggering feeling of being pulled out of your body, out of life itself had to have been terrifying. I cannot imagine your horror at realizing that you are dead. Then the waves of grief for your family, for the life you had planned to live with them were shattering. Then you grieved yourself. And then to hear that voice, talking about you in the third person: 'She's not ready.' How utterly bewildering! For some reason you were given the unusual option of deciding to leave or to stay. I would imagine that choice is not often given to people. This is a massive amount of trauma to experience in the space of a few moments."

"Yes, Tina, that's true. I realized that as I was fighting that wind, pulling me into death, that I did have a choice and someone was listening to me fight to live, to stay with my family. I'll never forget those moments, those timeless seconds when I made my love for my family known. And that voice saying to someone: 'She's not ready.' Wouldn't everyone who loves their family say that? Wouldn't everyone fight to live a whole life with everyone they love?"

"I would imagine that a large percentage of people would want to stay and would fight death. I believe that yours may not have been only about a choice. You had a body that you could reenter. Yours was an anesthesia death. You could be revived which created an option to continue life. If a person has catastrophic injuries, then the soul has to leave, no matter how traumatic their death may be or how much that person wants to stay with their family. I have spoken to those souls who died in this way and had no choice. There was no viable body to return to. Their grief is exactly what you are feeling.

"And I also suspect that it isn't entering the house of the Lord that is creating so much grief for you. Your grief is centered on leaving your family and being unable to imagine that they could live without you. Is that true?"

"Yes! They need me. I help them, I look out for them. If I weren't there, it would be so hard for them. How would they manage? If I left them, I would feel as if I had failed them, let them down somehow. I almost did. Maybe that's why I'm so afraid to go to sleep that if I don't wake up, who will take care of them?"

People who love their families with all of their heart are so conscientious about caring for them. They cannot imagine what would happen to their loved ones if death deprived them of a life together. But death comes at all times in a life and that can be very early, mid-life, very late – all for critical reasons we may not understand.

There is the concept of a life plan, when a soul is going to die and many people do feel death coming, but for other people it is a stunning, crushing surprise. Somehow, I have to find a way to help her to let go of the concept of attachment yet enable her to enjoy the rest of her life.

"When your dad died and you were only eight, you all had to manage without him, didn't you?"

"Yes, and I remember how hard it was. My mom had to leave us with relatives to go to another country to make a living. It was horrible. The family I lived with while she was gone was so cruel to me."

I could hear her sense of betrayal as the memory of her father's passing pierced her thoughts, reawakening old heartache.

"Yes, she did and had your dad not died, you would not be in this country, would not be married to your husband, live in the house you are living in, have these two wonderful children or be talking to me right now. I wouldn't know you. Your father's death opened a door for you that you could not imagine. Every death has a purpose, even if that person's passing creates a tremendous amount of pain. When we are in the middle of grieving someone we love, we cannot see that there is still a future for us or that we can ever find something beneficial coming from such tragedy. Does this make sense for you?"

"Yes, it does. I never looked at it this way. But what do I do about my fear of dying? I don't want to die. The part where I was yanked out of my body by this terrible wind is so terrifying for me, that... How do you know when your time is truly over or if you have a chance at a longer life? How do I ever sleep again?"

"Not sleeping will not forestall death. Death will come when it is the correct time, day, or night. Your family will adjust to your eventual death as you adjusted to your father's passing and then more recently to your mother's death. Part of living is adjusting to the passing of those we love. It is a critical lesson of learning to value life and respect death."

". . . . and my fear?"

"Remember that you can always ask for an angel to protect you in the sleep state as well as to assist you at death. You have the right to ask for help to transition. And I will help you. You can ask for me to help you at any time, in any dimension whether or not I am conscious of your situation – or whether or not I am alive or dead. You have more power than you realize in those breathless moments when you feel death coming. And I believe you felt death coming even before you sat in that dentist's chair. This was why you called your daughter. You were saying goodbye to her."

"Yes! I felt that I was saying goodbye to her and I was already sad and I didn't understand why. Does this mean that I already knew something was about to happen?"

"I think on a certain level you did know something was about to happen; you could feel it coming."

"So, I don't have to be afraid anymore? I won't die in my sleep? If I did die in my sleep, what you're saying is that whenever I do slip away that I will still be all right, that I can have help. I have to accept that my family will still be all right if I'm here or not?"

"Yes. They will miss you. They will struggle and grieve you for a very long time as you have grieved and missed your dad but you lived your life with the memory of your dad always in your heart. Didn't you?"

"Yes, that's true. So, I can relax and live? That death I almost experienced was terrifying, but what you're saying is that it didn't have to be so bad. That now I can know that I have the ability to ask for help. Do you think other people know this?"

"Well, if you allow me to share your story, they will know it. In this way you can be of service to others."

"I think it would be good to share my story. Was this a near death experience?

"Yes and no. You didn't move toward the light. You didn't feel that peace of release and have to return. You had a different experience. Yours was to value the life you are living and to understand a different facet of death and of life. Every experience is inherently valuable, but yours was priceless."

"Priceless, yes it was. Thank you, Tina."

Epilogue

I would love to know what it is about a dentist's office that causes more people than you would believe to have a ghostly encounter or a difficult experience. I suspect it has to do with the fact that some of the energy of the pain and fear of being in a dentist's office lingers in a location. Most dentist chairs are imbedded with the predecessor energy of fear.

Working on your teeth means that someone is deep inside your auric field and that person may cause you pain. The energy of pain has a tendency to linger in all the metal in that office space for decades, from the metal probes, file cabinets, chairs to the metal rebar in the walls themselves. The older the building, the longer the dentist or dentists have had successive businesses there, the more powerful the buildup of the 'tense/pain' energy is, and it saturates the walls and floors.

If a person is psychically sensitive to certain energies, then a visit to a dentist's office can be quite problematic. That energy will bombard the soul and it may be that as the anesthetic took effect, Elena's soul fled the toxic energy in the office but Elena had no idea what to do when this happened. It was also possible that the dentist gave her too much gas and it stopped her heart. Either way, it was a type of perfect psychic storm. But we know that karmically, no energy is wasted and Elena will have learned a great deal from this experience.

Elena chose not to return to that dentist. The dentist's attitude was appalling. His unfeeling staff did nothing to care for their patient except to quickly usher her out. I suspect that she flat-lined right in front of them and it terrified them. She may also have been out for much more than a minute or two. Thankfully, not all dentist offices are this unfeeling. Most dentists care a great deal about their patients.

Elena emotionally recovered from her dental visit, and she is now able to sleep at night. Her new appreciation for the love of her family is based on her knowledge of her near-death experience.

And finally, the reason that I told her that she could call on me whenever she needed to, is that once she makes that connection, she is also connected to my spiritual team who are always at the ready to help anyone.

The Lieutenant's Roommate

Where Do I Begin?

It's been many decades since this happened. Quite a long time since I was a very newly married lieutenant in the US Navy, stationed with my handsome husband in Naples, Italy. I just never saw this coming.

    Maybe I should back up: this story is as much about me, and how my psychic ability developed, as it is about the incident itself. You never think you will wake up to being able to do these things. Really, you think you are just like everyone else. You surely don't want anyone to know about it. But I digress. I need you to see how all of this unfolded, so back to Naples.

    We were two lieutenants with no kids, and no debts, living in a penthouse apartment that overlooked the sparkling azure Bay of Naples. It was a three-year honeymoon. Off of our bedroom balcony was a spectacular view of the isles of Capri and Ischia, and the moody Mt.

Vesuvius itself. We often watched clouds swirl around the volcano, its ancient threatening cone projecting a tenuous calm and illusory, dormant energy. The stunning, craggy cliffs of the Amalfi coast lay further south past the volcano, as we gazed at it from our rooftop terrace. We loved living downtown. The flickering lights that lined the Bay of Naples glistened in the distance by Castel dell 'Ovo in the harbor.

  Our elegant three-bedroom apartment came with 20-foot ceilings, terrazzo floors, no heat, and no screens to protect us from the flies with sticky feet that attached themselves to us like Velcro. Every arrival and departure meant stepping into the 3' x 3' square elevator that took us to and from our top floor apartment. We had to pay one Italian gettone coin (about 5 cents) every time we used it. Or we could climb up and down 14 flights of stairs to reach our happy home.

  I spoke fluent Spanish and my husband spoke French. Pretty soon we both spoke enough Italian to have a blast anywhere we went.

  The commute to work was not far. I was stationed at a Communications Area Master Station, meaning my command was responsible for all radio communication with all NATO and US ships and submarines operating in the Mediterranean. My husband, Troy, was attached to Submarine Group 8. His job was to manage the coming and going of submarines operating in the Mediterranean Sea. He also occasionally rode those submarines as an inspector.

The Lieutenant's Roommate

We were having the time of our lives. Italy was (and still is!) magical, every single day. I was in heaven. Naples was a daily adventure in delight: fabulous food, wonderful people, and shopping to die for. Then of course there was the adrenaline rush of driving in Naples traffic. We traveled everywhere - Rome, Florence, Venice, Amalfi, Sorrento, Salerno, were all just a couple of hours or a modest train ride away.

Troy had just left a tour as assistant weapons officer on a nuclear submarine. He would be at sea 105 days and home 90 days: exactly. You could set your watch by this unrelenting schedule. So, when we arrived in Naples, we were still getting used to being married to each other. We realized that that we had never lived together longer than 90 days in a row in the three years we had been married. This was going to be a real adventure. Maybe it was living together after that 91st day that triggered it.

Making 'Normal' Friends

When we lived in New London, Connecticut, I had worked hard building those precious friendships with the other wives because it was those relationships that got me though those long months when Troy was at sea. Even though he was at home now, I still enjoyed the camaraderie of the other wives and the roughly ten female Naval Officers stationed with me at that time. We all enjoyed various shopping adventures all over Naples and often bragged about the latest treasures we had discovered.

The friendships you develop when you away from home and outside of the United States are lasting. You are 'in it together' and you quickly learn to depend on, look out for, and help each other. It is a tremendous feeling.

One of those friendships was with a most intelligent lieutenant, named Connie, who arrived after I did. She was from Texas. Several of us took her under our 'wings' to help her get settled. She was one of the communication watch officers, which meant that she oversaw the volume of 'message traffic' that was coming and going from the participating multinational NATO ships and shore stations in the Mediterranean.

Getting settled in the Naples area is always something of a challenge, especially if you're not fluent in Italian. Yet, Connie was able to find a charming place way out in the country. Her small 'villa' with shiny, blue tile floors was bright and airy. There were no Americans by her; she was not in any sort of Navy community. She was pretty isolated way out in her little rural community of Licola. Yet, she did not seem to need anyone nearby; she loved her place. She was perfectly comfortable living alone.

The Resonance Issue

The buildings where we each stood a 24-hour watch were in a military location in Naples called AFSOUTH, or the headquarters for Allied Forces Southern Europe. These buildings were left over from World War II. The Italians constructed some of the office buildings, but the Nazis built most of them.

I hated those times when I had the duty and I had to spend the night in those buildings. My skin crawled. I could hear what I imagined were tortured voices and plodding, reluctant footsteps coming from the floors above me. I was sure that the communications building was haunted. I just knew it. But I'm a Naval Officer. Psychic things like haunted buildings and ghosts are not discussed.

But Connie knew it too and one day over lunch, she broached the subject.

"Hey, Tina, have you noticed how haunted these AFSOUTH buildings are?"

"Oh God, yes, Connie! I refuse to be in the admin building alone when I stand watch. I'm so glad to know that I'm not alone in feeling this. I thought it was just me."

"Have you heard those voices? I always get the creeps when I stand watch. I stay really close to the comm center offices and I always take a petty officer with me when I have to make rounds to the outer buildings. Have you had any 'experiences' like that?"

"I believe those buildings are seriously haunted. I've heard sounds, muffled voices, clomping. I think someone or maybe many people were tortured up there. And I always stay in the comm center offices like you do. I haven't seen anything, but I'm convinced that the Nazis built the building we are in, not the Italians. I don't know how we would know, but the admin building feels terrifying."

I shivered a bit inside. It was so good to be able to talk about this out in the open. Connie continued.

"I know. Do you do the grounds tour alone?"

"No, I take a Chief Petty Officer with me."

Connie also seemed glad to be able to talk about this.

"I think one of the upper floors in the admin building was an interrogation room. Sometimes I hear someone screaming. I can't make out if it's a male or female voice. I - I think I'm afraid that I'll see a ghost of some soul that was tortured-by-the-Nazis. Maybe I'm just weird."

I inwardly shuddered. I also had no desire to see any type of Nazi era ghost. Then I wondered if there were ghosts watching us. I left that chilly thought alone to answer her.

"I haven't heard the voices like you have, and I hope I never do. I guess it's time to get back to work. Hey, do you want to get together this weekend? Troy's got the duty. You could come to my place downtown, or I could come out to Licola. Got plans?"

"Well, it started out as a quiet, ordinary, day."

The Lieutenant's Roommate

So, we decided that I should pick her up at her place, go shopping and then just hang out that day. It was a quiet, ordinary day. Well, it started out as a quiet, ordinary day.

After we finished visiting the fragrant fruit markets brimming with summer apricots, peaches, watermelon, juicy cherries, grapes the size of my thumb, we headed for the abundant crates of crimson tomatoes, crisp beans, rocket (greens) and squash. These markets are so vibrant the aroma of this food is one of my happiest memories. Even the fishmonger offered fresh swordfish, calamari, eel, and fish I had never seen. The mountains of aromatic cheese and crusty bread beckoned us and we loaded up on these and then we brought these delicious provisions back to make a lovely supper at Connie's place.

Her villa was sparsely furnished, a simple kitchen table, a couple of chairs, a lamp, and a bed. After supper, we chatted. Military personnel who lived in Naples at that time seldom had a television. Few if any of us spoke enough Italian to keep up with translating a TV show. So, when people got together, they actually had conversations, took walks, and enjoyed long, lingering dinners.

Connie was ironing her uniform. I was absent-mindedly looking around her place as we chatted. There was a lull in the conversation as I glanced in a corner of her kitchen that was in shadow. That's when I saw him. I was so startled that I forgot to be afraid. Stunned, that was it: I was stunned to so clearly see a ghost standing in the corner.

He was about six feet tall wearing a dark brown, double-breasted wool trench coat fully buttoned up. He sported a 1940s Fedora, worn at a jaunty angle. His face was slightly hidden from me, but from what I could see he looked pale, pasty, and surprisingly handsome. I did not see his feet. There was not a mark on him. I say this because I also didn't have a clue how this ghost had died since his cause of death was not obvious to me.

I had a million thoughts racing through my head: does she know he's here? Does he mean her any harm? Is he a Nazi ghost who followed her home from one of the creepy buildings at the AFSOUTH headquarters? Could he harm me too? What if he follows me back to my place? Why hasn't he moved on? Is he trying to tell her something? Is he even watching her when she showers and sleeps? I shuddered inwardly at that last thought. How do I tell Connie that she has a ghost watching her or us?

He did not make a sound but it was obvious in that way that psychics know things, that he was well aware that I could see him and that I was quite taken aback by this turn of events. He was not aggressive toward either of us. I calmed down a bit, gathered my courage and broached the subject.

"Ah, Connie, you're pretty psychic, aren't you?"

The Lieutenant's Roommate

"Well, yes, sort of, I guess. Why do you ask?"

"Because there is the ghost of a tall man standing in the corner over there. I can see him quite clearly. He doesn't seem to be threatening, he's just lurking or lingering or watching. I can't be sure. Have you seen him? I mean. Well. How do I put this? Do you know you have a ghost watching you iron your uniform? Do you realize that there are three of us in this room?"

"You can see him? That's amazing! No one else has ever been able to see him; this is wonderful! Someone else can see him!"

Okay, this was so not the reaction I expected. I was dumbfounded.

"Um, yeah, I see him and it's very clear to me that he's watching you, not me. How long have you known he's been here in this villa?"

Get ready. Here it comes.

"Oh, Tina, it feels so good to finally tell someone, this is Theodore. He's been with me all my life. He loves me. I can't remember a time when Theo wasn't with me. He's my constant companion; he goes with me everywhere. No one else has ever been able to see him. Maybe he feels comfortable enough to allow you to see him, or maybe you are just that psychic. Isn't this wonderful! It's been so hard to keep this secret because who can I tell?"

Stunned. That's still the word for this situation that, for me, was without precedent to this very day. This was the first time I had come face-to-face with a ghost. Secondly, to be able to tell someone what I am seeing and receive validation that he was really there was tremendous; I was stunned. But Connie's reaction to my 'revelation' also left me bewildered and a little shaken.

"Connie, you're a Lieutenant in the Navy for God's sake! How can you have a dead man living with you here? How can he have been with you all of your life? I'm so confused. Help me to understand this."

"Tina, I love him. All I know is that I love him and he loves me and we've been together for, well, forever. I don't want him to leave. That's all I know. Maybe it's strange to you but this is my life and I have no desire to change this. Can you understand? Can you please try?"

Well, can I understand it?

I had to ask myself if I could understand a situation that was so outside my norm.

Clearly, I saw him.

Clearly, she knew about him.

Clearly, he was watching her, watching over her and loving her somehow.

Clearly, he was not threatening, not terrifying, not horrible. He was just always there.

I suspected he could feel my profound bewilderment and then instantly I could hear his thoughts.

"I do love her. Connie and I have been together forever and we're still there for each other. Death has not stopped that. Death does not stop love. She knows this; she knows me. It's been lonely for her, never being able to share our 'arrangement' with anyone else. Never being able to love me the way you love your husband. You know what I mean, don't you?"

Theo made the last statement with the intention of having me look at Connie with compassion, not confusion. All I could think about was how much I enjoyed the physical aspects of my relationship with my husband. Connie can never touch Theo, cannot kiss him, cannot hold him, or build a life with him . . . and Theo heard this and responded to me.

"No, she can't build a life with me like you have with your husband but our life is not for you to judge. If we are happy with our relationship, what difference does it make?"

"... who am I to judge my friend?"

Connie did not appear to me to be under Theo's spell. She was down to earth, logical, an exceptionally competent Officer, and she was my friend. So, I asked myself, as those awkward seconds ticked by between us: who am I to judge my friend?

"Please forgive me, Connie, I'm just a little surprised by this situation. It's also the very first time I have actually seen a ghost and had it validated. He is real. Wow. Do you communicate telepathically with Theo, like I'm doing?"

"Yes, well, I do both. I talk to him, but not often. Mostly we hear each other's thoughts. If I allowed myself to talk to him like you talk to Troy, well, you can imagine how crazy people would think me. So, I hear him, I feel him, I know him. It's a different life, you know? It's my life."

"Yes, Connie, it's your life. Your secret is safe with me. Frankly, you've been really helpful to me as we both shared what we were feeling in those old Nazi buildings. I can't tell anyone beyond Troy what I can psychically see and hear either. I guess the lives we are both living don't fit into anyone else's norm, do they?"

Epilogue

We never discussed Theo again. I had the impression that that psychic door was marked 'Private' and was now closed. While I could sense him with her many times, he never made his presence known to me visibly again. It was almost as if he wanted to allow Connie to have a spiritually aware companion with whom to share this secret.

I speculated that they both died in the 1940s but she returned to live a mortal life again, and he did not. He simply waited for her to be born, found her again and stayed with her. While there may be paranormal precedent for this, I believe it to be an exceedingly rare event.

One psychic event after the other happened to me while we were both stationed together in Naples, Italy. Connie was the one person who unfailingly helped me deal with each and every one. She was bright, intuitive, and extremely psychic.

Connie has continued to be my friend to this day. Her 4th dimension companion stayed with her through all of her duty stations. In fact, Theo saved her life while overseas in another country, warning her that she was suffering from carbon monoxide poisoning.

She never dated, and she never married a mortal man.

She was promoted to Navy Captain and had a dynamic naval career.

We each make choices regarding the lives we are going to live and who will live those lives with us. It was not for me to judge Connie's living arrangement; however, I knew that there was some very interesting karma attached to not fully living a mortal life with another person. There is karma attached to all that we do, all the choices that we make. Ghosts incur karma in the 4th dimension because they influence the lives of the living and Theo was definitely influencing Connie's life, consciously preventing her from having any kind of physical relationship with a living person. He also earned karma for not reincarnating and living a full mortal life himself. How all of that karma will play out over time is surely beyond my pay grade.

I would imagine that when Connie finally leaves this mortal life, that her afterlife reunion with Theo, may or may not actually happen. If she immediately crosses over, Theo will be quite alone again. Perhaps her crossing over will be the impetus for him to finally leave the 4th dimension, stop the karmic clock from ticking and cross over himself. Whatever happens to them both, will be absolutely fascinating.

I saw several more ghosts in Naples. However, it always felt as if someone or something was managing what I saw and felt, introducing me to new concepts and ideas. I was so grateful that I didn't see the millions of souls who have died in Italy over the centuries. Imagine wandering through Pompeii and Ercolano and seeing the dead from the Mt. Vesuvius eruption of 79 AD. That would have been horrifying. I would not want to live like that. I was allowed to see only what I needed to see to handle a paranormal situation. If you have psychic ability, you do not always get to understand why you see what you see, when you see it, sense, or feel it. I know there is karma attached to this process but it took me years to begin to understand it. Now I accept that I am shown what I need to do and I simply do that spiritual job at hand.

Ghost Stories from the Ghosts' Point of View Vol 3

A Hole in Time

Thousands of bloody battles defined the Civil War. Two thousand of those conflicts took place in Virginia. Everywhere you go in this state you have the potential to find some type of Civil War stack of time. Therefore, when my friends Don and Carla Dickerson called and asked for a remote view of their home and property in Newport News, Virginia, I was prepared for anything – or at least I thought I was.

Carla requested a remote view of their new house because she and Don had been having problems with dirt on their back stairs. She complained that no matter how much they cleaned the stairs to their second-floor bedrooms, overnight there would be mud, hard-caked mud on each step. There was also something on the walls as you walked up the stairs. It looked like someone had smeared something dark red. Carla cleaned up the mud every day. They never heard any noises, but there was always dirt there the next day.

I assured her that I would get back to her in a few days.

I was pretty sure this was simply a situation with a messy ghost and that assisting this soul would be no problem.

The Gingerbread House

Once I was able to locate her home in time and space, I found a new-looking Victorian two-story white house with the ornate 'gingerbread' style woodwork trim on all of the outside roof edges. This trim graced the eaves and added charm to this house. The house was a clean, crisp white and the rest of the trim was a soft gentle grey. A lovely wrap-around front porch, with red geranium plants gracing each front step, and a forest green set of rocking chairs created an inviting and welcoming feel. This was the type of porch that harkened back to times gone by when people actually sat in those rocking chairs and bid welcome to passing neighbors.

This style home reminded me of old plantations in the South where people rocked the evening away in the humid air. Their home was beautifully done. The yard was neatly kept and the Dickerson's would have been considered good neighbors in this quiet subdivision.

I 'stood' outside on the street and observed their home. The overall energy of their house felt new, clean, tidy, and ordered. These people obviously loved this house. As I began scanning their house by going through the front door, I immediately saw a long hallway with polished walnut-colored wood floors that led to the back of the house. Something about this hallway seemed to be beckoning me. I did not feel the need to scan any other room of that first floor.

I stood at the back screen door of the house and observed that there was a stairway to the right with white wood banisters that led to the second floor. There is a sense that on the surface, this house was physically clean, and well kept.

Occupying the Same Space in the Same Bent Stack of Time

I took a deep breath and sank into the energy of the house. Slowly, gently, I separated the energies of modern, 21st century time and allowed the other energies of the past to slip into my consciousness. It's like putting different stacks of time into slots in your mind so that you can sort out which energy is influencing the current era.

Patiently, as I was standing by that back stair I felt this tremendous pull to a different time, as if like Alice, I was being sucked into a hole in time, a portal to a different, very active time stack. Now I'm not merely separating stacks of time, I'm being sucked into what was a current stack of time in another time.

A Hole in Time

Once I know that I have shifted into a different historical time period, I feel my soul shudder as I take a deep breath and move up the second step as I climb that back stairway.

Instantly - I realize that there is no other way to describe it - a hole in time opens up to me. I can see the edges of my current time begin to blur into 1862. Once I am firmly on the third step, all vestiges of today are gone and I am squarely climbing the stairs of a farmhouse in an utterly different stack of time. The reason this is different from moving to a past stack of time is that I know that when you can slip into a past stack, that means that the current time has slipped away. A hole in time is different because it is actively operating on a daily basis and impacting the current time on a daily basis. The actions of that time are still ongoing, as if the present and the past are doorways that somehow eerily connect to each other.

Stepping up to the fourth step, I could now see fresh blood on the walls and clods of dirt on the stairs. A once proud farmhouse was now a shell of a structure. There is no family living in this farmhouse. It was long ago abandoned to the destruction of the War Between the States.

Staring out the window of the farmhouse, I can see and hear a Civil War battle – heavy casualties, smoke and acres of war dead, the colors of their blue and grey uniforms obliterated by blood, dirt, and mud. The name 'Antietam' comes to mind, among the bloodiest battles of the Civil War. 23,000 men died or were wounded that afternoon. But Antietam took place on the Miller farm in Sharpsburg, Maryland, not Newport News, Virginia. These two locations are not near each other, but hundreds of miles apart. I realize that I am no longer climbing the stairs in the Dickerson's house, but with the shifting of one step forward, I am climbing the steps of an abandoned farmhouse with a white front porch and a large second floor loft – in an entirely different location. I'm no longer in Virginia; I'm in Maryland.

Can time bend? Is that what has transpired here? Time, which does not necessarily flow in a direct line, can move in circles and bends, eddies, and pools.

This primitive place is a refuge of sorts. There is hay all over the floors to catch the blood of soldiers. Who put this hay here? Did someone anticipate that as the battle lines were drawn, that wounded men would use this house to struggle up to the loft to rest from battle before seeking out a field hospital? Some of them die in the loft. All of them are alive when they enter this loft.

However, as they climb the stairs to the loft, they are literally stepping through time and into the Dickerson's' 2nd floor bedroom in Virginia. Somehow there is a wrinkle, a distortion in time. As bleeding, wounded men, walk up the steps they pass through a time portal. There is even blood on the Dickerson's walls by the steps, the fresh blood of the wounded. It would appear that the caked mud and dirt on the stairs, and the blood that Carla complained about could be smudges of the blood from men wearing fatally soiled uniforms.

Somehow the transition is made on the stairs to the current time. By the time the soldiers enter what should be a hay filled loft, they are ghosts in the Dickerson's house. They are completely and totally confused because when they entered the farmhouse in 1862, they were not dead and when they get to the top of the stairs, they find they are now ghosts – but they do not know they are ghosts suspended in time. When they run down the stairs, they cannot go back to that other time – they are completely stuck. They are able to see around them a future time in an utterly different location. They are trapped in their confusion of time.

The men in this hay loft/second story bedroom are bloody Union and Confederate soldiers. At this point, none of them cares which side anyone is on in this confusion of time and space, the living and the dead, logic and the fantastic.

There is a very different kind of fear on their faces. There is the primordial chill of each of them realizing that they are all in a different time and space with no idea what they're supposed to do next. Some in the loft were not wounded at all and merely carried their comrades up to the loft to get them out of the battle. The able soldiers fully expected to return to the battle but found themselves stuck several hundred miles from where they started. They don't recognize their surroundings. This is a modern-day bedroom. There is no hay on the floor. The stairs they try to use as they think they can leave this place are modern and take them down into a future time. They quickly return to their comrades. Now they are all on the same side.

There is no way out, no way back and no explanation. They no longer hear the ruthless battles of the Civil War. They only hear the sounds of modern time and have no frame of reference. Nothing is familiar.

None of them speak to me. There are no names, only the grimy, bewildered faces of the eternally dead. There are dozens of them and they kept coming, they kept being displaced to another time and place where numbers do not matter.

Closing the Hole in Time

I have never closed a hole in time. It's one thing to encounter a stack of time, and to consciously move between one time and another, but it is an entirely different situation to face a hole in time and space.

I sought to separate out the concepts facing me. I was in one stack of time, a modern-day stack of time. As I climbed those back stairs, etherically, through my remote view, I realized instantly that I was in a loft during the Civil War based on the soldiers I could see. However, I was in a completely different location, in Sharpsburg, Maryland. It was as if these two locations were somehow connected through some common thread, which was, and still is a mystery to me. I could see the hayloft in Maryland as well as the guestroom of the Dickerson's house, full of ghosts. I could see what should have been there when the men climbed the stairs; and the men could see the current guestroom when they crossed time and space and ended up in the 21st century.

Was the homeowner one of the men who died at Antietam? Is he the connection? Did he die in that loft all those years ago? Is he the link between not just one location and the other, but one time and the other? We frequently reincarnate near where we died in a past life, or at least visit those places where we had a significant life. What if, in his case, he was the unwitting connection? I know in my heart that we will never have an answer to this question but for now, we have brought the issue to the surface and are dealing with it.

Einstein's theories state that all time exists at the same time. If this is true, what about location connection? Can time bend to accommodate this time connection? I believe that this has happened here.

Finally, I gave up trying to attach a logic trail to the situation and began to focus on closing this hole in time, for all time.

My first step was to request an angel to assist me to open a Divine doorway. Together, we opened a Light Bridge and facilitated the transition of hundreds of exhausted soldiers, to the Heaven World.

My next task was to correct this distortion in the time/space continuum – which I cannot do without help from the Heaven World. Sometimes it would be so helpful if this job came with a handbook for these uniquely bizarre situations. But there is no handbook. There are no guidelines other than the absolute dictates of Spiritual Law. So, recognizing my own limitations, I requested spiritual assistance. The Heaven World does realize the mundane boundaries of their mortal field agents and they readily provided a specialist to help rebalance the energy of the location.

The work begins and I feel as if I am an apprentice to a wonderful angel who is patiently walking me through the odd realities of the situation. Time and space are dependent on gravity to exist.

Time and space and gravity are required for the 3rd dimension to function, for us to have the physical time and the actual space to work through the karma of our lifetimes. We are often unaware of the pleasure we receive for the happy 'times' we get to enjoy. The sad 'times' are just as powerful and we have to have the 'time' to fully appreciate that experience. Gravity anchors us in time and space. It is the critical element.

Apparently, there was a distortion in the etheric Ley lines (or Earth Energy Lines, see Glossary explanation) on this specific piece of property. Either they were wrinkled, or there was a problem with the magnetic field or there was a time connection changed by these Ley lines. I was directed to realign all the etheric Ley lines on the property, and to loosen the energy grid on this property only. This then was supposed to enable me to search for the 'time gate' to find a way to close it. However, I was unable to do that or to even find the 'time gate.' What I did find was a further distortion in the field.

This situation is not unlike pulling a sweater thread and discovering that the more you pull it, the more it unravels. This was the case here. The more I began to work with these force fields, the more I realized that this situation was larger than I originally perceived. This forced me to request further Divine assistance, to smooth out all these additional distortions. Sometimes tasks are just beyond my capabilities, so I simply asked my Divine advisors to finish this job. I appreciated the opportunity for further experience, but at some point, I just needed them to fix it. I also provided additional healing for the property, including the house itself.

Epilogue

There is precedent for this concept. A wormhole is basically a space-time shortcut that connects two locations. This can take place in space and cover vast distances or exist on Earth. Using the theory of relativity, Albert Einstein and Nathan Rosen proposed that bridges (hence the concept of the Einstein/Rosen bridge) do exist between two locations. It is not seen very often, but it does exist.

The modern-day family never stepped through this wormhole themselves when they climbed the stairs, nor did they ever sense the hundreds of Civil War dead when they entered their back bedroom. The only hint that there was a problem, were the clumps of dirt on the stairs and the smeared darkened blood on the walls as they climbed the steps. They never heard a sound, sensed a ghost, or felt ill at ease in their house. The dirt was an irritation that they simply wanted fixed.

Once the dead were removed, the hole in time closed and the energy grid/Ley lines repaired there was never another instance of darkened blood on the walls or clumps of mud on the stairs.

Don and Carla were pleased: for them the job was done and now they had a clean house.

All the soldiers were blessedly released to the healing hope and restoration of the Heaven World.

The Earth was rebalanced and the hole in time closed.

It was the experience of a lifetime for me.

Echoes of the Inquisition

The sad part for me is that I never got to talk to her, never got to discuss what happened to her. I only know that the end result was beneficial. However, the pain that she endured will stay shrouded in her memories, forever shuttered from conscious recognition. She closed the emotional door, refusing to discuss it further. She moved on, hopefully to happiness.

Reluctantly, I respected her wishes.

The Classic Frantic Phone Call

"Who's calling you at 12:15 in the morning?" my husband demanded as I quickly answered the phone. I did not have time to answer him. When your phone rings in the middle of the night, it's never going to be a social call. It is always going to be something difficult.

"Hello?" I answered, half expecting to hear a relative on the other end.

"Tina, is that you? Can you hear me?"

"Yes, I hear you just fine. . . um, Marcus, is that you?" I thought I recognized the voice of one of my neighbor's sons on the phone. How odd, I remembered thinking, that he would call me at this time of night. I could swear his mom told me he was in Spain. Maybe I was wrong. Funny how many thoughts run fleetingly through your head as you fully awaken. People do not call you in the middle of the night without a specific reason, and it is seldom good news.

"Yes, it's me, Marcus, and I really need your help!"

"I thought that voice was yours. Is everything alright?" I queried.

"No, I'm desperate for you to help me and my sister Meghan. You know we came on this trip to Spain together. We were having a great time, but now we have a serious problem." His frantic voice made me feel as if one of them was in real danger.

"Ok, so you and Meghan are in Spain. What time is it there? I mean, it must be almost, what 8 in the morning?"

"Yes, it's almost half past 8 and I've tried, really hard, but I can't seem to help Meghan. She can't stop throwing up. She looks green; I mean she's really sick. You have to help us. I've tried to help her all night and nothing seems to work, so I know you do this remote viewing thing. Can you help us?"

His request was so desperate sounding but I hesitated.

"Son, did you call your Dad? Did he give you any ideas what to do? He's a physician for heaven's sake and he would seem to be your first line for advice."

"Oh, I did ask Dad, he said he could prescribe something but that will take a lot of time to resolve with a Spanish pharmacy and he suggested that I call you."

"Ok, glad to help, but I need to ask a few questions first. How long have you been in Madrid?"

"About five days. We've had a great time, but yesterday she got sick, all of a sudden."

"What did you eat that day? Did you each eat something different?" I always try a process of elimination first.

"No, that's what's so weird, we both ate exactly the same thing. We had, what I thought was a great day and now she's so sick."

I could hear how helpless he was feeling.

"Marcus, you know I'm going to do everything I can to help her. What are her symptoms?"

"She's vomiting and then she is having this diarrhea. I'm so worried that she is becoming dehydrated and she is too, but she doesn't want to go to a Spanish hospital. And it's weird, it's like she is crying at the same time. Her stomach hurts so much. She can't even keep water down. You have to hurry and help her."

"Marcus, you know I have to ask this, has Meghan given permission for me to work on her, to find out what happened to her and what's going on in her body?"

"Yes, I told her you would ask and yes, she has given permission for you to look at her. Please hurry. She looks so bad. I'm real worried."

"I'll begin work immediately. Call me back in about 4 hours. Hopefully, she should begin to feel much better before then."

The Perpetual Energy of Horror

Remote viewing is the act of projecting your energy through the ether, or 4th dimension and working on the etheric location or the etheric body of another person. There is no time or space or gravity in the ether. Distance is not a factor. The person or location can be across the galaxy or in the next room. [. . and this is the basis of String Theory. . .] Distance is irrelevant. In this case, even the hotel address was unnecessary. I simply followed my aka cord connection to Marcus to reach his sister.

Moving effortlessly through space and distance, I 'stood' in the hotel room and gazed at her body. I became a wisp of psychic substance barely enough to feel the energy her pain-wracked body was projecting. And when I did, what I felt broke my heart.

I see things that are with a person, whether it is a ghost, dark beings, or emotions. In her case, I saw that her body was encased in this dark shroud of sickening terror. Her panic was so great that without relief, I am not sure how she would come out of this paralyzing energy. I can see why it made her want to rid herself, from every orifice, of the energy that had invaded her body.

Before I could clean away this terrible darkness, I had to find what was generating this towering fear. Although her subconscious had seemingly completely shut down, I coaxed her inner self to help me to help her. It was at that point that I could see that she, the subconscious part of Meghan, was cowering in pain and terror.

I brought in angels to help me with this daunting situation. I was still trying to determine what was causing her to feel this panic, this poisoning feeling of destruction. The angels immediately brought light to this dark etheric area and began to mitigate the dread she was feeling. I needed her to tell me what happened to her. I was now convinced that her physical symptoms had absolutely nothing to do with food and everything to do with an event.

Emotional Haunting

I provided immediate healing to her body, an etheric anti-emetic to stop the vomiting, and enough life force for her body to have the resources to begin to heal itself. I also provided the energy of comfort and safety to her by allowing her subconscious to see the angel, to feel the relief from the crippling nausea and the sense of helplessness that diarrhea caused her to feel. I also provided assistance to immediately stop Meghan's abdominal pain.

Once Meghan's subconscious began to calm down, I asked her as gently as I could, to show me what event caused this terrible reaction. Slowly, hesitantly, she began to talk to me.

"I had reservations about coming to Spain, you know? But I wasn't sure why. It was illogical to not want to come on a trip with my brother but I had this vague sense of unease. I couldn't put it into words. I didn't tell anyone about it, I just put on a happy face and got on the plane. Papa bought the tickets for both of us as a special gift. I didn't want to disappoint him by not going on the trip, but as the time got closer, I kept feeling uneasy. It wasn't logical. Nothing seemed logical.

"At first, we had a great time, went to the Prado, saw the art there, had Paella, saw the Flamenco dancing, and did the usual sight-seeing. I was okay, not great, but okay until this last tour."

"Meghan, you're doing really well. Remember that this angel is standing here. You're safe. Nothing can happen to you now."

"I – I know, but it was so real, you know? Like it wasn't 2002, but 1582 or something. Marcus suggested that we wander around this plaza in this cool area of Madrid and explore these amazing buildings. We toured several rooms. But the closer we got to certain rooms, the worse I felt. It was like my anxiety was rocketing to the surface. I wanted to scream, to run out, to escape, but I said nothing. How do I explain this to my brother?

"But I felt it happen, that creeping sense of fear begin to take me over, gag me inside just like they gagged me during that time. I died in one of those rooms, after I was raped repeatedly by these supposedly pious men. It was during the Inquisition. I don't know what I did to be punished so . . . They tied my hands and feet. They were so cruel. I think I died there, but I can't be sure. I remember the torture though. It – it was horrible.

"There were paintings in this building of people being tortured. I knew exactly what some of them were feeling. It was as if 'now' fell away and I was back in that room, having horrible things done to me, and I felt that it had never ended. I guess I was tortured and then maybe blacked out? I was there. It was real. I felt the fear. I saw myself being raped. I could see their faces again and again. It was like some video that keeps replaying. Maybe for a moment I couldn't tell what was real.

"All the emotions of those horrible minutes came back, drowning me again and again in that pain and horror. We weren't in that place long, but it was clearly long enough for me to be yanked back to that time, as if there were no time, as if it was happening right then. When Marcus tapped me on the shoulder to leave, I jumped. I came back to the 21st century feeling defeated. This is so real, so painful, so terrifying. I want to scream and cry even now but I can't.

"Oh, you asked me when the vomiting started. Well, we went to dinner but I couldn't eat much. I felt this huge bubble-like feeling welling up inside of me. I told him we had to leave because I wasn't feeling well. I threw up on the street as we left the restaurant. We got back to the hotel and I clung to the toilet and just kept vomiting again and again. Pretty soon, even my bowels let go. It was horrible. Poor Marcus. He had no idea what to do with me or how to help me."

"Are you beginning to feel better?" I felt that just telling someone what happened, was, in and of itself healing. I was not sure she consciously had any idea what happened to her.

"Yes, but why was this so real?"

"Certain past lives haunt us because they are so powerful, so influential in how they change us for lifetimes to come. For your subconscious, time does not exist, only the energies that are manifest at the moment. The energy of the Inquisition was still in the walls, the floors, the furniture, the paintings, everywhere. You were not only bombarded by your experience, but also by the energies of all the others who were tortured in that building, or who were burned at the stake in that plaza. You don't even have to be psychic to feel it.

"Are you feeling better? Do you understand that that time is over? You're safe now. You don't even live in Spain, and you are leaving in a day or so. You will return to a safe place in the States."

"Yes, I know that's true. It - it was so real . . . Will I remember this conversation when I wake up?"

"I doubt it. I will tell Marcus what happened, that you don't have any physical illness. He'll ask you if you want to know when you awaken. If you don't want him to tell you, that will be fine. You can heal now."

"Can I keep the angel with me the rest of the trip?

"Of course, you can. Rest now."

Rescuing the Tortured

I proceeded to provide healing to her entire body, making sure that she would be able to function within a couple of hours. I tried to mitigate the intense level of fatigue she would naturally feel after that much retching and evacuation of her body. Her acute level of terror also heightened her fatigue. Fear is exhausting. There was also a part of her that was grieving that this even happened to her, that she had to see that happening to her body.

I also worked to dilute the high level of adrenaline she had pumping through her system. An adrenaline overdose can also make you vomit. The body can only handle so much at a time, enough to get you to a safe place, but if you don't see yourself escaping, then that adrenaline just keeps pumping and making you sicker and sicker.

What made this situation so severely painful was that her subconscious did not merely remember the event, her subconscious could see it happening to her during that time and at the same time, could feel the torture as if it were happening in real time, as if the centuries fell away and she was there again.

No one rescued her then. Her poor subconscious became paralyzed with the terror that this could happen to her again and that again, no one would be there to save her. The challenge in this situation is that you can know logically that you are in another life, that you are in 'modern' times, but to your subconscious, you are still a tortured prisoner and there is no escape.

Relief

True to his word, Marcus called me back four hours later. It took me almost that long to help Meghan because the damage from the toxic load of paralyzing memories was so great.

"Hey, Tina, it's me, Marcus."

"Hi, so glad you called back on time. How's Meghan now? She's going to be sore all over from the endless retching she did, but she should be turning the corner now."

"She has stopped vomiting, thank God! The diarrhea has also ceased and she is sleeping now, looking almost peaceful. I figure she'll be pretty much out most of the day. I don't think we need to go to the pharmacy. Dad said that if you couldn't stop her vomiting and diarrhea that he would prescribe something and help me navigate the Spanish pharmacy down the street. I checked it out just in case."

"That's great that she has physically calmed down. Sleep is what she needs. I'm so relieved. Sometimes it can take a bit of time to move healing from the etheric to the physical, but in this case, it seemed to happen pretty quickly. Be sure to keep her hydrated, even in her sleepy state."

"I will. I'm dying to know, what did you find? Can you tell me?"

"Did you guys visit any type of Inquisition Museum yesterday?"

"Um, let me see, I know we toured all around and then we went into this one building that had all kinds of rooms and I believe on one of the plaques there was something about how the Inquisition conducted interrogations in some of the rooms. Why do you ask?"

"Did you happen to notice if Meghan had any reaction to any of the rooms?"

"Yeah, now that you mention it, one of the last ones, well, I guess it was the last room we were in, she seemed to feel uncomfortable and said she wanted to leave. Why?"

"Because that seems to be the room that triggered her physical reaction. I believe that she had a horrific experience in that room. I believe she was tortured by the Inquisition in a previous life and that terrible memory brought back all of her physical pain from that moment in time. Even though you can logically say that it shouldn't affect her because she is living in modern times, the truth is that the energy of that room and her just being there was so toxic that she felt it and I'm guessing it triggered her memory. That sickening memory caused her all of this vomiting and other stuff."

"Wow, that's unreal! Can I tell her this? Do you think she knows that this is what happened to her?"

"No, I don't think she has any idea. I'm also hazarding a guess that she may not want to know what caused it."

"Should I ask her to talk to you about it? Can I tell her what you told me?"

"No, actually, you can't tell her. She has to want to know the cause and because it was so physically painful, don't be surprised if she never calls me and never wants to know. Her pain has stopped. That's all that may matter to her. It's also possible that this event happened to her at this same age. The synchronicity is a little too chilling. Wait and see what she says to you. If she says nothing, let it be. There's no compassionate place to go with this."

"No problem, I get it. I'll just be here for her and then maybe we'll go to Seville or Barcelona on the train and see something outside Madrid. You know, take her mind off of this experience."

"Sounds like a good plan. You did a good job, helping your sister. Your dad will be proud of you."

"Thanks, Tina."

Epilogue

Meghan was able to move about later that day and they did tour other cities in Spain. And just as I suspected, she never called me. Marcus told me that when he offered to tell her what I found, she held up her hand and said she didn't care. She didn't want to know. The retching had stopped and that was all that mattered to her.

We come into mortal life for experiences and some of them are horrendous. Because death by torture is so traumatic, the soul has no time to process it. This leaves the soul in a place of an extremely low frequency, which lands them in the darkest places of the 4th dimension. The soul then reincarnates from this dark place and tries to work through the previous life trauma while living through their life in the current life. But sometimes, there is a type of past life 'break-through' that plunges that soul into the darkness of the past with no way to understand the mental and physical emotions that are flooding them.

Meghan may have felt so much better after those toxic emotions were released from her subconscious whether or not she knew it. I seriously doubt that she will ever return to Spain.

All of our experiences accompany us life after life, stuck to us as part of our soul experience and seldom if ever cleared. If a soul is experiencing severe emotional and physical reactions, it is very likely that he or she reincarnated from the 4th dimension. The only way a soul can clear the experience fully is to cross over into the Heaven World at death. Then the great Beings who help us all there can facilitate processing the life just lived. Then when this soul reincarnates, he or she is not burdened by the past, but is enlightened by the experiences of that previous time. This is why it is critically important that all souls be assisted in crossing over into the Heaven World.

Ghost Stories from the Ghosts' Point of View Vol 3

A Rainy Night of Tears

It was January 1988, and I was a Commander in the US Navy, stationed in Virginia Beach, VA. I had a rather unusual job. I was the Assistant Chief of Staff for Force Physical Security, Anti-Terrorism and Law Enforcement for Commander Submarine Force, US Atlantic Fleet. My job was to protect 86 Submarines, 9 Submarine Tenders (the ships that repair submarines), 3 Submarine Rescue Ships and 3 Submarine Bases from terrorist attack: well over $100 billion dollars in Defense Department assets. This includes safeguarding the large number of nuclear weapons and other armament associated with each submarine. Needless to say, it was among the most challenging jobs of my life. I traveled all over the world, relentless in pursuing every possible device and idea to protect the fleet. I was eventually able to develop enough procedures and devices to protect all of these assets, to the point that all of them are still used by the fleet to this day.

I was also a Navy wife, as well as a mom to our two young children. My husband was the captain of a Submarine Rescue Vessel, USS Kittiwake, ASR 13, one of the many ships I was charged to protect. Life was crazy busy for all of us.

I was so preoccupied with the dynamics of my life and was flying so constantly (I was gone a good two weeks or more a month) that perhaps that is why I was completely unprepared when it hit me.

The truth is, there is no way you can adequately prepare for this – this event, this moment. It 'smacks' you. It can hit you at any time, day, or night. It's never convenient and it is among the loneliest feelings any human being can experience. I knew I was somewhat intuitive, but I had a staggering responsibility to protect our submarine fleet and frankly, anything psychic was seldom on my mind.

The Seven-Minute Stop Light

Heading home from my office one bitter cold and rainy January night, I was thinking about the trip to Sandia National Labs in New Mexico I was scheduled to make the following morning. Trying to get last minute things done, including reading all the latest terrorist threat reports, meant I left the office later than usual. You always have to steel yourself against imagining the horrors of what any terrorist could do to the fleet you are dedicated to protecting. It can be daunting and distracting.

Focus, I told myself.

Focus on doing your job because thousands of lives, both military and civilian, depend on just how well you do your job every day.

Focus on keeping nuclear assets safe, every single day. I sighed.

It was pouring rain. I was tired, thinking about my trip the next day. My mind wandered to what I would pack for New Mexico, and what would be going on with my children. My husband was at sea.

Almost home, I told myself as I stopped at the stoplight on Diamond Springs road. That is a seven-minute stoplight. It's so long that I timed it once.

Little did I know as I watched the rain pound my windshield, that I was about to have an extraordinary experience, one that haunts me to this day: one that as long as I live, I will never be able to release.

I came to a stop at that stoplight and then the very next thing I remember was feeling like I had been hit with a tidal wave of gut-wrenching, staggeringly horrific grief. I was literally slammed by an energy I could not identify. It was so powerful that I struggled not to throw up in my car. I physically felt something I can only describe as an energy wave hit me.

A Rainy Night of Tears

That seven-minute stoplight changed to green, but I could not move. Someone behind me started honking at me to go. I could barely see through my tears and the pounding rain. I moved slowly through the intersection and found a place to pull over. Then I began the most profound, heart-breaking sobbing I had ever experienced in my life. I cried so hard I could barely breathe. I gripped the steering wheel tightly as if somehow, I needed to be anchored in time and space. Something terrible had happened and I was praying it was not my husband, children, or family. I had no idea what it was for what seemed like a long time, but I believe it was only a few minutes.

As I continued pouring out my grief, I closed my eyes. Suddenly, I could see it: burning wreckage, smoke, and carnage. I could smell burning electrical insulation, and smoke, charred thatch, and unidentified objects. I could sense people screaming but there was no sound. Ever intensifying waves of revulsion swept me.

My mind's eye showed me a man holding on to a shredded briefcase. He had on a tattered brown suit and was covered in blood. He was standing in what looked to me to be the destroyed remains of some type of thatched house.

Nothing made any sense. I continued to concentrate, trying to understand this bizarre scene.

There were smoldering fires everywhere. The man looked like he was standing in hell. I could smell the smoldering ruins and burning flesh.

"You've got to help us!" He demanded. "Do it now! We need help! Can't you see what's happened to us? Don't you understand what happened here? HELP US ALL!"

He screamed this at me as if he thought I was somehow in charge of making sense out of his situation.

"Don't you see the little girl in the row ahead of me?"

"I'm so sorry, but I can't see that row. There - there isn't any row. All I see is you in shredded clothes and what looks like wreckage all around you."

I tried to wrap my brain around the fact that I am attempting to explain this to a man I can only see in my mind. I am having a conversation with – a – a dead man. I came to that realization with a sudden chill that brought on more throat-choking sobs.

"You've got to see her," he insisted, "she was in the seat ahead of me, a child about five years old, in a red dress. Help her. She shouldn't have died this way. Help all of us!"

"Oh my God, sir," I tell him through unrelenting sobbing, "I – I don't - - I don't know how to help her, or you or any of you. I can just barely see the outlines of other people."

"Look, can't you see the wreckage of the gigantic 747? What's wrong with you? You're the one who's supposed to help us. Why else would I be talking to you?"

A Rainy Night of Tears

I think at this point part of me went into a type of shock. Why was I seeing this? What did he mean I was supposed to help him? "You're the one who's supposed to help us." Oh my God, what does that mean? What if I cannot help them? How can I fail at something I do not know I can do?

"Help us!" he kept screaming. "Help us find our way home. Help us understand what happened to us! Where are we? Why didn't the plane land? Where is the plane? Did we crash? Why are all of these people just wandering around? There isn't anyone but you to help us! Please help us!!!"

"I'm so sorry. I'm so terribly sorry, sir, to all of you, I have no idea how to help you." I voiced this through more griping sobs.

"But you have to. We weren't supposed to die this way. Our families will miss us. We never got to say good-bye to them. We miss them already. I'm so confused. All we can see is you and each other. Is this what death is like? Why isn't anyone helping us? Why can't you help us?"

"I can't help you because I don't know how to help you. I'm so sorry. I'm so sorry. I feel - feel so bad. I feel your grief. I feel all of your grief to the very core of my being. I'm - I'm so sorry. I want to help you with all my heart, but I just- I just have no idea how to do this or whatever it is you think I'm supposed to do. I don't understand how you can see me or how I

171

can see you or how any of this works. Dear God help me, I wish I understood."

That Utterly Inadequate Feeling

I had no idea how to help him but I knew with that deep, dull, sickening sense of unrelenting dread, that I was seeing all the ghosts of this plane crash. At this point in time, I could not fathom how to help him and all of the passengers and crew of that crashed airplane cross over into the light. But none of them could see any light. I did not know how to make this happen for them. All they could see were what must have seemed like the fires of hell and for some reason, they could see me. I felt such guilt that I could not help them. Threading my way home through the flooding tears and the rain, I was overcome with the grief and shock of scores of dead passengers and I did not even think of using the 23rd Psalm. However, I got the impression that he believed that I had some elevated ability to help them way beyond saying the 23rd Psalm.

Once home, I tried to explain to my mother [who managed our children at the time] what had just happened to me. I asked her what plane crashed today. She said none had been reported, certainly not a 747 jumbo jet. That would have been news. It was then I realized that this emotional event must be some kind of premonition. I tried to explain to her that I was having a premonition.

Even though she knew I had some measure of psychic ability, she had no idea how to help me, nor did she understand the concept of a premonition – if that was in fact, what this was. Since my husband was at sea, there was no one to turn to: I was utterly alone with the most devastating emotions I have ever experienced. I cried wrenching, grief filled tears for the rest of the evening and into the night. How do you process the grief of hundreds of people all at once? I could not tell if I was grieving them or I was experiencing their grief at their own deaths. Because as I did eventually learn how to help the dead, I learned that the dead grieve their own death, their method of death and those they leave behind.

I could not get on my flight the next day. I cancelled it. I knew I would have a hard time explaining to my boss why I had to cancel my flight, so I told him that I wasn't feeling well – which was true. He graciously gave me the day off.

I spent the next day in bed trying to make sense of the event, breathlessly watching the news. Surely that plane crash would happen any moment, I thought as I desperately waited for validation all the while battling the dread of grief for what it would mean if validation came. But it did not come. No planes crashed that day, or the next. The heaviness of the grief of those passengers was still with me. This was real, this wrenching pain, this towering sadness was real.

Then as I was coming to terms with this terrible plane crash, I realized that this surely had to be the premonition from hell because no 747 jet went down that day, or the next, or the next. I surmised that probably a 747 jet is going to crash into some houses with thatched types of roofs. Hundreds of people are going to die. Probably there will be a bomb on the plane.

Somehow, I knew this with a nauseating, sickening certainty based on the condition of the wreckage I could see. Could it be that what I saw was a premonition of an event to come in a future farther out than I could imagine? Next week? Next year?

Those Heartbreaking, Unsettling Questions

In the days that followed, in those occasional quiet moments when I was driving to or from work, I kept churning the unanswerable thoughts and questions over and over in my mind.

These people had no idea that they were going to die on that flight.

They would have had no idea what hit them and that was why they were coming to someone like me for help.

How did they even find me?

'Someone like me.' What does that mean?

For God's sake, I kept asking myself, why did they come to me?

Surely there are much better, more competent psychics than I am. Surely helping them was someone else's job. Surely . . .

Oh my God, I don't understand. What is happening here?

'You're the one who's supposed to help us.' That statement haunted me because when that man said that to me, I believed he was dead. If you are dead, what is the mechanism that enables you to connect to a living person, a person you don't know, have never met and who has no idea how to help you.

What did all this mean?

But none of these people were dead – yet.

How can I feel people who are going to die?

How could a dead person from the future contact me?

What did they think I was going to do to help them?

What did they think I was going to do to help them when they haven't died yet?

I had had a premonition; of this, I was sure.

What was I supposed to do with this information?

Do I tell someone about this?

Who do I tell?

I know they'll (whoever 'they' could be) think I'm crazy.

'What flight is it?' they'll ask me.

What day of the year will this happen?

Which year?

Over what country will plane wreckage and bodies fall out of the sky?

What airline will have this catastrophe befall them?

What leg of which flight?

How can I warn anyone if I have only the tiniest handful of questionable impressions?

Not being able to help in any way but being given this fragmented picture was torture. How can I help if I have no idea how to apply the information? Why was I shown this?

Even saying the 23rd Psalm was of no use here because none of these people were dead yet. You cannot cross over a living person.

Overwrought, in a confusing turmoil of grief and guilt I wondered: was I supposed to know what to do? Had I failed these people? Or would I fail them in the future when this plane comes down? For I knew with a sickening sense of unrelenting dread, that this plane was going to explode at some point in the future.

And then there was the worst question of all: would I, or someone I love, be on that flight?

Finally, Horribly, I Know

It took me several days to begin to feel normal again. The scene haunted me for months. I was still flying all over the world, but with an uneasiness that never left me.

As my time in Norfolk ended, I looked with a sense of satisfaction at the number of devices and procedures that had been successfully put in

A Rainy Night of Tears

place to protect the Atlantic Submarine Fleet. I received a Meritorious Service Medal for my work there. It was time for my next assignment.

Finally, with our time in Virginia over, we were transferred to sunny, cheerful, San Diego, California.

By November of 1988, I had taken over as the Executive Officer for the Fleet Ballistic Missile Submarine Training Center at the Point Loma Submarine Base, in San Diego. My husband was the Executive Officer of USS McKee (AS-41), a Submarine Tender.

The busyness of moving our family across country had been a huge distraction. Getting settled in a new job was all consuming, and I allowed that haunting premonition to slip into the recesses of my mind, but it never left my heart as the months passed.

On December 21st, 1988, I was driving home from the office and I heard on the radio that a 747, PANAM flight 103 blew up 31,000 feet over Lockerbie, Scotland. It exploded a mere 38 minutes after leaving London. Two hundred fifty-nine people and 11 people on the ground were instantly killed.

Then I knew: that explosion was my January premonition. And I knew it with a certainty that went to the core of my being. I could see those souls all over again walking through the wreckage and destroyed homes in the green fields of Scotland. This time, however, I did not feel their grief. I felt that dull sadness that lingers around your heart. I said prayers for them. I asked God to love and keep them and to give them the help I could not give them that day.

When I got home, my mother, who moved to San Diego with us, began to tell me what she had heard about that terrible crash. Validation had arrived, I told myself sadly. 270 people died today. This was not an accident; there was no mechanical failure, no pilot error. With a detached, sick feeling, I mechanically explained to her that there was a bomb in the luggage, and that terrorists bombed this plane. My mother could not figure out how I knew for sure what caused the plane to crash. Reminding her of that chilling day in January when I saw the victims of the crash in a horrifying premonition caused her to understand a bit more. I tried to get her to understand that I inherently knew why it crashed: the event was so profound that it must have already existed in the future, in time and space. Knowing that a big jet would come down this way and having no way to warn anyone rushed a new level of grief into my heart. Without concrete dates, times and flight numbers, the information I had, was just a wisp of the future shared with me in a moment. Sometimes you're not going to be able to do anything about what you are forced to see will happen in the future.

Yes, It Smacks You

It has been over thirty years since PANAM 103 blew up. In that time, I have learned that people who will die in the future can come to a psychic and ask for help with their transition prior to their death. It happens on a subconscious level, perhaps on a spiritual level. I do not pretend to know how this works.

This psychic feeling of premonition can strike anyone at any time or place, although until 2012, I had never heard of anyone else having quite this experience, but there is always a first time.

My friend Sandra was returning home from a trip to Michigan in August of 2012. When I saw her number on my phone, I presumed that she was calling to chat about her trip. But the woman's voice on the other end of the phone was someone I barely recognized.

"Hi Sandra, have a few minutes between flights?"

"Oh my God, Tina, you have to. . ." gasping for breath, "you have to help me! I'm so dizzy, and I can see and feel that I'm surrounded by thousands of dead passengers from planes that have crashed over the decades and planes that will crash in the future. It's overwhelming! It's like an electric shock racing through my body. Help me, I can't focus or function!"

"Absolutely! Stand by."

I instantly dispatched an entire team of Angels of Transition to her location and directed them to move on the souls of the dead and to create a safe, spiritual space for what I have come to term: 'the pre-dead', those people who will die in the future. I knew they were there because I could feel them. Not all ghosts are already dead. Then I stopped the physical and emotional onslaughts that she was feeling; now she could participate in the process and still feel sane.

"Sandra, I completely understand. Are you feeling any better? Can you tell me what happened and oh, goodness, when does your plane leave?"

She took a deep breath and gathered herself together.

"I've -- I've stopped shaking and I'm not dizzy anymore. Thanks. I'm in the Denver airport waiting for my Southwest flight to San Diego, and I was typing on my iPad when I felt this electric shock hit my back. I thought that was weird and I wondered if there was a short in the electrical outlets on the floor, but there were no outlets that I could see. I looked behind me, but nothing was there.

'Then I felt it again, but it was different. This time I felt a huge electric shock go down my back, and with it, this wave of intense panic and fear. And then it got worse and worse. It was like something smacked me.

"I then felt like my back was breaking in two places. Tina, it felt so real, so staggering, crushing. I began sweating and shaking like crazy trying to figure out what was going on. I almost don't know how to describe it. I looked around and I was not in my 3rd dimensional world. Suddenly I could see hundreds of people from all of these downed planes, United, American

Airlines, Delta and foreign airlines surrounding me. Why was I seeing this? Was it a premonition? This gnawing sense of panic engulfed me. Between seeing these dead people and scanning for my Southwest flight, I was wracked by indecision: should I board or not? Any minute now I just know they're going to start boarding. Tina, I don't know if I can get on that plane!"

"Check the board again. When does your flight leave? Do you have time to tell me a bit more? I can see that the angels have removed them all now. Keep going you have to get this out."

"Thankfully, my flight has been delayed for about 20 minutes. I can talk to you; I'm still really shaky though. It was almost beyond description. At first, you know, I didn't see any people, just tons of wreckage, and it was wreckage from many different plane crashes. Then I got so dizzy. The next thing I knew, I was free falling out of the sky! I was having the sensation of free falling, but I could see my feet on the ground. How can this be real?"

I sighed.

"It can be very real, Sandra, and indescribable. I'm glad I can help you before you board the plane. You'll be alright but go ahead and describe what you were feeling."

She took a deep breath before continuing.

"This was all happening so fast that I couldn't figure out my reality. I slipped over to a more private waiting area, but I barely made it there. I was sweating and shaking so much I could hardly hold onto my things. As I was walking, I felt like I was continuing to free-fall and was sinking beneath the floor. I could see my feet on the floor, but I was free falling. Then, I felt like every fiber in my being was being crushed because the free falling had stopped. My body felt completely destroyed. The pain . . . Tina, it was unbelievable. I wanted to move them on, but I couldn't think straight or function, the pain was so intense. And the fear: I now know what paralyzing fear feels like.

"I feel so alone with this. Their grief, oh my God, their grief, and their agony! I could see hundreds of people with horrific damage to their body; they were so confused. The people who died in those crashes, don't know what happened to them or what to do. I think some of them are from plane crashes that haven't happened yet. They're all in so much pain, the same pain I was feeling."

"Sandra, did you have any conversations with any of them? Did they give you any specifics?"

"I have little recollection of my conversations with them. All I know is that somehow these plane crash people are from the past and the future. I have no idea how that works.

"I have to board now but my subconscious self is screaming 'don't get on that plane' while my higher self is saying that 'it will be all right . . .' It's really hard, you know. Bet I'm the very last one to board the plane. I don't think I will ever look at flying the same way again. Tina, thanks. Who else could I talk to about this and get help? I'm just grateful you were there. I'll call you when I get back."

Epilogue: The Nature of Premonitions

It is possible that there are two kinds of premonitions, the kind you can do something about, and the kind that you can do nothing to prevent.

Over time, as I continued to analyze my PANAM 103 premonition, it became clear to me why I was shown that particular plane crash. Perhaps because I was in resonance with some element of terrorism, although my job was to prevent a terrorist act from harming our submarine fleet, I was the quickest link before and after the plane blew up. I would care about them because it was my job to care about people, to keep them safe from terrorist harm. Or maybe it was because at some point in the future, I would be assisting thousands of ghosts to cross over into the Heaven World.

Once the premonition had happened, I asked myself why I had not questioned that man about which flight he was on, which leg, what day this happened and what country. And yet I knew that answer: in that moment when I was slammed with the emotion of the event, I believed it had already happened and it never occurred to me to question him on those details.

Still, I tortured myself with the nagging cruelties of "what if and if only."

What if I had asked more questions?

If only I had overcome my profound grief and had more presence of mind, could I have prevented that crash?

Did I fail all those people? I have long pondered this question in those private moments of anguish that any person would feel who had foreseen tragedy and could not stop it.

But this was not mine to prevent. Some things are going to happen, and no one can stop them. Throughout history, individuals have been shown tragic future events, events so tremendous that the power of their occurrence echoes forward and backward in the slipstream of time. Presidents Abraham Lincoln and John F. Kennedy were both warned that their deaths were imminent and that they should be careful. President Kennedy was specifically warned not to go to Dallas, Texas in November 1963. The tremendous shattering effect of their deaths could be felt even before the assassinations took place.

My premonition experience in 1988 fueled an intense longing to find a way to help the dead, even in the future. Working with Sandra in 2012 showed me how valuable it is to be able to help those who have just perished as well as those who will die in a future event.

Maybe that was the point of Sandra's experience in the Denver airport, with the dead passengers and those who will be dying in the future. If this happens to anyone else, I would quickly advise bringing in teams of angels. Assign an angel with specific directions to immediately accompany any soul to the Heaven World when death comes in that horrific instant. Play the video of The Crossing Over Prayer if you are too overcome to speak. Once I learned how to help the dead cross over into the Heaven world, I made sure that all of those souls from the crash of PANAM 103 were blessedly crossed over.

Now I will know with peace in my heart, that when a businessman in a shredded brown suit begs me to help him, and the little girl in the red dress, I will know how to help them, and all those passengers find their way home to the light of the Heaven World when death does eventually come.

A Soldier's Heart

"Hi Tina! I know you've visited my little house in the hills above La Jolla Cove and it occurred to me that maybe I should have you look at it, you know, to make sure that there's no one there. When you were here a while ago to Feng Shui it, did you feel anything?"

I thought back to that Feng Shui consultation some months previously. Her house was a very sunny house: a two-bedroom, one bath, living room, dining room and a small kitchen. The back yard is small with a grassy fenced in area, colorful outdoor table, and umbrella. Not a great deal to care for but enough to enjoy the sea breezes that drift up from the cove. It has a garage with windows around two thirds of the structure.

"No, Helen, I didn't feel anything. But remember, that doesn't mean that there couldn't be something or someone there through stacks of time. I just didn't sense anything that was having a deliberate, overt effect on your house. I only remembered thinking that it was a charming place. Are you feeling anything now?"

"No, not specifically. It feels great when I'm here, a bright, happy house. I don't think there's anyone here, and it doesn't feel to me like anything bad happened here. But I want you to check it out to make sure that there aren't any lingering ghosts. This house was built in the late 1940s and it has a lot of sweet elements, you know hard wood floors, a sunroom of sorts for plants, arched doorways, and an efficient kitchen. I just love it and again, I don't sense anything but then, I didn't sense anything in my house in Pasadena either and you found four ghosts in that one, so I'm not taking any chances. Can you please take a look and let me know what you find – or hopefully – don't find?"

"Of course, I'd be happy to look around."

The Jewel

There is a reason that some of the wealthiest people in the world live in La Jolla, California. It's stunning. The ocean views, the small town/village feel make this a jewel of Southern California. Torrey Pines line the streets, graceful with their outstretched branches enveloping the scenes give an almost European feel to the small town of La Jolla.

Prospect Street winds you into the downtown village; perfect for walking around. Wonderful restaurants that serve some of the most unique and original farm to table food in the world offer a delicious range from authentic Mexican to Thai, Italian and of course the fresh California cuisine. Many overlook La Jolla Bay with its view of seals, kayakers, and surfers. The shops, some of which have been here for decades are filled with stunning art, world-class photography, designer clothes and decorator items.

La Jolla has been a playground for many who love living here as well as those who only come to visit. The cool ocean breezes keep this inviting community at a perfect temperature most of the time. Multi-million-dollar estates sit side by side with 1920s vacation cottages that neatly parallel the coastline. The fragrant jasmine and sweet ocean air fill the La Jolla hills with a peaceful nostalgia for times gone by or maybe it is just that time does not pass as quickly here as much as other areas. The homes have often stayed 'in the family' for generations. Property is pricy for that reason, in addition to its enviable location.

I have walked La Jolla village many times, enjoying these attractive, tree-lined streets for the years I lived in San Diego. But even lovely areas carefully guard their secrets. Property changes hands and history is often buried under new construction. Memories of times gone by are often lost in the salty sea breezes.

Such a Tiny Cottage

A Soldier's Heart

It took me quite a while to sift through the stacks of time for this neighborhood. At first, all I could see was Helen's pretty house set way back from the sea, up a hill far from the cliffs. It felt clean and peaceful, but first looks can be deceiving. Then, Helen's house left my view.

I finally found her, the lone ghost from another time and place. She was not in Helen's house; she was in another house that was perched high on the bluff overlooking the sea. In this stack of time there were no other houses around this very simple white clapboard house with black shutters. It was a very traditional almost East Coast style summer cottage. It had one bedroom, a tiny bath, a small, functional kitchen, and a living/dining room combination with only a fireplace for heat. It also had a many windowed, one-car garage (very much like what Helen has now) about 100 feet away from the main house on a lower level. It took many steps to reach the garage. This seems unusual now, but then things were different in the 1920s. This was the era I was sensing, based on the visual cues plus that indefinable sense of time.

I had the feeling that someone owned several acres here and had built this little summer cottage high above the churning sea. It was set way back from the jagged cliffs, but the wind would still have been stiff on certain days, ruthlessly stealing away sound, and perhaps some memories that are better left unremembered.

This was not Helen's house. Her house hadn't been built yet. This was another dwelling that pre-dated Helen's place but was subtly influencing the surrounding area. All predecessor energy influences us, even if we have no idea that it is happening. We are also attracted to certain predecessor energies, which is why we are drawn to some properties more than others. We are totally unaware that we are in resonance with some aspect of that energy from another time.

Beaded Satin and Velvet

Once I had established that this was the stack of time having even albeit a faint influence on my client, I focused here. I entered the house through the white wooden front door and searched the few plain and tidy spaces that were there. I found her standing in front of a floor length mirror admiring the sweet, pretty, youthful image reflecting back at her. She was wearing a crepe, cream-colored, beaded evening dress that hung in sensuous, body-hugging folds down past her knees. It had a sculpted collar with emerald bugle beads and a bright blue sash was tied around her narrow waist. But it was the dress that she was holding that was the key to her story. I gingerly approached her as she stood swaying back and forth with her dress.

"Excuse me, I hope you don't mind if I admire how lovely you look in this dress. Are you trying to decide which dress to wear? Are you going somewhere?"

I hoped that by engaging her in a discussion and focusing on her dress, that I could get her to tell me why the back of her head was smashed in and her cream dress was stained red with her blood as it eternally dripped down her back.

"Oh yes, Tom, my husband, and I are going to a dance in the village tonight. I love to dance and wear pretty clothes. I'm so excited to feel Tom hold me in his arms again. It's been so long. I waited for him every day. Every minute that we're together is a sweet pleasure for both of us. I love him so much! But I can't quite decide between this buttermilk cream, beaded dress I'm wearing, and this dusky, blue velvet one. I loved the swishy triangles with the pretty sequins on it. Both hug my body so elegantly and move with me as we dance. This will be such a wonderful evening. I want to show Tom my dress but I . . . I . . . don't want to go outside."

"What does Tom call you?" I decided to keep focusing on Tom and come back to the question of what lay outside. She would have blushed when I asked her this question if she had had any blood left in her body. She seemed shy about answering me. She slowly swayed back and forth holding the dress in front of her, softly humming to herself as a permanent distraction. She finally answered me in a dreamy, almost far away voice.

"He calls me his sweet Eleanor. I love that: his sweet Eleanor. We're so happy. I want to show him my dress and ask him which one I should choose. I'll sort of model it for him although I'm not quite ready to change clothes. I'll just take the dress with me and give him a peek at how wonderful I'll look tonight! He's in the garage tinkering with the car. He's some kind of amazing mechanic. That's what he did in the Great War: he was a mechanic for all the trucks. I couldn't believe he lived through the Great War, and that even after all the fighting in Europe, he came back to me. I love him so much. We were married just before the war. I nearly went mad with fear that he wouldn't come home. But when I found out he made it and he was coming home I cried grateful tears of happiness and relief!"

Then her face changed and like an unwelcome evening chill, sadness draped her shoulders.

"It's just that when he came home after the war ended, he wasn't quite the Tom who left. He . . . was . . . different somehow. He was Tom but not the fun-loving Tom I knew. That Tom never came home; never held me in his arms the same way or looked at me with the same bright sparkling eyes. His eyes are dull now and when he holds me . . ."

It was as if this part broke her heart. She wanted the man who left to be the same man, the same Tom who came home, to be who he had always been to her. But war forever changes a man and the Tom who came home in 1918, would never be the man who said goodbye in 1914.

"It's 1920 now and he's been home for two years, but he's still so distant. I thought that this dance would spark the joy and laughter that I remember in him, the lightheartedness that captured my heart. I keep trying to find it. Maybe I'll find it tonight at the dance. We're still young: he's just 26 and me, well I'm only 24. Maybe for a few brief moments the old Tom can return."

"Eleanor, did you show him your dress? Did you go outside? What were you doing when it happened?"

I needed her to come to terms with what took place, to get her to accept the finality of her moment. But she was stubbornly determined to avoid it.

"Did you see my closet? I have so many clothes! I must have seven beautiful evening dresses! Come and see them."

Closets in the 1920s were small. Seven dresses would have been a large number during that time. I looked at her closet with her and noted that dozens of garments were not something people in this era routinely had. She proudly showed me the sky-blue dress, the deep cut velvet eggplant colored one and the pink one and on and on. All were in a similar style: velvet and lace, body hugging elegant dresses. They seemed innocently, yet seductively designed to win back her husband's heart and mind. She hoped that as he slowly ran his hands down her lithe body as they swayed together to the light summer songs that he would remember how it used to be for them – before the Great War.

"They are all indeed so beautiful, so winning. Are you trying to win his heart back?" This seemed to stop her briefly, and her manner changed.

"Yes. I guess that's it. I'm trying to get his heart back. They said when he left the Army that he had "Shell Shock." I know in the Civil War they called it "Soldier's Heart." After my grandfather returned from fighting for the Union Army, they said that he wasn't the same either and they called it "Soldier's Heart." It feels like Tom's heart is not here but over there, in Europe, stuck on some bloody battlefield. I can't explain it. It's as if he can't ever be happy again. He never wants to talk about it. So, I accept that. Then I try to distract him with happy things, but he can't seem to let himself be happy. Maybe he keeps remembering his friends who died and maybe he feels guilty that he made it back here, back here to me, to our life together in this pretty place."

She turns back to me now, her light strawberry blonde hair in a stylish twist or it would have been if her 'updo' were not so soaked with blood.

"Please don't make me go outside."

"Look over here, Eleanor, I have this soft, comfortable, golden colored shawl that goes perfectly with your dress."

"Thank you."

She said this flatly, without enthusiasm as if she knew that once I touched her with this embracing light that she would have to face going outside.

"Please show me what happened. Let me help you."

She begins to cry, using her new shawl to wipe her sad green eyes.

"I wanted to show Tom the dress I had chosen for the dance. It was almost time for him to come and get cleaned up before we went to supper. It was such a simple thing. It was another excuse to give him a kiss, to distract him from his work on the car. Sometimes, when I come into the garage, he brightens and he always gives me a smile and for a moment, just a moment, he's happy, and he's my sweet Tom again."

The Color of Cement

She moves with me to the front door, slowly, inevitably as if she is beginning to accept the next steps on her soul's path.

The door opens.

She sees it.

She sees what happened and she tells me through choking sobs. I know she has to get this part out. I know it helps her to let go. I know this, but it doesn't make it any easier for this heart-broken soul. She repeats to me again why she left the house, as if it's important for me to understand, so that I won't judge her.

"I – I was so excited to show him my dress. I was looking toward the garage. I came out here many times a day, to call him for lunch, or supper, to drag him out of the garage to see the pink and honey colored sunset or to get ready for a dance. How could this happen to us?"

"I know it's hard Eleanor, but it's important for you to tell me."

"I came out of the door carrying the blue velvet dress and you see those steps? There's three that go down toward the hill and another seven more that lead closer to the garage. I always skip down the stairs. I try to be 'happy' for him. I wasn't paying any attention because I was carrying my dress, but then I never saw it, and I never heard it either. It didn't make a sound. You'd think it would warn me, but that didn't happen. Maybe I came upon him too quickly, you know? He was the exact color of the cement.

"As I came down the third step to the landing before the next seven, I stepped square on a huge rattlesnake. He must have been sunning himself on the warm cement. I guess he never even had a chance to shake his rattle at me. I saw him too late to pull my foot back and as I stepped on him, he reared up to strike me, and he sunk his fangs into my calf so deeply that he had a hard time getting his fangs out of my leg. It's strange, I guess, that I remember that part so clearly, the hideous face of this timber rattler sinking his fangs into my calf and my looking down at that horrible creature, as if I saw everything very slowly, like, you know, like time almost stood still.

"It hurt so badly I screamed and screamed and I was still screaming when I completely lost my balance and fell backwards and smashed my head on the edge of the first step. Then, instantly, I was standing next to my body. My screaming brought Tom running from the garage. By the time he got here, I guess the snake was gone, but Tom could see the fang marks in my leg. Then he collapsed next to me and felt for my pulse: he knew I was gone. It was horrible.

"I watched him break down into sobs that I couldn't believe came from him. He scooped me up and wrapped his arms around me and sat on that step rocking me back and forth, kissing my face, smelling my hair, holding my limp, bloody, body and just sobbing until it got really dark. I was dead and I was standing beside him crying too. I could see where the dress I was going to wear, the dress that was the whole reason for me to go outside, was sort of crumpled next to the steps.

"I couldn't believe that he survived the war and I couldn't survive a walk to the garage to show him my dress. I died! I'm dead and he's alive without his 'sweet Eleanor.' How can he ever heal now?

"I watched him sob for what felt like an eternity and then it was as if something snapped in him and he carried me into the house and ever so tenderly, laid me on the bed. Then he went and got the Sheriff and they took my body away. Tom never came back to the house. I figured he stayed with friends until the funeral and then I think maybe he left the area.

"I stayed with the house. I went back to the bedroom and my dress. If I could just be there, I could pretend that it never happened and I was still going to go see him and kiss him. I – I didn't know what else to do. I couldn't face being dead and not being with Tom, so I returned to the time before my death so that I could still feel happy. Is that bad? I'm so guilty! If I had only been more careful, looked where I was going but the snake . . . the snake was the color of the cement, I never saw him, he didn't rattle – is it – is it my fault?"

I felt a little stunned that she felt guilty for dying when clearly this was not anyone's 'fault.'

"No, Eleanor, it isn't your fault. It's just what happened. There is no blame here. There's no need for guilt. You've been mourning your death for roughly 85 years, though, and it's time for the grieving to be over. Once you go with this angelic guide I've brought you, over the Light Bridge, he will help you to find your true love. I know this is so hard but it's time, it's finally time to let go of this tragedy."

"I know I need to leave but I can't seem to stop crying. It hurts so bad to have left him, to not have had that life with him. I feel like I abandoned him. I feel that I hurt him so much with my death. Will someone help me? I guess I should thank you. Maybe I had absorbed the sadness of the Soldier's Heart inside of me and maybe I couldn't take it anymore. I don't know."

She paused and took what would have been a deep breath.

"I'm ready now."

Epilogue

My client Helen, felt so badly for Eleanor. Helen may have sensed her elegantly attired ghost on only the subtlest levels. There was no overt haunting going on in Helen's house.

'Shell Shock,' 'Soldier's Heart,' and 'Post Traumatic Stress Disorder' all boil down to the same thing: deep, severe, trauma brought about by the unspeakable acts of violence. It's as if part of the soldier's very soul has been splintered apart. There is no pill, powder, or procedure that can erase this trauma. Only time wedded to the stability of love and hope have a chance of helping a person to reunite and heal the shattered parts of their soul.

Unfortunately, with Eleanor's death, Tom would have emotional trauma added to heart shattering injury. Tom may have suffered from war trauma, but there was no doubt that he truly loved his wife and was trying to heal from the war. It is also possible that Tom suffered from survivor's guilt, now, exacerbated by the added trauma of surviving his wife's stunningly sudden death.

How wonderful it would have been to report that Tom met Eleanor when she crossed over, but alas, he did not meet her. Guilt and grief hold many a precious soul in the 4th dimension. Tom's trauma and possibly survivor guilt may still be holding him in the 4th dimension somewhere.

As hard as this situation was to assist, I was glad that Eleanor was finally able to leave the bedroom and find the light. Mostly, I am heartened that she will be able to heal her own sad heart. Hopefully, she will also be able to find Tom with the help of her angelic companions, and then, finally, she can help him to heal his tragic, soldier's heart.

Can You Help My Daughter?

It's late in the evening and, as I'm about to go to bed, the phone rings. As I go to answer it, I recognize my accountant's phone number. "Why in the world would he be calling me at this time of night," I wondered as I picked up the phone, "it isn't even tax season."

"Hi, Harry, how are you?"

"Hi, Tina. I know it's late but I was talking to one of my clients about a family problem, and I realized that you might be able to help him."

"Okay. What's his problem?"

"Well, actually, it's his daughter. I know it's late but he's so desperate. He just needs some help and I thought that maybe if you talked to him that you could - I don't know, do something to help him make the situation better? I tried to explain what you do but you are hard to explain. Can I give him to you now? He's right here, I'll just hand him the phone and go into another room. Is that okay? You're his last hope."

No pressure there! I'd be alarmed, but then I realized that either I can be helpful or I cannot. There is no middle ground. Harry knew I would tell his client truthfully what the situation was – whatever in the world that could be.

"Sure, Harry, I'll be glad to talk to him. What's his name?"

"It's Yee, Tom Yee.

The Desperate Mr. Yee

"Hello."

Mr. Yee took the phone awkwardly from Harry, as if he wanted to talk to me but was reluctant to hear whether or not I could be of any assistance. I could tell from his voice, even in that one simple word that he was under great emotional strain.

"Good evening, Mr. Yee. Do you know what it is that I do? I gather Harry tried to explain."

"Ah, yes, he did. I know that you do some kind of psychic work and since we've tried everything else, I guess you're our last hope."

"Alright Mr. Yee – may I call you Tom? Can you tell me about the situation? I have no idea whether anything I can do will be helpful to you or not. We'll have to see."

"Yes, of course, please call me Tom. I don't know. It's been awful. It's about my daughter, May."

"How old is May?"

"Our daughter is 23 now and it's always been hard with her, even from the time she was a child. She is miserable every day and now she is in the hospital in a coma and I don't think she's going to make it. Her mother and I are so worried – I guess it's more than that, we're facing her death and we don't know how to do that. We can't believe that someone this young, can die like this."

Tom's words tumbled out quickly and I would have thought that there would be more emotion, but his voice was flat. He sounded completely numb, as if he had no energy or emotion for the situation anymore. He seemed completely defeated.

"What is her diagnosis?"

"They say that she has terminal cancer. How can you have terminal cancer at 23? But that's what they're telling me – the medical people who surround her constantly but don't make her any better. She refused chemo, any form of treatment. She has lapsed into a coma now, and it - her death, I mean - could be any day now. Her mother is with her night and day. I know I should go to the hospital room but I – I had to have a break from the hopelessness of it – of her dying."

A million thoughts are racing through my head.

"I'm so sorry this has happened Tom. What would you like me to do?"

"Well, um, Harry says that you can do something where you look at her body and talk to her. Can you - can you really do that?"

"Yes, I do something called Remote Viewing where I can look at a location or a person and get a sense of what is really happening. However, the person has to give me permission to either look at their property or their body. Your daughter has free will. I can only approach her if I have her permission. Since she is in a coma, the best that I can do is to speak to her subconscious. The subconscious of a person never sleeps, sees everything. This is the part of your daughter that I can contact. To be honest, sir, if she says no to me when I first approach her, then I must leave. I cannot violate her free will."

"Like I say, we've tried everything else. Can you please try for us and for her? We have to feel like we've done all we can before. . ."

"Before you let her go?"

"Yes," he takes a deep breath here, "Before her mother and I, her family, before we can let her leave us. Your children aren't supposed to die before you. Please help us."

Tom didn't cry with this last statement but I could feel the pain of tears crack his voice.

"Of course. I'll do what I can and I'll tell you honestly what I find. Do you have the hospital address and her room number for me?"

Crying for a Lifetime

Can You Help My Daughter?

When I hung up the phone, I focused my thoughts. Then I began the remote view. I found her hospital room rather quickly and took a minute to observe May and her surroundings.

I was instantly struck by the dominating presence of a ten-foot Angel of Death* standing patiently in the corner of her room to greet her when she left her body; he nodded in acknowledgement as I entered the room. The prayers of so many loved ones blanketed her. A sister, possibly a deceased twin sister, was also standing beside the Angel of Death – waiting for what they believed to be this beautiful young girl's inevitable end.

She was waif-like, thin to the point of emaciation, and a pale grey pallor left her looking bleached, as if all color had drained from her body. Her lips were white and her stringy black hair looked thin. Her mother had nodded off in a chair next to May's bed, yet even in sleep this grieving Mom was holding on to her child's skeletal hand. Once I assessed her physical condition, I began to evaluate her etheric body. Instantly, I could see her subconscious standing, looking at the bed looking down at her own body. She turned to look at me. This spiritual part of her looked to be about sixteen, but I could not be sure. She was so sad, as if she had been crying her whole life.

I pondered for a moment what kind of grief, even beyond depression, would cause such a lovely young woman to be sad to the point of willing herself to death. I addressed her subconscious directly.

"May, I have been sent by your father to talk to you about the choice you are about to make. He has asked me to provide you with healing to forestall your death. Will you accept this help? If you say no, then I will leave."

"I want to leave! I hate living! I hate being here every minute. Life in this body is a torture. Oh, please let me go! Don't give me anything that will prolong my suffering here!"

Her highly animated response caught me off guard. She may have been dying but she was powerful in her will to die.

"I understand. I will not prolong your suffering. Will you accept assistance that will help your transition after death and will facilitate your spiritual healing once you cross over into the Heaven World? I'll also be providing you with guidance for that as well. Will you accept this type of healing?"

"Yes, you can do that but nothing more." She responded flatly.

"May I ask why you are so sad? Will you share that with me?"

"I hate being in this body. I miss the feeling I have out of my body. I miss those who have left, and don't tell me I'm grieving. This is far beyond any grief that anyone has ever suffered. Let me die."

"Very well, then I shall begin."

It appeared that spiritual rigor mortis had begun to set in. This means that emotionally/spiritually the soul is already in the process of dying. Everything begins in the spiritual and then is made manifest in the physical. Spiritually, she had already begun the dying process. Yet, even at this point, she could be healed: she still had the opportunity to turn back toward living. Spontaneous healing is possible but it has to be something that the soul desperately wants. But May did not want healing on any level.

"There is No Hope in Life"

As I scanned her body my heart ached for her. She saw herself as full of darkness and heartache. I had never met someone who so despised living as much as she did. Her deep and abiding sadness stemmed from soul crushing grief and self-loathing. Her self-hatred was manifesting in cancer that seemed to be located within her reproductive tract and every organ of her body was filled with thick sticky darkness but her heart seemed to have the most density to its darkness.

Who broke her heart? How did this happen? I could see that there were several deaths in her young life and each one plunged her deeper and more completely into total despair until she perceived death as the only avenue out of her pain. Her twin standing there looked to be about sixteen. Perhaps the loss of this twin was one of the initiating causes of her profound hopelessness. But this was not the only loss. Someone she loved, a boyfriend, had also died but he was not present there. I could only feel her longing for him. I got the strong sense she would not speak of the causes of her sadness.

By cleansing her body just prior to death, it will make her transition to the Heaven World after death much smoother. Any healing and/or prayer assist the soul even if it is just prior to death.

I got the impression that this woman despised herself so much it became torture to continue living in a mortal body. It was that simple, that plain, that tragic. I could hear the echo throughout her body of her saying:

"Please. Let me go. Let me leave. Death is my only path. There is no hope in life."

That Tough Conversation

"Tom, this is Tina. I have completed my work with your daughter. I am so sad to tell you that she would not allow me to provide her any healing to forestall her death. I wish I could tell you something miraculous, and hopeful, but she did not want to live any longer. She begged me not to prolong her life and I had to obey her wishes. All I was able to do was to give her a type of healing that will facilitate her transition into the Heaven World upon her physical death. And I believe that her death is imminent. I'm so sorry."

Mr. Yee was silent for a moment, as if he already knew what I would say.

"That's alright. Did she tell you anything?"

"Yes, she told me that there is no hope in life. She asked that her life not be prolonged an extra minute. She saw nothing in life worth living for. I know that's awkward to say but that's what she said repeatedly. She kept telling me about her despair and that she could hardly wait to die. All I did was to alleviate some of her pain at the point of physical death. Spiritual death had already begun when I got there. Her physical death will be very soon: the cancer has consumed her entire body. I - I wish I had better news for you. My heart goes out to you and your family."

"Tina, these are the exact words she has said to us over the last many months as we watched her waste away, as we watched her body become full of whatever this cancer is. I know you talked to her because these are exactly the things, she has said to us. She knows how much it pains us but she never wavered. She seems angry that it is taking so long to die."

Epilogue

May died two days later without ever regaining consciousness. She never said goodbye to her parents. They never saw her smile again or offer them any solace as she abandoned them. The emptiness of her passing left them emotionally exhausted and bewildered.

I had provided an Angel of Transition to assist her as she began the crossing-over time. Souls that are filled with despair and self-loathing are often extremely reluctant to move into the light. They feel they deserve only the punishing, dark, cold void that is the 4th dimension. However, the energy of healing just prior to death and the presence of an assigned angel ensured her crossing the Light Bridge to the Heaven World.

Her dad called me to let me know. I thanked him.

While I was working on her body, I was aware that the light side was giving her an opportunity to choose to stay. Up until the very last moment, she had a choice and she still chose to leave.

The hard part is that she will have to reincarnate again and learn to live with despair. Karma never lets us avoid lessons that can only be effectively learned in the three-dimensional mortal world of a physical body.

Her next life will surely have its challenges. However, because she was transitioned into the Heaven World and because she will have had Divine counseling and healing, there is hope that in her next life she will have much better emotional coping tools to be able to live through these lessons. Such is the blessing of crossing over, of finally receiving Divine assistance.

*The presence of the Angel of Death would seem to mean that the soul already has an angel to assist them in death. The presence of this great one is not what that means. An Angel of Death is present in many places, especially in hospitals. They help a soul leave the physical and move into the 4th dimension but they do not cross a soul into the Heaven World, because the soul has free will to do that on her own. It is always helpful to assign an Angel of Transition to assist a soul's transition into the Heaven World. Anyone can ask for this assistance for a ghost or a person dying.

The Aviation Museum

The Sticky Psychic

A friend of mine's college-aged daughter, Lexi, visited the Military Aviation Museum in a funny-named community called Pungo, near Virginia Beach, VA. Giant hangars house rare, World I and II aircraft, from the American, British, German, and Japanese air forces, fully restored to their original design, unique paint job and mechanical capacity.

Lexi, a lovely, young woman is beginning to know when there are dead people with her, and although she never goes out and 'hunts' ghosts, she has discovered that they seem to be attracted to her. She has learned the tools to deal with the occasional ghost, but something about this place made her feel uneasy, so she called me.

"You know, I saw airplanes (including Nazi aircraft) from all sides of World Wars I and II.

The Aviation Museum

They looked so colorfully innocent in all the hangars with those caricature-like painted faces over the fuselages. But I know those planes were instruments of horrific death. It was hard to reconcile their presence as almost 'toy-like,' yet knowing they rained carnage down on thousands of people. Now that I'm home, I'm feeling unsettled, and I have a headache. I wonder if I 'picked-up' anyone when I was there."

"Can you tell me a bit more?"

"Well, Tina, this privately owned museum was started by a guy born here in Virginia in 1948. He was never in the military, but he's obsessed with collecting these WWI and WWII planes and cars. He still flies and repairs all the aircraft. I know we've talked about past lives before and I thought of that when I was walking through this museum. It felt to me like this owner may have lived and died during one or both wars. Does that make any sense?"

"Oh yes. We're all familiar with people who reenact their deaths in Civil War battles. Some past lives are so profound that some people need more than one lifetime to process the energy, emotion, and trauma from that life. So, that could be the case here."

"Are there cases of people who died in World War II who returned already?"

"Indeed, there are stories of men who returned in as little as 2-5 years after dying in World War II. Some of them had recurring dreams of dying in battle, on airplanes or in submarines. We have no way of knowing for sure, but it's a definite possibility that the owner died perhaps early in World War II and turned right around and reincarnated."

"I'm wondering, you know, did I pick up any ghosts when I was there? My headache's getting worse. Could you remote view my house to see if anyone came home with me?"

"Absolutely. I'll get back to you."

The Dog Fight

Sometimes it takes me a while to sift through stacks of time to find what is influencing a person, place, or object, but not this time. As soon as I began to remotely look at Lexi's house, I was immediately shown open blue skies and found myself observing an intense aerial battle.

They called them 'dog fights,' those relentless chase games played in the air over France and other countries, during World Wars I and II. I was pretty sure that the specific acrobatic display that I was witnessing was during World War II, based on the make and model of the airplanes. Two planes in particular were in a death fight.

I got the impression that this deadly battle was between a British pilot in his 'Hurricane' fighter, who was intently trying to shoot down his German adversary. For some reason, I can hear the thoughts of the British pilot.

"Got him! They don't call me an ace for nothing. That's three planes today alone. Three planes who won't bomb Britain, now on to the next fucking Nazi. I'm homing in on him. I don't think he sees me. I think I've got him! He's in my sights now! No. Wait. Where did he go? I thought I had him. Where is he? German bastard. You'll never take Britain, not while I have life left in my body. There are so many planes, but this guy: I've got to get him; I'm going to get him.

"Wait, oh my God, what's that sound? I've been hit! SHIT! Where did he come from? How bad is it? I think he hit my gas tank. I can smell fuel. What's that taste in my mouth? I'm spitting blood. Damn, he got me! Maybe I can bring the plane down in a field. Oh my God, I've got no control over the ailerons! No rudder controls! My engine's gone! I'm going down! FUCK! That sound . . . Oh my God, that field is rushing toward me . . . Damn. I died."

I watch, helpless as this battle takes place. The British pilot crashes in a farmer's field on what looks like the coast of France. He is a ghost of himself as he stands beside his crushed and crumpled plane.

"How can I fight for England now? I let my squadron down. I died. FUCK!! If I had paid more attention! How did I miss him? I needed one more maneuver to get that other guy. Guess I didn't see this other Nazi coming up behind me. Maybe if I had just been a better pilot, I wouldn't have died! I want revenge! I want to get that Nazi. I'm so angry! I died too early; I wanted to defend England from the evil Nazis. I - I failed."

I could not help but wonder if this British pilot reincarnated and became the aviation museum owner. No way to know for sure. Maybe it was the intensity of the energy of the battle or the power of this pilot's rage but I was exhausted with this much remote viewing. I had to stop and resume the next night.

Healing the Dead in the 4th Dimension

When I resumed my remote view, I could still see aerial dogfights. Like a video loop eternally playing, I watched the same planes crash again and again. I scanned the land and sea to get a better look at the surrounding water and beach areas and to see if there are other elements of the story.

The ability to remote view carries with it the peculiar additional capacity to glimpse where souls ended up in the 4th dimension. And the picture I am seeing is horrific. The symbolic water off the coast of Europe appears thick, black, and gooey. It is as if it is a mixture of soot and water, making for a black, tarry, thick mess. As I scanned the beach area, it appears to be filled with black oil, which is on fire. As I move closer to those fires, I can see people screaming in pain because they are on fire. This oil is a combination of fuel and gasoline. Are these the cries of the pilots who burned to death in their planes as the fuel and oil blew up? There appear to be thousands of pilots there. I cannot tell which side of the conflict they are on and at this point it matters not. Each tortured soul requires assistance to stop the continual inferno.

But it's not just the pilots I see. There are also people on the ground who died when planes crashed, who died when bombs were dropped and fires swept through buildings and across property. An ever-growing horrifying roar of pain and agony erupt from the screaming and crying people who died this way.

I immediately stopped the 'repeat' action of all of the on-going dogfights and bombing runs that inflicted so much suffering. The healing process for all of these souls began. A healing station was quickly created with showers so that people could (symbolically) wash off the oil. Clean white towels, new clothes were provided to begin the restoration process. Food, and coffee began to nourish them. Angels set up healing stations to repair their still savagely raw wounds. Finally, all of their pain ceased.

Healing prior to transition to the Heaven World facilitates crossing over. The soul sees and feels the scars of illness or injury from the life just lived. Once in the Heaven World, more comprehensive healing is applied not only to the physical scars of war that damage souls, but also to the emotional and spiritual wounds that are not as visible, but that are so often revisited upon a soul once they reincarnate.

Healing Prior to Crossing Over

Once the healing stations were arranged in the ether or 4th dimension and the soul's provided assistance, I sent out a mental message. I called upon all people who were injured, by whatever means to come into the healing circle and receive help. As soon as this massive energy of hope and healing began to be broadcast out to all these souls, I began to see that people from more than one stack of time were responding to this call.

I could now see people from WWI who were also suffering horrendous burns from mustard gas injuries. The angels immediately bathed them in a special soothing rain to instantly stop that pain and shock. This will help to heal and restore them. Thousands begin to slowly pour into this healing station. This is a deliberate and arduous process because all are bone weary, and shell-shocked.

Some people, both military and civilian victims are unsure what has happened to them, but they do know that they were in a war. These are people from World Wars I and II. Some were in action and some were non-combatants. There are men, women, children, and animals that died from the bombings, shelling, and field combat. World War I used a large number of horses so that may be why I also saw them there. There were also many soldiers who were flying planes and driving trucks and tanks. Some soldiers had been walking when they were fired upon from the skies. They are groggy, dazed, and disoriented. They stumble into the healing circle confused yet desperate for relief. It is time for all of these people to move toward healing.

The Voices of the Dead

Since most of them had no idea that they died, I gently broke the news to them. There is shock and awe, disbelief, and relief that the war is finally over. Their haunting voices start to penetrate my heart. I am hearing bits and pieces of their thoughts, fears and hopes. Even in death, the truest nature of the soul comes forth.

"... that Messerschmitt* ripped up my body with bullets. I - I thought that I just kept going... did someone tell my girlfriend that I died?"

I would imagine that more than one British pilot voiced this lament.

"I wonder if my girlfriend married..."

"I wonder if my wife remarried..."

"My mama is going to be so mad...I should have run away and joined the circus. At least I could have visited my mama."

"What were we fighting for, do you know?" A bewildered young German boy did not understand the war he was in. "I know what they told us, but I never understood why we hated so many people."

"Why did this hell rain down on us? What did we do? What did we do?" A French farmwoman tending her fields wanted to know.

"I hope that I killed a lot of Nazis," Said an Allied soldier.

"I know I killed a lot of Brits... I did the Fuhrer proud. I upheld German pride."

". . . Killing. Never . . . never saw myself as a murderer. . . how did this happen?" A German pilot asks this question while witnessing the horror of what mustard gas bombs did to the bodies of innocent civilians during WWI.

"I keep seeing the faces of the people I bombed..." Many a young soldier voiced this concern.

Another pilot feels remorse for his role in the war.

". . . we make murderers into heroes. But we're all murderers. Why do we keep murderin' each other?"

An American pilot flying with the British asks this question, his decidedly Georgia accent distinguishing his nationality.

"I don't know how to escape this hell. How can God welcome any of us after what we've done?" A pilot who climbed out of the black muck from the beach asked this out loud.

"What have we done? How many lifetimes will it take us to atone?" Another soldier cried out.

"I don't care how many Nazis we killed, there will never be enough dead Nazis to pay for what they did . . ."

"Those bastards, I'll bomb them into smithereens for what they did. . ."

". . . hate, they filled me with hate . . . I guess it's never really over, is it?"

"I don't know who I have become. How can I ever go back to church and how can I look my minister in the eye?"

"Are civilians innocent? Do they deserve this hell because they elected a mad man?" Asked an American pilot trying to make sense out of the insanity of war.

"I hate myself for what I had to do . . . hate them for putting us in this position . . . hate is what keeps me going."

"How many children did I kill? How many orphans did I make? How much hate will come back to me?"

"Who are we that we are okay with so much death?" A German pilot asks this in a deep introspective moment.

"Is there another way to fight tyranny, without mountains of murder?"

"The glory books never warned me how bad I would feel inside . . . I see an angel and I can never be deserving . . . judgment day is my eternal hell."

"I think I'm glad my plane got shot down so I don't have to kill anymore . . . how many fathers did I kill? How many widows did I make? No one tells you how to handle these thoughts. I know I'm going to be haunted for eternity by the misery I created. I don't deserve a wife and family. I'm sure that I'm going to hell."

"I was an altar boy . . . how can an altar boy become a murderer over night? And yet I wanted to do this . . . I wanted to stop the Nazis..."

"I wanted to prevent the Kaiser from taking over the world. I hope whoever invented mustard gas spends an eternity in hell . . . I'll probably join him for spreading the torture with my bombs."

"Where can you possibly send me where I can understand the unfathomable cruelty of war?"

"And here we are together; both sides in the end are together . . . what is the sense of it? Why do we let our leaders get away with it?"

The inner reflections go on forever. The concentrated anguish of their emotional torture seemed a universal theme. They felt they had to stop the aggression; but the price – the price of peace was so high and it cost so much death. None of them could reconcile it all.

Nor was it for me to reconcile either. My job was to transition them. Eventually all of them will understand what happened in those brutal times; but right now, there is little I can say to help them understand their roles in this litany of carnage.

Epilogue

Usually, as the angels help to cross souls over to the Heaven World, there is an emerging feeling of brightness, of hope among the dead. But not this time: this time there was a dull, empty, desolate feeling. Even the angels were not smiling as the despair of the murdered and the murderers took their toll on all the participants.

I began feeling sick to my stomach. Emotions came crashing over me in a sickening flood of sadness, guilt, and grief. The darkness and the horror were inescapable to them: they were each stuck in the blackness of their despair. The sticky, gooey, tar on the beach represented the volume of guilt these souls were feeling.

Poor Lexi had indeed picked up more than enough emotion, tension, and pain for her pounding headache. When I related how many thousands and thousands of souls were helped by her request on their behalf, she became quiet and introspective.

"Tina, did we do the right thing helping them all, even if they were Nazis or soldiers of the Kaiser? It seems wrong for them all to move into Heaven, much less with the Allies. Don't those evil souls deserve to remain in hell? Why would you move all of them on together? Did you separate them out so that enemies wouldn't have to be together? Do you know what I mean?"

Her question is such a natural one.

"Lexi, perhaps in the end, it was simply an element of birth that one pilot was German or American or British. Each soul, including the 'innocents on the ground' had become swept up with the energy of fighting of that time. This is not an excuse, merely an observation. Some Germans did leave the Nazis and flew for the British. I understand your question. Let me assure you that each group went with their people. The French were not with the Germans. The Brits and the Americans went together. The Germans also stayed together. I'm not sure if the Axis and the Allied powers ever saw each other. They were so focused on their own shock at finding out that they died and that now they could see that the war had ended. I moved them all on seemingly together but the Angels did a masterful job of ensuring that each group stayed with others like themselves.

"All souls are moved into the Heaven World without judgment on my part. Had I sought to separate who was deserving, to enter Heaven, and who was not, even if it was obvious who each was, that would have immediately put me in a position to judge each soul. I can never do that."

"But Tina, don't the Nazis deserve that 4th dimensional hell?"

"Yes, but they also reincarnate from hell often in the same frame of mind they had at death. When does it end? How can anyone help the world to heal if we keep reincarnating with the same belief in hate and death? Look at all of the Neo-Nazis around today? Where did they come from? Why are they here?

"My job was merely to cross them over so that they could have the benefit of Divine counseling, something they will never receive in the lower astral environs of the 4th dimension. Maybe this time when they reincarnate, they will come in with a slightly different view. Each soul earns certain karma for every action taken; none of us are in a position to judge the karmic path of another. The karma created by certain actions engenders reincarnation into horrific places on Earth. The law of inevitability is relentless, never forgets and is eternally balancing all actions."

"I never looked at it that way. Justice will prevail. Is that what you're saying?"

"Yes, Lexi, justice always prevails even if we don't get to see it in our lifetime. Karma will always balance the scales."

"Thanks for helping me with my headache. I don't think I'll ever be comfortable returning to that museum. I think too often, wars are romanticized, glorified, and admired. But I know that they are all hell. Thanks for the help today."

*The Messerschmitt 109 was Nazi Germany's primary fighter plane in the Battle of Britain and was a worthy adversary to the British Spitfire and Hurricane.

The Twins

"Hi Tina, can you help me with -- I mean do you work with kids?"

My new client blurted this out before she told me her name or anything about her situation.

"Yes and no, let's start from the beginning: how did you find me?"

"A friend of mine said that you remote viewed her house here in Charleston and she was convinced that you could help me with my, well, rather unusual problem. She said that she had these ghosts in her house and that after you helped her, her ghosts were gone and she was better or maybe I should say that her house felt so much better. She said that she couldn't think of anyone else who could possibly help me with my – um – my problem."

"Well, I may be able to help you. What's your name?"

"Janet, Janet Howe. I'm sorry, it's just that I've been so absorbed with this for so long and I haven't had anyone to talk to who doesn't think I'm crazy. I believe what's happening is real but I feel that among adults I'm so alone with this difficulty that. . . after a while I begin to doubt myself. Do you know what I mean? Please forgive me for dumping all of this on you all at once, just as we meet."

"It's alright Janet. You aren't the first person to tell me these types of things. Yes, I can help with children. And I won't think anything that you tell me will be weird. You can't imagine the strange things I've heard. No need to be shy; it's all part of my unusual world. So, how many children do you have?"

"I have twin boys, Josh and Jeremy, who see ghosts sometimes and then they see these dark evil things in the house. . ."

"And the boys are how old?"

"The boys are only four years old, but they are super smart and I'm not just saying that because I'm their mom. Oh, and they're also super sensitive, too.

"My husband thinks the boys are schizophrenic and that we should put them on drugs so that they'll be 'normal.' How can four-year-old little boys be normal on drugs? How long do you have to be on drugs to be considered normal? I'm sorry, that entire concept so upset me that we couldn't talk about it anymore. My husband can't stand it when he sees the boys talking to an empty room. He becomes insanely angry.

"I tried discussing this with my Baptist minister but he said that there aren't any such things as ghosts and that the boys could be possessed by the devil. Can you believe that? Ghosts don't exist in his mind but four-year-old children can be possessed by the devil? Unbelievable! This made me so mad and my husband was embarrassed by the thought that our boys were evil. It was appalling. How can four-year olds be evil? We pray to Jesus every night. This is crazy! Are my kids crazy? Am I a bad mother? Should I put them on drugs? What should I do? I'm so confused!"

Dark Evil Things

"Okay, let's back up. Go ahead and describe in as much detail as you can, what the boys see so I can get a handle on the dimension of the problem."

Janet takes a deep breath and begins to calm down. I suspected she was terrified that I would think she was crazy or even a bad mother for voicing her concerns about her sons.

"My boys see dark beings. I don't know what else to call them, spirits? Ghosts? What else is there to call them? Is there more than one type? This is overwhelming. I mean they see ghosts in the grocery store, wherever we go and they don't seem afraid of those ghosts. But when they are here at home, they're afraid of the ghosts they see. They tell me that the ghosts are scary, mean. Nighttime is especially hard for them; they always want to sleep with us. Sleep is a nightmare in this house for all of us."

"When did all of his start? How old were your boys when this began? When did you really notice what they were seeing? Let me be specific, when did you first notice that they were seeing ghosts? Do you remember the first time you realized what was happening with them?"

"I guess when they were eight or nine months old, I could see that they were watching – I don't know – something. Sometimes they would stare at things and then burst into tears. My husband is an engineer so he discounted what I thought the kids saw. Other times the boys seemed to see other kids and would be playing with them. Ted, my husband, and I had no explanation for what the kids saw. It wasn't too scary at first. But now, the feeling in the house seems to be getting worse and more evil. Sometimes I'm terrified. To be honest I can feel ghosts too. I can see things out of the corner of my eye. I'm afraid for my sons. My own house creeps me out. I feel powerless. I wish we could all leave here."

The Energy of Dissention

"Do you and Ted fight over this?"

"Yes, I guess the truth is that we fight constantly. Sometimes we scream at each other. One day, Ted was screaming at me, grabbed me, and shook my shoulders so hard he shocked himself. He isn't a violent man but the look in his eyes wasn't him; I was terrified. I think his behavior surprised him. I was stunned; he's never done anything like this before."

"How old is your house?"

"Well, it was a foreclosure. The previous owners went bankrupt and they fought all the time (according to the neighbors), and I think one of them used drugs. Why does that matter? I'm not sure of the age, I think it's close to 100 years old."

"Did anything happen in this house before you moved in here, that you know of, or perhaps that your neighbors told you? Please bear with me. I'm going somewhere with this."

"I don't know, other than we think that drugs were used in this house. Why does this matter? I don't think anyone died here but how would I know?"

"It matters because you are dealing with two very specific issues. One is predecessor energy, which I can feel quite clearly just speaking with you on the phone, and it is very dark energy. The other is that you have two very psychic children. Your boys aren't crazy. They really are seeing things, both the ghosts and the dark things or Lower Realm Intelligences. That is their correct name."

"What do we do? Can you help my kids? Do I turn them over to you now and you can maybe get them to stop seeing these things? Can you do that?"

Parental Responsibility for Psychic Children

"Janet, I want to explain to you that you never, ever turn your children over to any psychic to 'work with them,' even to me. I never work directly with someone's children because it is actually a violation of spiritual law or the 'children's rule.' This means that you cannot expose a child to information beyond their karmic ability to use the information with good judgment. Even a teenager would still fall under this rule. This is an aspect of understanding that there is karma attached to all of this psychic/spiritual knowledge. This is why it's important to honor this information and a child doesn't have the judgment to do that, certainly not four-year-olds."

"Oh my God, this sounds serious. Is it serious? Are my boys in danger? They're only four!"

"I don't mean to scare you. I'm only telling you the truth to protect you from exposing your children to anyone who might be unscrupulous. You don't want someone to give your children information that would cause them to use their ability in an incorrect or harmful-to-others, manner. My focus is teaching you and your husband how to help your children learn how to use their ability for the greatest good. When you have kids this psychic, their ability may only increase. You have to be trained in how to help them to handle who they are and the ability they came in with, in accordance with spiritual law."

"You mean that they are psychically gifted?"

"Janet, with all that's been happening, does this feel like a gift, to you?"

"Oh no. It feels like some cruel nightmare, for all of us. Alright, what do we do, I mean what do I do?"

"You need to learn how to help your children, how to clear your house and how to look at your world differently. Let's go back to the beginning again."

"Okay, Tina, it feels daunting. But finally, I have someone I can talk to about this and maybe I won't feel so powerless when the boys see things."

Opening the Door to Hell

"The reason, Janet, that I asked so many questions about your home is because of something I mentioned before called predecessor energy. This means that the energy of all the people who lived there over time is still having an influence on that house, whether you realize it or not.

"This is especially powerful if there were individuals who used drugs. Any drug use, including marijuana, heroin, crack, LSD, methamphetamines, and prescription drug use, (if abused) can open up a doorway to another dimension – a very dark place indeed. Meaning that this dark place has more than ghosts: this can be a doorway to hell and can open your home up to creatures called Lower Realm Intelligences. These are what you referred to as little devils. They can torment the dead and the living. The reason that drugs were used in your home is that something else really dark took place in this house or on this property, and that was the original initiator that created this opening to the dark side."

"What else other than drugs could have been worse than this? Oh my God, was someone murdered here? This is just sounding worse and worse!"

"I know this sounds dramatic but this is the explanation for what has been happening. These terrible beings are also extremely active at night, which explains why you aren't getting any sleep."

"Can't you just do what you did for my friend, Joan, at her house, you know, clear it and then we'll be all set? Why isn't it that simple for my house?"

"I will be glad to remote view your house and remove everything that is here. I'll do that tonight, but you have a much bigger challenge than Joan. Joan doesn't have twin psychics acting like potential ghost magnets. Oh, did Ted also give permission for me to work on your house? It's important that he be on board with our plan because when I am psychically wandering around your home, his subconscious will see this."

"Yes, I did tell Ted about Joan and her house. Joan talked to Ted and told him how much better her house felt and that she can finally get some sleep now so he was alright with my calling you."

"Good. Here's the plan: I'll work on your house and get back to you. Then we can focus on your boys after that. Sound good? Could you please share this with your husband?"

"Yes, will do. We all need some sleep!"

The Remote View

Charleston, South Carolina barely has a square mile of land that is not haunted by someone, from Native Americans, and colonials, to plantation owners and slaves. Then, of course, there are the thousands of Revolutionary War, War of 1812 and Civil War dead that haunt streets and neighborhoods and even parklands. There are also the people who died by natural and murderous causes that populate the endless stacks of time that define this deceptively calm and now, seemingly peaceful area of the United States. You would think that Charleston would be full of bad places, but so many people have loved this city and have continued to rebuild and refurbish it that the energy continues to be refreshed on many levels.

And this was true of Janet's property. The house was lovely, but even a lovely house can have a past that needs clearing. There were several stacks of time represented on this small piece of land, including one where several runaway slaves had been hung from trees in the yard once the Civil War was over. The Civil War may have liberated the slaves but it was at least 75 years before many of them actually felt free from the terror of the Ku Klux Klan.

I also found a wounded Confederate soldier who made it through the war, only to die of infection not long after his wife welcomed him home. His grief was heartbreaking. He felt so cheated to have died that way and not gotten to spend a lifetime with his beloved.

Once this property became in resonance with murder and death, the frequency of the land was lowered and difficult things continued to happen here.

I quickly offered healing to all the souls who were still stuck there. They were silent as I crossed them over. Their emotions of grief and sadness, anger and hopelessness would still be felt on the land on subtle levels had I not mitigated that energy.

I asked several ghosts if they could see any little boys where they were in the dark void of the 4th dimension, but none of them could see the children. And although the boys were invisible to the ghosts, that did not mean that the twins could not see these dead men. I could imagine their terror as they saw those men swinging from trees, their faces horrifying in the ravages of death.

Once they were transitioned into the Heaven World it felt as if the sun came out. Then

I closed up the ominous portals that were opened by dark acts. I cleaned and cleared the house from the drug usage, which took place there in more modern times. I waited several days to give the energy a chance to settle and then called Janet.

Psychic Parent School

"Hi Janet! I've cleared your place now, so you should all be able to sleep so much better. How are your boys? Are you and Ted still arguing?"

"Oh wow, Tina, we're doing so much better! What a difference! The boys are finally sleeping in their own beds and they don't seem to be afraid anymore. Ted and I have stopped arguing. It feels like this nightmare is over for us. Can this be true?"

"Ah, well, yes and no. The doors to the dark places are now closed, but that doesn't mean that your boys will stop seeing ghosts any time soon. Some children do grow out of this ability, meaning that the veil comes down and they stop seeing things. However, that may or may not happen for Josh and Jeremy. You still have to deal with the ghosts that the boys see wherever you go. You live in Charleston, after all, and the entire area is haunted. It's like you live in 'ghost central.'"

"You mean there is more for us to do?"

"Oh yes. You have to learn how to help your boys; how to get them to understand how to help these ghosts or you will do this for them."

"You mean I have to help the dead? Ah. . . no . . . . ah, I don't think I can do that."

"Yes, you can. You have to learn how to do this. You have two very psychic kids and they desperately need you to step up to the spiritual plate and show leadership and courage. I'll teach you how to help them and remove the dead. I've made it easier than you think. Parenting always has unusual challenges."

"Yeah, Tina, but I couldn't have imagined this."

"The first step is to begin documenting all that the boys are seeing. Get a book that will become your journal of their experiences. You will want to be looking for patterns."

"What kind of patterns?"

"Do they always see the same type of ghost?

"Do both boys see the same things all the time?

"Is one child more or less psychic than the other?

"Do they seem more psychic in the morning or the evening?

"Do they sense the same thing in the same location every time?

"What causes them to be fearful or friendly toward what they are seeing?"

"But what do I do when they see a ghost? I've tried telling the ghosts to leave. I burned sage. Nothing worked. Do I just call you each time?"

"Yeah, sage is worthless for removing ghosts. No, I have a much better solution that will give you power in this situation and yet will be of tremendous service. I'm giving you The Crossing Over Prayer©. Keep it on your phone, ready, at all times. When the boys say that they see a ghost, say the prayer out loud or play the video of the prayer which is on my website www.TinaErwin.com. You can also get the book, The Crossing Over Prayer Book© which is available on Amazon and Audible. You can play the prayer on the audio book or look the prayer up on your Kindle on your phone. Eventually the boys will learn to say this themselves. If saying it out loud isn't appropriate, say it in your mind. Then ask the boys to tell you when the ghosts are gone. Also, say the prayer every single night before the boys go to bed to keep them safe in the sleep state."

"Seems like a lot to do. . . Can this be it for today? I feel like I'm overwhelmed."

"Janet, it's just a simple prayer and it really works. Use it. There is more to do. But this is enough for now."

Psychic Service and Organized Religion

"You know, Tina, I feel so much better today. It's wonderful how much clearer you can be when you get a night's sleep. Even my husband is amazed by the change in all of us. He wanted me to share that prayer with our minister. I told him I had to ask you first. I also wanted to know if this is about religion because my minister says that there is no such thing as a ghost. How can my minister be so wrong?"

"Your minister has a belief system. Your children's ability is beyond what he believes is part of that system. It's not up to you or your husband to change his mind. Your minister is wrong about ghosts because he is denying basic physics: energy is neither created nor destroyed. What happens to the energy of a person when their body dies? Where does that energy go? It goes to the 4th dimension. Your minister may feel safer not believing in ghosts because he does not know how to deal with them. It's not your job to change him.

"I get the feeling that your husband either wants your minister's approval or wants to prove him wrong. Don't share the prayer. Make your own spiritual path. Connect to God. You don't need an intermediary, just love God, and believe in your connection to the Heaven World. You are taking charge of your life, starting right this minute. I'll be happy to talk to your husband and explain all of this to him.

"Believe your boys. Believe in your children. Every single time you say The Crossing Over Prayer© you connect to God and you teach your children to do the same thing. This is perhaps the best psychic protection that you

The Twins

could possibly have: connection to God through prayer and service. You can also teach your children to ask for angels for help in every situation.

"Fill your home with photos and statues of angels. Silently in your mind, ask for angels to fill your home, too. The presence of these Divine beings shifts the energy of your home permanently and makes all of you feel happier. But do not use angel cards, because they are tools of fortune telling and divination and will not help the energy no matter how many angels, they put on them.

"The key issue is to educate yourself in how to connect to the Divine and the dynamic of spiritual service. This is a powerful lesson for your boys. Teach them, as they get older, that they only need their connection to God. They do not need Tarot Cards, Ouija, séances, to connect to the psychic side of life."

Janet took a second to take all of this in and process it.

"I never looked at psychic ability this way. I thought it was a powerful gift that people on television and in books had. I had no idea that there was any responsibility to it, much less service."

When Janet said this, I felt an inward shudder. There is an ocean of well-intentioned people out there who think this. It meant everything to me to open her up to the possibility of spiritual service to the dead and to her own living children.

"Janet, can you imagine how you would feel if you were stuck in a cold, dark and scary dimension? Imagine (God forbid) if your boys were stuck there. Wouldn't you want some kind and caring person to help you or to help them? Can you begin to imagine the power of compassion they would feel coming from you? This is the true gift of psychic ability: the power to be of service to the living and the dead.

"Helping ghosts creates positive karma for you and your sons. I can only begin to imagine the respect your boys will have for your courage and leadership in guiding them as their ability develops – if it does. You will be so proud of your sons for helping others. This ability can build character in all of you."

Epilogue

Janet was true to her word, a conscientious and courageous mom. I spent many hours building her confidence in guiding her boys until she simply no longer needed me.

She taught her sons the meaning of service to others and they began to help the dead. Josh and Jeremy did see dark things sometimes and bringing in angels helped them every time. They also avoided violent television shows and negative things. Slowly but surely their life took on a very different rhythm, the rhythm of working on both sides of the veil: the 3rd and 4th dimensions.

The patterns that Janet observed with her boys helped her to know how to help her sons handle a variety of spiritual situations. She learned to understand what they needed from her and how to help them to grow with their psychic ability, which, by the way, never left them. They built a special communication system so that when they saw a ghost Janet was able to quietly play the prayer on her phone to remove the soul. They were discreet and successful. That teamwork built tremendous respect between mother and sons. Even Ted got in on the act and placed the prayer on his phone for times when he was alone with his sons. There were no more screaming matches and, blessedly, the boys were never placed on drugs. The parents were fully confident working with their sons. I smile every time I think of this successful family.

Ghost Stories from the Ghosts' Point of View Vol 3

The House of the Dark Arts

Living in San Diego is gorgeous every single day. I lived in one of those pretty bedroom communities outside of San Diego, called Mt. Helix. Houses of all shapes and sizes ring the mountain with stunning views of San Diego and its harbor. On a good day, you can even see the islands off the coast of California. At the very top of the mountain is the Mt. Helix cross. We live in the shadow of that beautiful cross.

And so do many other homes that nestle into the mountain. Our yards are filled with every kind of fruit tree: citrus, avocado, fig, pomegranate, and guava. When we have water and are not in a drought, everything grows here. It is inherently an extremely positive place washed in glorious sunlight and cool breezes from the sea.

Perhaps one of the reasons this area always feels so good is that no wars of any kind have ever been fought in San Diego County. No one has ever attacked the city except for the creatively dressed superheroes and aliens who show up for Comic-Con every summer. The community is in an upbeat place with tremendous diversity, opportunity, and variety. The constant military presence of several bases fosters a subtle feeling of safety.

So, with all of this sunny energy surrounding homes in San Diego, plus specifically being in the shadow of the cross on Mt. Helix, it takes quite a bit of work to destroy this delightful feeling. But with insidious determination and a thoroughly black heart, goodness can be systematically destroyed on any property. You do not have to believe in malevolent intent for evil to affect you.

The Routine Call

"Hi Tina, my name is Della Willow. You don't know me, but I got your card from one of your neighbors. You worked on their house and now they actually enjoy living there. Do know which house I mean?"

"Yes, I know it well. It was one of the most negative houses in the neighborhood. Three different owners went bankrupt living in that house, and since I was allowed to clear it, thank goodness, that terrible pattern is over. How can I help you?"

"Well, I bet my house is worse. Can you do something do you think?"

"I never make any promises, but I have cleared some tough locations. And before I clear a location, I always make sure that the homeowners are in agreement with me doing this work. Della, are you married?"

"Yes, and my husband, Derek, said whoever I could find would be great. But he said he didn't want any more weirdo, Tarot reading, hippy psychics with long hair and blue eye shadow working on our house and, for some reason, he wants to meet you in person. Is that possible? I mean could we visit you before, um, before you actually begin the work on our house?"

"Sure, when do you want to come over?"

Dark Foreshadowing

Della and Derek came to visit me one Sunday afternoon. They sat in my living room on opposite sides of the room. I remember this detail so clearly, as if something huge separated them. I expected them to sit huddled together on one of the sofas, united in their desire to remove this terrible blight from their lives, but they were as far apart as they could possibly get. The awkward feeling in the room seemed to grow with each passing moment. Derek immediately decided to start the conversation even before I could offer them a cool glass of tea.

"Nice place you have here, and thanks for meeting with us. We've had quite a tough time. I don't even know where to begin."

"Let me interrupt you, Derek, before you launch into what you've been experiencing. If you tell me too much, you'll never know if what I'm clearing is because of what you said or because I really cleared the things that were genuinely causing you problems. What I will ask is that you both give me your permission to begin work and that you understand that this process can take several nights and that I do charge for this work. It takes tremendous energy to clear any home and my fee balances that energetic expenditure."

"Okay, Tina, I get it. As much as we want to pour out all the crap that's been happening to us, to that house, we'll wait and see what you can do. But I do have one question. We contacted one weird psychic who told us that she could clear our house for free but that we had to buy $5,000 in 'special psychic candles.' Do you use candles to clear property?

"Okay, $5,000 in candles? Are you kidding me? No, I never, ever use candles. That's just outright theft. Also, I remote view your location; I won't be going there until it is fully cleared and then only if you choose to invite me."

There was an awkward silence for a few moments. Then Della began to speak for the first time. She had been oddly silent until now.

"Has there ever been a house that was so bad, so horrible that even you couldn't clear it? If you have encountered such a place, what did you do? I don't mean to be disrespectful, but –

but I have to ask. We've been through a lot of psychics and we're only here because you do come highly recommended."

Della's question, so innocently stated, gave me very subtle chills.

"So far, I have a pretty good track record of clearing houses but it can take me quite a bit of time. If it turns out that I cannot clear the house, I'll tell you, and I'll also tell you to move. I usually only recommend that if you moved into a house where crystal meth have been cooked and used. However, karmically, that's not as easy as it sounds. What I mean is that as bad as this house is, you don't want to pass it off to someone else so that they experience the difficulties that you and your family have felt. It is terrible karma to deliberately pass something harmful to another person. So, this house needs to be cleared, no matter what.

"By the way, do either of you do Ouija, Tarot or play violent video games? Do you participate in séances? Do your kids play with those things?"

"No, no we don't do any of those things and our children are only two and four years old, so no, those things are not part of our lives."

Della took a long breath.

"Okay, Tina, go ahead and see what you find in our house from hell."

A Chilling Level of Evil

The next day, I began the process of working on one of the most difficult houses I have ever cleared.

It did not take long to find this house. I did not see it in 'real time:' I only saw its etheric structure, rather like looking at the auric field of a person and not necessarily seeing the person's body, only the energy that surrounds them. The energy surrounding this house looked like someone had dumped an oil tanker's worth of black, oily, tarry, oozing mess all over the house. It looked like it was dripping darkness. I could not imagine living in such a place.

While that was terrible, what was significantly worse was the feeling of evil I have seldom encountered. I was convinced that this house must have some type of portal to hell open somewhere on the property.

When you remote view a home, you always start at the front door and then move into the house. The front door in Feng Shui, is the mouth of chi or energy and what blocks or welcomes you there will influence all that happens in the house. And at this front door, there was a sentinel 'thought form' that reeked and oozed evil. He was terrifying looking, about 8' tall, wearing black, greyish shredded clothing, and he had red, scary eyes – but he was merely a thought form.

If you are not familiar with the concept of a thought form, let me explain. All thoughts are forms of energy, even if you cannot see them with your physical eyes. Some thoughts are so powerful that they can physically manifest as semi-visible objects and, in some cases, can be projected as physically visible to anyone. You may see them as orbs, or they may seem to be ghosts, or scary apparitions. Psychics who are well schooled can see them in the 4th dimension. Sometimes white magicians create them and they can look like shafts of bright light. But the more common types of thought forms are the ones created by black magicians in either the 3rd or 4th dimension. They can appear to be something terrifying, either in human or non-human animal-like form. A favorite black magician thought form is a terrifying wraith-like being. Visualizing salt raining down upon them removes them for they do not have strength in their shape. Salt destroys negativity and visualizing salt raining down will psychically cleanse any location. Before you remove them, it can be unnerving the first few times you see them.

This thought form was deliberately designed to be horrifying, scary and intimidating. A thorough dousing in highly concentrated salt quickly dispatched him and the salt also cleaned the threshold of the front door. I was unsure who had created this creature, but eventually, I would find out.

The Walls Started to Talk

Sometimes the walls in a house 'talk,' and you can feel and hear the story of what went on in the house. The emotions that people have experienced, their traumas, fears and nightmares seem to become imbedded into the very structure, the wood, metal, and stone of the house. And what this house had to say confirmed my suspicions that a malevolent energy had taken over this dwelling. If energy is neither created nor destroyed, then the energy that a family feels and experiences has to go somewhere. Usually, all the substances in the home absorb that energy. If the essence of the house started out positive and now it was negative, there had to be an operating force that changed the very nature of the life force in the dwelling. My job was to discover the source of the negative charge, stop it, clean up after it and restore the proper energetic balance to this home: an extremely, daunting task.

The 'house' told me that this couple had had chronic car problems, including a water pump issue, dead batteries, flat tires, even a hole in the radiator: all representative of energy draining away. Mechanical things in the house were breaking down with no reasonable explanation: a broken dishwasher, refrigerator, computers, and heaters. There were constant plumbing problems, toilets and pipes leaking yet never successfully finding the source.

I could sense that their financial problems had left them on the brink of bankruptcy. They could see money was coming in, yet their bills never seemed to be paid.

This house would have felt filthy all the time, no matter how much it was physically cleaned: a clear sign of detrimental psychic interference.

The vermin that infested the house would have defied any exterminator. Rats, mice, ants, wasps, black widow spiders all found their way into this seemingly dammed house.

One family member after the other was sick with a cold, the flu, chronic allergies, and they would all suffer from a feeling of such tremendous fatigue, that they could each barely make it through the day. No matter how much they all slept, it was never going to be enough.

Nothing could get done because they felt so constantly fogged in their thinking that they could not focus on what they had to do next. When they were not struggling with their blocked thinking, they were arguing with each other over petty little things that made no sense. I would have imagined that their behavior began to change over time. I guessed that they reached the point that they felt madness was setting in for all of them. They thought moving into this gorgeous, 6,000 square foot, two-million-dollar house on Mt. Helix would be the answer to their dreams, but from the moment they moved in, I could feel that their lives started circling the energetic drain.

The Superhighway to Hell

This is a massive house, covering four floors of space on a two-acre lot that steeply sloped down in the back. That slope alone would almost immediately drain their resources, but with Feng Shui that could be improved. That slope alone would not have explained the sheer volume of nightmarish problems this couple had and I suspected that the couple before them had had as well.

After psychically scanning the entire property and finding dozens of things to repair, I turned my attention to the two massive vortices that were on either side of the perimeter of the property. These looked to me like someone deliberately opened them to drain away any energy this couple originally had. I quickly closed them up and then placed etheric mirrors over them to return that 'draining' energy to the original creator of this sophisticated level of black magic.

The longer I spent in the house, the more I began to get a sense of the black magician who had targeted whoever would own this house. This deliberate malicious effort was quite cleverly crafted; this magician was no entry-level dabbler in magic. As I worked from room to room, I began to feel a very strange resistance to my being there, as if I was constantly being watched. Was someone nervous that his or her energetic food supply of negative energy was about to be severed?

I tried to determine how long the energy in this house had been there. There were no stacks of time to sift through. All I got was a feeling of fire energy, as if another house had been here some time ago and burned to the ground. After quite a while another house had been built, but there were decades between houses. This much work was exhausting, so I set up my own spiritual police to watch the house and I stopped for the night.

When Evil Stalks the Halls

When I resumed my work the next night, I wore protective clothing even in the ether because of the dangerous level of psychic toxicity in this house. There was so much evil there, it was hard to fathom. I was amazed at how this family was still alive.

Moving methodically from room to room, I became aware of someone watching me closely, as if I had invaded her territory, probably a ghost. Ghosts are curious when someone enters their space.

Although this woman was not overtly making her presence known, I could feel her, and the more I felt, the deeper that sick feeling of dread became.

Was someone murdered here? Was I sensing the victim or the murderer? What if no one was murdered here? Who then was this watcher being?

As if on cue, a lonely gaunt woman in shredded clothes came down a flight of stairs in the center of the house. A female presence, old, conniving, and manipulative with a sense of supreme power smugly followed me as I cleaned up the horror and fear I found in every room. She looked like she was made from crumpled crepe paper, ashen as if the life had been sucked out of her. Her sparse hair, long, soiled fingernails and hideous features would have terrified anyone who saw her. However, in death, it would be hard to tell if a magician caused this or not; maybe she was the magician. I was unsure. But her evil smile told me that she was indeed the dead magician, and she acted like she owned the place.

She was eternally sucking energy from this house and whoever lived here. This was the house of a very powerful, female, black magician – one so full of wickedness and hate that her terrible energy had permeated the walls and the very ground upon which the house was built. She was watching over 'her' property, making sure that she got their energy, which would help to maintain her own dark energy level, even in death.

She had no wish to speak to me, so I quickly moved her on to the appropriate realm. Her karma alone would determine where and how she would end up as finally the energy of light triumphed over her dark world. She was definitely not happy that she had lost all of this power and, when I at first attempted to move her on, she tried to resist, but the powerful angels and spiritual police that I brought in as reinforcements quickly dispatched her.

This evil woman knew that the homeowners would try to 'fix' the house, to cure it of the evil they could feel. Ever the clever mastermind, she completely booby-trapped the entire house so that long after she was gone whoever bought it would continue to suffer and suffer. This was the first time I had ever seen a house so deliberately constructed to cause harm. No amount of cleaning or decorating would ever rid this family of this much evil without powerful spiritual help.

Inside the walls, under the house, in the ceiling in places where anyone psychically clearing a house would not think to look was exactly where she laid her perpetual traps. Even if you cleared the ghost, and closed the vortices, you would not expect to find so many black magic time bombs imbedded in the walls and floors. It was quite an education. Had I not had my own spiritual team with me, I would not have found them all.

The magician's family also practiced the black arts so that whoever bought this house, no matter how many times it changed hands, the current owners would continue to feel harassed, thereby supplying the magician and her descendants with energy for eternity, both in the 3rd and 4th dimensions. I suspected they lived nearby. Again, this was an extremely sophisticated level of evil.

I made a note to have the owners collect all of their closing documents for the purchase of this house, and place them in aluminum foil, shiny side in, to stop the energy of that dark transfer from emanating.

Part of me wondered what would happen to the still-living, master magician who had taken over from the previous magician that I crossed over, and who was still maintaining the level of evil of this house. If this level of evil was returned to her, I realized with a chill, it could potentially make her deathly ill.

The Toxic, Terrifying, Tedious Cleanup

Etherically, the house was a disaster. There were so many portals open to the lower astral realms that I almost told them to move, to have the house destroyed. But financially, I knew they could not afford that and then eventually someone else would build there and this would start all over again. No, this had to be cleansed. Even tearing it down would not have cleared the terrible energy.

I had expected to find more dead here but I realized that the magician had no desire to share the energy, so she would have cleared those souls out of the house, a rather ironic twist, and sent them further into whatever hell she choose for them. They were not available for me to help, although removing the magician might enable those souls to be able to cross over eventually.

I cleaned off the black goo covering the house. It was as if the house had been on fire and all that was left was smoldering, smoky ash with a covering of this black goo.

I disabled all the perpetual poison machines hidden in all the walls. This would have explained the chronic illnesses and allergies that everyone suffered.

Systematically, I closed every single portal to the lower astral, effectively closing the door to all the Lower Realm Intelligences that were so freely coming and going. These beings are about three feet tall all black with red eyes and claws. If you have to live with them, they will make your blood run cold because you can 'see' them out of the corner of your eye and they can make themselves visible to you in the sleep state. The more miserable they make the family, the more negative energy they create; this is the only source of sustenance the magician allows them.

The remaining Lower Realm Intelligences that patrolled the house for the magician were also removed and sent to the appropriate realm. These 4th dimensional creatures haunted, tormented, and gave the family endless nightmares ensuring that they would never receive a night's sleep. These beings would taunt the homeowners into quarrels, then fights, and then who knows what. In a private moment, several weeks after the final remote viewing conversation, Della admitted that her terror was complete one morning when she discovered a butcher knife under her bed on her side. She knew she had not put it there. Neither she nor her husband knew how it got there, but it caused her to begin to suspect her husband. Perhaps this is how some of these terrible murders take place where one family member murders an entire household. Now I understood why they were sitting so far apart from each other when they visited me.

And although the original magician herself was gone and had passed on the vicious torch of power to her daughter, I had the distinct feeling that she had left additional living heirs to guard 'her' property by some method. I did not know who they were or how they were working to continue to harass this property and these owners.

I knew that cleaning up this house would help this family, but there was also the subtle karmic effect of helping the nearby community. When a home is this horrible, on unseen levels, it affects the entire neighborhood in a negative way.

So, after two long weeks of work, cleaning, clearing, and filling this house with light, it was time to go back and talk to Della and Derek.

Oh My God, the Difference!

"You know, Tina, we've lived here for almost four years. Four years of pure hell. Our house isn't that old, it's been here for only 28 years, not that long when you think about houses on the East Coast where Della and I are both from and yet, it must have been really haunted."

"Derek," Della interrupted, "we can talk about that later, I'm dying to know: what did you find?" Della sounded better than I had ever heard her.

"I'll get to all of that but first, are things any better for all of you? Have you seen any differences, any improvements? How are you sleeping?"

This work is so esoteric, so surreal that your only real 'proofed pudding' is how they are all feeling.

"I – we . ." Derek started.

"Let me tell." Della interrupted him.

"No, I want to tell her since I was the most skeptical."

"Guys, I want both of you to tell me. Derek, you go first."

"Okay, I, we are all sleeping so much better. The cars worked this morning and nothing was wrong with them. I couldn't believe it. I feel human again, like I can think, like this fog lifted and the sun came out."

"Great, now Della?"

"I can sleep at night and there are no more nightmares of these horrible, terrifying beings coming to strangle me. The kids were sleeping with us because they have been terrified. They now sleep in their own beds. It's amazing. Our daughter told us the scariest thing this morning: that 'she's alone inside of herself this morning.' I have no idea what that means but it sounds like something let go of her??"

"Yes, it feels like she can be a kid again. So glad she is sleeping and feels safe in her own bed. It sounds like your daughter had experienced what is known as, an attempted possession, possibly by those Lower Realm Intelligences that I removed. I'll explain those later. How is your son?"

"He sounds like a normal child. He giggles and laughs like he is finally comfortable here. I had no idea what that was like because I was pregnant with him when we moved in and then he was born with cleft palette. Do you know what it feels like to think that your house has harmed your children? That's how it has felt and no matter what we did, nothing worked." Della's anger at her house and her situation were not leaving overnight.

"I'm thrilled that your son is behaving like a normal child. I'm sure you almost forgot what that happy chatter sounds like."

"Yes, Tina, we feel like a family again. It's amazing. What else did you find in the house?"

"As I worked through your house, I had the impression that you have the following issues: chronic sleep deprivation since those Lower Realms would torment you in the sleep state. Growing financial problems to the point that you could be on the verge of bankruptcy. Car troubles - even on a new car - would be a chronic problem because the sooty darkness of the lower astral clogs everything. Plumbing leaks with no reasonable explanation would be coming from every area, representing financial drain. Continual mechanical failures of house appliances must have driven you nuts. Vermin would plague your house that you couldn't get rid of, even with an exterminator. I also sensed that your house felt filthy dirty all the time no matter how much you cleaned it. Finally, your relationship would feel like it was failing with the constant petty quarrels that would lead nowhere. Does that sound familiar?"

"Yes," Della said, "but there is so much more to tell."

The Litany

Della took a deep breath, and Derek handed her the phone. He said:

"Go for it honey, tell her the hell we've been through."

"You have no idea what it's been like for us. Yes, all of those things happened to us that you mentioned: cars, leaks, and mechanical problems. But it's more than that. Everyone told us that our house was evil, even people who don't believe in anything psychic told us this. One of the nannies for our kids told us that our house was so bad that we should move right away. As you know, I'm a University professor and she helped me with the kids. I felt horrible leaving them every day, especially when the nanny was terrified to be in the house. She eventually quit. Before she left, though, she asked if her priest could do an exorcism on the house."

"Did that happen?" I asked. Della continued.

"Yes, her priest came but after two hours of working, he also told us to move, that the house was so evil that no one could clear it. So, I tried a variety of psychics and they all came over, but none were successful. One of our gardeners showed us an area on the property, which had obviously been used for devil worship. That was the first one; after he found more, he quit too.

"One by one our friends simply refused to visit us at our house anymore. They all said the house creeped them out and that they could feel the evil coming through the walls. What was I supposed to do with that? This is a two-million-dollar house! You don't just walk away and no one - no one - had a clue how to help us – until you came along. But there's more.

"We did have rats and mice and we could hear them at night. It was like living in a special hell. Finally, my parents felt we needed more help so they moved out here. But not long after they got here, my dad died of a heart attack. Then, as my mom was grieving him, she started feeling really terrible and she was diagnosed with double breast cancer. I – I feel so guilty that I have put my parents through so much. I lost my dad! I'm so guilty for this! How can I ever forgive myself? I feel like my house killed my dad and created my mom's cancer. My mom is recovering but she couldn't come over here anymore – we all knew it wasn't safe for her.

"There was the endless quarreling between Derek and me. We felt as if our entire marriage was beginning to fall apart." Derek picked up the thread of problems.

"Then there were the constant business failures. Do you realize that we have had five businesses fail? We're facing bankruptcy! This is the nightmare that doesn't end. But maybe now, now we might be able to get out from under all of this mess.

"You mentioned you thought we might have had car problems? The starter broke. Then, at only 120,000 miles the engine on our Honda – A HONDA – blew up. The mechanic said these things had no explanation; he said these were not normally problems to be found on such a reliable car at such relatively low mileage. Oh, and at only 40,000 miles, the transmission on our Cadillac crapped out and then the battery went. I almost forgot, I went out one morning and all the tires on the Honda were flat and the door handle fell off. You can't make this shit up. . .

"Our new TV quit, the heater broke and it was also new.

"Our two dogs and two cats seemed to be sick all the time so we had constant vet bills.

"Oh, and there's more."

As Derek was completing his litany and before Della could begin on the next set of catastrophes, I had a vision of a black magician smiling smugly at her many successes at seeking to destroy this family. I had made a huge dent, but I had a sick feeling that I had not found it all, not yet at least.

Gateway to Hell

Several days later, they asked me to visit them because they wanted to show me something.

"After you did so much clearing, we found 'it.' Come with us and we'll show it to you." Derek said this confidently as he led the way out of the room.

We wandered down two flights of stairs to a lower bedroom area near his daughter's room. It looked like this area of their home had become part house, part cave as it connected with the granite of Mt. Helix behind the wall. They thought it was just a wall, but they found that there was a door.

"We call this the hidden secret closet or the door to hell. We can only show it to you briefly. We realized it was deliberately walled over but it was definitely a room. Look inside this room – quickly."

I took a deep breath before I peeked into the room. I scanned the room as Derek directed and there, on the inside of this cave-like room was this thick tarry stuff on the tile. It looked like a portal to hell. I could sense and see black mold creeping the walls of this room. Surely this house cannot get any worse.

"Della, this is a portal. Do you remember that I told you that the black magician had booby-trapped the interior of the walls? Well, this looks like her main portal, which ironically you were able to find once I removed the evil witch who was haunting your house. I would strongly recommend that you bring in a cleaning crew to thoroughly scrub this space, open it up to the light and change the entire energy. You will need to pack it with salt too. Burn the resin of Dragon's Blood, Benzoin, and Frankincense to cleanse it psychically after they have removed the mold and black tarry substance there. That could also be black candle wax as whoever set up this house did some dark occult practices to set this home up to be the gateway to hell."

"Well, that would explain why our daughter had endless nightmares, why we felt there was an attempted possession of her. She was constantly anxious. And she's so psychic, even as a baby, she could see these entities. Then she began to have sexual nightmares. I felt there was something so evil about her bedroom but we never knew about this horrendous room until you cleared the house."

I began to think that now that they could think more clearly that could actually see or find this and maybe other weird things in the house.

"You both need to know that I did an extensive clearing but with a house this challenging, more is required. I strongly suggest that you let me come back and do a Feng Shui consultation. Feng Shui dramatically shifts the energy in a house from the moment the consult is scheduled until the 'cures' begin to go up, a shifting process begins. It's pretty amazing.

"It takes concentrated effort to make a house feel this horrible. And it takes serious work to clean them up. You need to have someone working with you who believes you – who can see what you're up against. Now it's time to follow-up with Feng Shui. There is so much more to do to shift the energy because while I changed things on the etheric level, you have to look for the physical elements that can create darkness in a home. This is why doing Feng Shui will add another element of clearing as well as bringing balance to your entire property, inside and out. I suspect that there are more things here you don't know you have that are facilitating the perpetuation of negative energy in this house."

The Astounding Power of Feng Shui

Della and Derek invited me to visit their house to Feng Shui it after things began to feel so much better. They wanted to build on the positive feeling by changing physical things in the house.

The Feng Shui consult began outside and the more I shared with this couple and their children that they could do to bring in positive energy, the more excited and happier they became.

We burned the resins of Dragon's Blood, Benzoin, and Frankincense while the consultation was going on. We carried it around the house. These resins will instantly shift the energy in any location. Dark entities have to leave and generally they do not come back.

Feng Shui mirrors are the aspirin of Feng Shui because they reflect back the energy of negativity that was somehow being aimed at the house. They are the most powerful tools that you can use to bring almost instant balance to any space. And this house needed several-hundred of them. I did warn them that if there was still a living magician focusing energy on their home beyond the dead one that I removed, there was the possibility that the sheer volume of this darkness would be returned to the sender: magnified. This has been known to cause the demise of the offending magician. I have seen it happen before. When a living person is sending dark energy to another person, family, or location, you cannot focus on the magician. You can only bring your attention to fortifying the dwelling to make it strong enough to repel the magician's attacks.

Then I began to get them to focus on the little things in their lives that could be creating problems.

"Okay guys, here we are in your dining room. Are there any problems when you sit down together?"

"Yes," Della replied. "Dinner time is battle time, find fault time: we all dread meals together. Why do you ask?"

"Because you have this massive painting of a horrific battle scene that faces your dining room table. This is a gorgeous room and this painting is setting a tone I'm not sure you realize you have set."

"But I like this painting and I'm not going to change it." Derek was most definite about this.

"Hey, I get it, it's an amazing painting. Would you be willing to do an experiment? How would it be if you moved this painting to your office? Then you could look at it all the time. Put a painting of luscious fruit or flowers on this wall, which will facilitate positive eating habits and happy conversation. Wouldn't this promote beneficial family communication? Isn't this what you really want?" I directed this to Derek and he got it.

"Yes, of course. I see your point." And with that, he immediately removed the painting.

We eventually visited their master bedroom. And in a glass cabinet squarely facing their bed, were about two hundred Hummel figurines of small children.

"Alright guys, how can you possibly have any type of intimate relationship with 200 little kids watching you? I mean the symbolism of this is just weird!"

"Well, my parents gave us those and my mom expects to see them when she visits." Della said defensively.

"Let's put them in a hallway. No way these belong in your bedroom. Will this work?"

Della agreed and I could immediately feel a difference in the room as they decided to move those tiny 'watchers.'

"Alright Derek, talk to me about all of these swords, and antique weapons here in your personal den. So glad it's not near your bedroom."

"Well, you know I was in the Army and I have an interest in these things. Is that bad?"

"No, but the symbolism is that you are constantly fighting an invisible enemy or that these items are actually being used against you. It's a bit too strange and it feels like you're always in combat. I guess my suggestion is to put these away for a while and see if things begin to calm down."

"I can do that, anything to help this house."

The Feng Shui consultation lasted four long hours and so many things changed that they could begin to feel it even before I left.

Epilogue

Della and Derek implemented 100% of the Feng Shui cures that I suggested. The atmosphere of their home continued to improve. Their nourishing sleep enabled them to come back into energetic balance and their arguments ceased, business improved for them and their friends felt that they could visit their home again. They also noticed that their health improved; equipment stopped breaking down;

the vermin vanished; leaks ceased and their cars run just fine now.

And then it happened. I got a call from them, about 30 days after they finished implementing most of the Feng Shui cures. Their next-door neighbors, who had always been pretty nasty to them, informed them that their elderly mother had suddenly died of unknown causes. I had been waiting for this. I had had a feeling that the current, living black magician, who was the daughter of the ghostly black magician I had found in their home was living very nearby.

And all these things were the good news. They should have been so much happier and yet. I found myself waiting for the other shoe to drop. One of the more esoteric aspects of Feng Shui is that once you begin making these powerful improvements anything that is karmically out of balance will immediately come to the surface. Removing the extraneous aspects of the outside interference enabled them to realize that their marriage was truly shaky. One of the key factors, the elephant in the room was why this couple was attracted to all of this negative energy in the first place. I had asked them what attracted the to this house and they said it was the amount of beautiful light that poured into all the windows, the open concept, and the pretty front yard. They admitted that the back yard was pretty rough.

Despite all of their work, the couple discovered that one of them had some very dark elements to their personality, which was the attracting resonant frequency. They finally sold the house without taking a loss and not long after that, they divorced. It was how it worked out. Clearing the house enabled them to see the real issues and free themselves of their binding relationship, which had become sadly toxic. They were able to part as friends. Now, more than just their house has been cleared.

Ghost Stories from the Ghosts' Point of View Vol 3

Ghost Stories from the Ghosts' Point of View Vol 3

The Wrong Side of the Tracks

The Business of Living

Hank has so many properties in Virginia and I swear that I have remote viewed and cleared all of them. He is quite the landlord. But this story is not exactly about Hank. He's part of it, a willing part of it, but he is almost incidental. Each call I get to clear a location opens me up to the stories of the dead I am honored to help. Each living person/client who helps a dead person seems mildly, somewhat absent-mindedly glad to participate. Usually, they just want the energy to calm down so that they can get on with the business of living.

    The business of living is what it's all about – it's what we all do. We ceaselessly and mindlessly wander and intermingle with the dead who are often still there, their essence still lingering like faint perfume after the soul has passed. It is the energy of that essence that calls me to help them, to find them and to send them on their way.

Hank had some storage units on the Eastern Shore of Virginia. He was having trouble renting them out and he wanted me to remote view the area, clear his property, and then offer him some Feng Shui tips to enhance his business. Straightforward, simple – or it should have been. But it was anything but simple and it was unlike anything I had ever done previously. As I gaze back at this time, I am grateful to have played my part and been able to help all the parties involved get back to the business of living, wherever that would be.

Making Feng Shui Notes

Hank's two-acre property was on the outskirts of the tiny town of Exmore, Virginia. It seemed lonely and untouched by modern day energies. Perhaps that feeling stemmed from the density of the depressing darkness that enveloped that area in the ether, the 4th dimension. The bar next door to the storage units was certainly not enhancing the energy of my client's business. The bar's decrepit exterior and the ghosts lingering outside made me shiver because I could see all the Lower Realm Intelligences and barroom ghosts inside, urging the living patrons to drink more and more. I removed all the drunken ghosts and any Lower Realm Intelligences that had wandered on to Hank's area. But let's make matters even dimmer: there was also a graveyard nearby full of ghosts. They all seemed to be fighting each other over some element of fundamentalist religion. Each ghost wanted the other ghosts to reform to their version of the 'correct' belief in God. The irony was that they were all equally dead, all equally stuck in the darkness of their own anger and none were seeking the light.

Pulling the Thread

The next night I returned to the Eastern Shore to clean up the rest of this storage unit area. Since Hank owned all the units, I had permission to clear them all, no matter who had rented them. Spiritual cleaning ladies still have to scrub darkness out of areas, remove the Lower Realm Intelligences and brighten the place up. It is amazing how quickly you can feel the difference once that is done. So, I set about my work of cleaning as I was sweeping in and out of roughly 30 storage units. People put all kinds of 'stuff' in storage units, things they don't need, things they have no place for and things they do not want anyone else to see. There is no way for me to know what someone wants hidden, what deep secrets someone is trying to conceal. Well, unless what you are hiding is a body. . .

My main focus was removing any dark or negative energy. If you remove dark, toxic energy you will find that your business improves and you welcome better clientele because you have inherently raised the frequency of a location. If you continue to raise that frequency you should always have good business and positive clients/customers.

Is '7' a Lucky Number?

About halfway through my cleaning project I swooped into a storage unit with the number 7 on it. Could have been 27 or 7 or 17. The only number of any significance that stood out was the number 7. I found myself standing in this unit and sensing the energy of an 18-year-old girl.

"Can you see me? Can you help me? I think I'm dead, but you know I'm not sure. I kind of woke up after, after that party I went to at school but now I – I don't understand."

I could see her pretty hair, her clothes, and that overall, she was that typical adorable blond co-ed beginning her freshman year in college.

"Yes, I can see you and hear you too. Do you know what happened to you? What's the last thing that you remember?"

"I'm in a sorority at UVA - oh, that would be the University of Virginia. I guess I'm not too sure who you are or how I can talk to you. But anyway, one of my sorority sisters invited me to a mixer party at one of the houses on fraternity row. I had never been to one of those parties before. I – I wasn't sure what to expect. They had a band and it was super loud and this guy offered to get me a drink and then we went outside and sat under the trees near the house so that we could talk. He was really cute; said he was majoring in business. That's all I remember, and now. . .

"Now I'm here, wherever 'here' is. Where am I? Am I dead? I don't understand what happened to me, or how I got here. I guess maybe he put something in the drink he gave me. But I'm confused. . . Who are you and how can I talk to you?"

"I'm a psychic who clears homes, businesses, and property. I was hired to clear this storage unit of negative energy and ghosts. I'm Tina. What's your name?"

"Julia Stuart, or I used to be."

"I wish we could have met under better circumstances. How do you feel? Are you in any pain?"

"Am I dead? If you're dead, do you still feel pain, because I'm having a lot of trouble breathing?"

"Yes, the dead still feel pain but it is generally not as intense. How intense is your breathing problem?"

"Pretty tough, like I'm all wrapped up. It's like I still have a body but yet, I feel separated from it. Is that weird? I know I need you or somebody to help me. I can't imagine how worried my family and friends must be. I think this happened last night but I have no sense of time here. It's always dark and I can talk to you but I cannot seem to move, like my arms are bound up, and at the same time it's as if I'm

The Wrong Side of the Tracks

separated from 'me,' or who I am somehow. Do you know what I mean? Is any of this making sense to you?"

I paused for a moment and pondered what she was saying. This was not the typical ghost I would expect to see. Something else was happening here. What if she isn't dead?

"Julia, I'm bringing in an angel to stand by you, to help you. I have to investigate your situation a bit more and see if there is something more going on here, something unusual."

"Go for it. I have to get out of here, wherever here is but you know I don't see my body either, so am I dead? Are you supposed to see your body when you're dead? Is my body somewhere else?"

"Julia, honey, right now, I don't know. I don't usually see the person's body; I see the soul so my not seeing your physical body isn't that unusual. Most of the time, the dead cannot see their physical body. So, again, I have to investigate this situation. I've brought this bright angel to stand by your side and give you the courage to face the situation you're in – whatever it may be, you're in quite a dangerous situation whatever it is, especially if you are separated from your body. I'll get back to you."

I looked at the bright angel who was shaking his head, meaning he could not take her to the other side. Oh my God, she's still alive? Now what?

Getting Very, Very Complicated

Julia's situation left me completely perplexed. If she was not dead, was she in a coma? Was that possible? What if it was something else? What part of her was I talking to? Was it her subconscious? Was there part of her crying out? What was her connection to the storage unit in the middle of nowhere? So, I called my sister Andrea, filled her in on Julia, and brainstormed the problem.

"What if she isn't dead, Tina, what if she's missing? Could that be a possibility?"

"Anything's possible. Is there any way to look her up? She's not in the storage unit. I mean I'm virtually positive her body is not there but somewhere else and that is a very strong feeling. Something happened and she is disconnected from her body. I'm pretty sure of that, but I get the impression something of hers is in that unit and she is connecting to that or she was there for a while and they – whoever 'they' are – moved her. Could be a locket, a scarf, something, and she is tied to it through the aka cords. Maybe she was in the storage unit for a while. Maybe he or they thought they killed her but she wasn't dead? What if they moved her somewhere else?"

"So much we don't know. I'm searching now on the missing and exploited children website for Virginia and she isn't listed. Here, let me try the one for Maryland. The Chesapeake Bay Bridge Tunnel connects directly to Maryland on the far end. Oh look, here she is! I see her:

cute, blonde, age 18 and it looks like she went missing nine months ago from UVA. Oh, Tina, I bet her parents are frantic."

"Andy, you know, I think there's a chance this girl is alive and her body is somewhere else and something she owned is in this storage unit - something I can't see. Seeing in the physical is a bit tough for me."

"So, what do we do? Do we call them?"

I shuddered.

"It's the right thing to do but you know when a psychic is involved, they always suspect the psychic of participating in the crime. Let's not go there."

"Well, it says right here that you can make an anonymous call."

"Yes, Andy, but they can trace the phone."

"Not if I go to a pay phone and call. I think the airport still has those. I could make the call. What do you think?"

"What if we're wrong? What if I made a mistake? But what if I'm right? Andy, I spoke to this girl. She is real to me. This is so bizarre. I can feel the minutes ticking by and every minute that goes by increases the danger, the risk to this girl. I can't tell anything about the owner/renter of the storage unit. Only Julia's presence, her energy is visible to me. We have to do something, you're right, and soon."

"Okay look, I'll go make a quick drive to the airport and give the hotline people all that we have: the name of the storage unit, that there is the number '7' above the unit and that she's still alive and something in that unit will connect them to her. That's all we know, isn't it?"

"Yes, Andy, that's it, that's all I know. Let's pray they don't ask us how we know. Let's pray that they find this girl alive. Oh goodness, Hank! What about Hank? We need to warn him!"

"Oh, Geeze. Yeah, you better call him. I'll call the hotline for Maryland's missing teens. I'm leaving now. I'll call you back."

I had a foreboding chill of doubtful fear sweep me. No, I'm not wrong about this I reminded myself. I could not live with myself if I did not take the action of my convictions and my psychic ability.

Our Secret

"Wow, Tina, that's some story. So, you think she's alive?"

"Yes, Hank, I do. I think there's a very slight chance her body is in this storage unit but more likely there is something that connects this girl to her body. My feeling is that she's not there but her subconscious is in the storage shed for some baffling reason.

"Hank, I need you to please keep our involvement a secret. They won't tell you how they picked this unit or why they know. They may just tell you that a 'tip' came in and here they are. It's possible that they won't find anything. It's a risk I'm willing to take to help this young girl. The fact that we found her name and picture on the missing teens website and that we have this connection is baffling, but for now, please keep this our secret."

"No problem, I'll be glad to hold on to our secret. I wonder if anyone will come, you know? I'll be standing by. How much detail did you give the hotline?"

"Andy told them the name of your storage facility, and the exact address and that Julia Stuart or something about her is in a unit with the number '7' on it. That's all they have to go on. I wonder if they will have a search warrant or will they just ask you to open it up. Maybe nothing will happen. I have no idea how this will work out. Needless to say, we all hope that Julia can be found."

"Of course. Glad to help. I'll let you know if we see any action in our quiet neck of the woods."

Hank Reports

Hank's call later that same night was bursting with excitement.

"Hey, Tina, just had to let you know that the police called me and asked me if I would cooperate in an 'on-going investigation.' They said they had a 'tip' about something. I met them at the storage unit and let them in as they arrived in three police cars with two cadaver dogs. The lead investigator said they had a hotline tip about one of my storage units with the number '7' in it! Can you believe they are taking action on your tip?"

That same chill of fear swept me again. Was it fear or was it the excitement, the hope of helping the authorities find someone's daughter?

"Wow, that's . . . that's, I don't know what to say. I'm hoping that they find a clue that will lead them to this young girl. Thanks so much for keeping me posted. Did they break the lock for any of the storage units? Are you there now with them?"

"Yeah, I'm in my car. They said that they wanted the cadaver dogs to help them to determine which unit to open. Oh, now, they are focused on one and they even have an ambulance here in case, I guess in case they actually find a body."

"What's happening now? Can you see anything?"

"Just a sec . . . they're entering a storage unit and it has a '7' on it! Now they are running crime scene tape across it and have posted officers outside of it. Oh, Tina, they are removing a rug. I wonder if there's a body in that rug! I'll go ask."

"Thanks, Hank."

I waited with growing hope that they would not find a body but a clue for Julia's whereabouts. I did not have to wait long.

"Hey, Tina, they wanted me to give them all the information I have about the guy who rented this space. Apparently, the dogs alerted on something. I have to head to the office to get it. They only said that there is no body there but that they found 'things of interest.' He said that like it was suspicious and like I said, they used crime scene tape and they aren't packing up to leave. If they had found nothing, they would probably have left by now. So, I'll get them the info. I'll let you know tomorrow if I hear anything else. I haven't let on that I know about how they got the tip. It's our secret for sure."

"Thanks, Hank."

No More Contact

I went back that night to remote view the storage unit and try and connect with Julia again, but I no longer sensed her energy. Something had changed. I was so hopeful for her, praying they would find her alive. I called Hank back the next day but all the police told him was that this was 'an on-going investigation' and they couldn't tell him anything more.

Faith was all I had. Faith that our call made a difference, faith that something positive would come. Andy and I continued to pray for Julia and hoped that providing her subconscious with the bright angel would make a difference.

About two weeks later I called my sister to discuss the storage unit situation.

"Andy, what do you think happened?"

"I don't know. They must have found something."

"Why don't you go ahead and check the website. See if she's still on it."

"Okay. Checking, checking. I've typed her name in repeatedly and now there's no record of her, her picture is gone, everything about her case is gone. I dare not call again. They probably can't tell me anything or they won't under privacy rules, and they don't know who I am, so they wouldn't share anything. This feels so anticlimactic. I'm dying to know if they found her. Hank hasn't said a word to you has he, Tina?"

"No, Andy, he promised to call me if he did hear. I bet he's as anxious to know as we are. At least we know that the dogs alerted. I bet that they feel that the 'tip' was valuable and since they took her off the website, I bet they found her. We just don't know if she was found alive or not. This is such good news. Maybe at least there is closure for her parents. I think we know she isn't missing anymore since she's not on that website. We did all we could. Maybe we have to be content with that."

"Yes, but I really want to know exactly what happened."

The Torture of Not Knowing

"Hey Tina, now that you're coming out to visit next month, do you want me to set up a lunch with Hank? Could be interesting. At least we can commiserate about the storage unit."

"That would be great. It's been six months. You'd think we would have had some way to know what happened. Let me know what Hank says."

A month later, Andy and I met Hank at an elegant Italian restaurant in Virginia Beach. We talked about all the properties I had helped him with and how the Feng Shui had enabled him to improve his business. Finally, I brought up the storage unit, figuring that he still didn't know anything but it never hurts to ask.

"You know, Hank, I still can't get over that remote view of that storage unit. I saw Julia, but I wasn't sure she was dead. Usually, the dead are easy to cross over, but something about her was unnerving – I know – even for me and I began to believe that she wasn't dead. Thank you for keeping our secret. Andy and I would still love to know what happened to her. Bet you would too."

"You mean I didn't tell you? Oh geeze, I'm so sorry I never called you. The detective called me about two months ago to thank me for being so cooperative in the investigation. He said that he was happy to report that they found Julia – alive – in Florida. Several men were holding her captive. Oh, and they didn't just find Julia, they found several other co-eds who were being held captive, who had been kidnapped from various colleges on the East Coast. They uncovered evidence of other kidnappings in that storage shed but they seemed to have the most from Julia, maybe because she was the most recent girl they took. I got the impression from the detective that it was a group getting ready to put these young women up for sale in the white slavery market. She and all of them were rescued and returned to their families. That detective was really grateful. Wish I could have told him about you but I kept your secret like you asked. You ladies did good, real good."

YOU FORGOT TO TELL US????? I screamed in my head. But with some effort, I responded in a controlled fashion.

"That's fantastic! Thank you, Hank, for closing the loop on this. No, you hadn't shared that wonderful outcome. Seems they found more than just Julia there. I guess we can only speculate on what those items were but this must have been a huge missing link for detectives probably in several states. Thank God we were all able to help; we all played a part in her rescue and the rescue and reunion of all of those girls. All of our prayers were answered."

Epilogue

Who was I talking to in that storage unit? Julia was not dead, so I was not speaking to her ghost. I believe that her subconscious had separated from her body at the shock of all that was happening to her – and I will never know all that happened to her. Maybe I don't want to know. I have a suspicion that when they wrapped her up in that rug and she felt her arms and legs bound, she may have separated from her body and that would be the last thing she remembered. Maybe they took her out of the rug, drugged her in that storage unit, and then took her out of the unit and moved her to Florida. Maybe they changed Julia's clothes in that storage unit, maybe they kept a piece of jewelry as a token prize and she connected to that. I will never know. Andy and I are forever grateful to the powers that be that enabled us to help the police find Julia and the other girls and return them safely to their families.

My sister and I both have daughters. We had to control our feelings, imagining the anguish Julia's mother must have been feeling after her daughter was kidnapped. How can you live this way? Never knowing what happened to your precious daughter – an utter nightmare.

I was grateful, as well, for the signal from that angel and that I trusted 'my gut instinct' that she was not dead. It was as if her subconscious was screaming out for help and found us. I do not know how it all works. I only know that it did work, she was found alive and returned. Every time I think of her reunion with her mother I smile inside.

There are those moments when it would be nice to have concrete proof that remote viewing and psychic ability have a tangible result. That a psychic in California can project consciousness to a storage unit 3,000 miles away in a remote location in Virginia and sense the energy of a kidnapped girl is (even for me), astounding. Now we know that those skills did make a difference. We are forever grateful that we could be a part of something so life-changing, so lifesaving. My sister and I felt blessed that we had a hand in helping so many young women get on with the business of living – in this dimension.

There was one final irony here for me. We were able to anonymously call the Missing and Exploited Person hotline. We did not tell them that a psychic had provided the information. We just offered a tip. We were believed enough to get the police out there and get the case solved. Several years later, I had another case where I plucked up my courage and went to the police with information about a cold case murder. I had spoken to the girl who died and she told me who killed her. After I crossed her over, I gave the information to the police who had been asking the public for help in solving the case. One detective listened and directed me to call back in five days. I did so, but another detective had been assigned to the case and he thought any information from a psychic was worthless and told me so. That murderer is still out there; that case remains unsolved.

The Pony Express

Long before California became a state, people were making their way here to start a new life or escape a life with too many dark memories.

My clients lived in Alpine, California, about 35 miles east of San Diego. Solar covered roofs catching the sundrenched energy of 300 sunny days each year dot the rugged, scrub hills and mountains that line I-8 East to an elevation of over 4,000 feet.

Kennedy and Gerald Millhouse purchased 134 acres of desert scrub to create a health spa and emotional and spiritual retreat. It looked absolutely empty. They planned to put up an adobe style ranch house or inn, a stable and create trails among the native plants of this desert landscape. It sounded like a lovely idea. However, they kept having problems with whatever they tried to do on the property.

"Tina, do you want us to tell you the problems we're having? Is that what we're supposed to do?" Kennedy asked me when she and her husband called.

I marvel that it is usually the wife who begins the conversation with me when it regards the supernatural. Thinking back, I have seldom had a husband start the conversation about what a house or property was experiencing.

"No, that isn't necessary. I would rather find out what is happening without any prior knowledge of the property history. Too much information can cloud my psychic vision, so the less the better. You are more than welcome to tell me all that has transpired here when I have finished my work. In fact, you should feel a type of 'shift' once I have begun and definitely once I have completed the cleansing of your property."

"Hi Tina, Gerald here. Will you be coming out and burning sage on all 134 acres? Isn't that a fire hazard? Yeah, listening to myself, I'm a bit skeptical and nervous about fire out here."

"Oh, heavens no! Sage is worthless for removing any negative energy and you are absolutely right to be worried about fire in any area that has scrub vegetation. No, I do something called remote viewing. I won't be coming to your property at all in the physical sense. Let me explain."

"I so don't get this. How can you clear property without being here?"

"All thought is energy and there are those of us who have the ability to project energy to a specific location, evaluate what is there, and then clear the etheric energy of that place, all from the comfort of my own home. Some people call it psychic vision. The Secret Service, the CIA and the Russian/Soviet KGB all used it during the Cold War. You can look this up. The Italian terrorist group, the Red Brigade, kidnapped Brigadier General James Dozier, in 1981. The CIA used in-house remote viewers to locate him. Their accuracy was stunning. It is a well-accepted practice in many spiritual and oddly, intelligence circles."

I could feel Gerald was still not buying it.

"Yeah, this is just - just too strange for me. But nothing else we have tried seems to work, so I guess go ahead and do your thing."

The Echo House

Finding the property was uncomplicated, and at first all I could see was the kitchen of the present-day bungalow where they were living while the main ranch house was being built. Pretty soon, that seemed to fall away and I was able to find the outline of a previous structure, almost like it was an echo of an earlier house.

As the former dwelling and surrounding land unfolded, this unchanging desert area looked no different 100 years ago than it did in the present day. The only difference then was a two-story wooden structure on the property, which I see from a distance. There were corrals for horses and a companion barn close by and what looked to me like a blacksmith shop.

As I drew closer, there was a sign that said Stagecoach and Pony Express Stop on the front of the building. It had a green tin roof above the white painted house. I could see what may have been called the rider house, where riders for the pony express could stop and spend the night. The two-story building was lodging for those passengers when the Stagecoach line stopped there. There was a restaurant inside the white building and modestly appointed rooms upstairs. You could see clotheslines outside behind the building with billowing sheets drying in the hot desert air. A windmill near by pumped water to the buildings for people and horses.

So far, there was nothing raw or violent there, just the early elements of young California as this way station in the desert helped people to make the transcontinental crossing to the Pacific. The energy of some of the transient guests was less than stellar but nothing that would create problems . . . except for this one gorgeous red-haired woman.

The Escapee

She was stunning, her red hair glistening even in the beleaguering darkness of the 4th dimension. She approached me first.

"Can you see me? Hey, you, bright lady, can - can you see me standing here? I haven't seen anyone to talk to."

"Yes," I responded. "Yes, I can see you. What gorgeous hair you have!"

"Well, let me tell you, this hair hasn't done me any favors. I used to love my hair until it became a liability but you know I just couldn't cut it. I half wonder if that would have made a difference. My name's Libby, Libby Hughes."

"Hello, Libby. My name's Tina and I've come to help you out of this place. Would you like to tell me what happened to you? How did you come to be at this Stagecoach stop?"

"I escaped. I plotted and planned it and then I left that devil, who had enslaved me. I saved enough money and sold clothes and jewelry and then I got a ticket on the stage for points west. I told him I was visiting my aunt for two days because she was ill. My aunt helped me out but I knew he would eventually find out what happened. I couldn't keep it a secret forever. I had hoped that I could disappear out west and that no one would ever find me. I even changed my name. I guess my name doesn't even matter now, does it? I reckon I'm stuck in this desert forever."

"How long were you married or were you married to him? What was his name?"

"I'd only been married to him for about a year but it was a year of pure hell. I hated him – Reginald, he called himself. He was a beast, a pig, a slob – an abomination who didn't bathe and delighted in raping me whenever he felt like it. He had no business having a wife. I was his slave. I should have guessed when people whispered about his other wives. He claimed that they all left him because they were selfish women but that I was different. I wasn't any different: I was available. At first all of his gentlemanly attention was flattering, but once we were married, a totally different man emerged, one so evil, so cruel that I knew that I had to get away.

"I piled my hair up on my head and wore a hat so people would not remember this infernal red hair and I could slip maybe unnoticed, but the fact that I was traveling without a man by my side made me noticeable no matter what I did."

"How far did you get? Where did you come from? What state?"

"I was living in Philadelphia, Pennsylvania. I kept changing stages, I changed clothes, hats and even tried to pay a guy to pretend I was his wife but no one would help me escape Reginald. I felt I was getting pretty far ahead but then one of the coaches broke down and we lost several days in Oklahoma. I took this route, this southern route over the mountains even though he would have expected me to take a train to either San Francisco or even Los Angeles. I tried to be clever. I knew I was running for my life that if he or his goons ever caught up with me, I would be dead. I now know that he must have killed his other wives. Maybe they ran off too, but I know he tracked them all down and killed them making sure no one could ever leave him. I planned my escape the best I could; I tried so hard; you know? But I had no idea his men were so close."

"Do you remember how it happened? Did you know they were in the building?"

The Pony Express

"No. I didn't know what his goons looked like. He had so many shady men working for him that I would not have known who was looking for me. The last thing I remember is that I was brushing my hair – now that I was alone in my own room - and three men broke through the door and shot me. I remember my horror and fear as the bullets ripped through me and then suddenly, I was standing there looking at my blood soaked, bullet-ridden body.

"I heard one of them say: 'See, nobody ever leaves Reginald.' I thought to myself: and neither will any of you, now that you have committed murder for him. Murder for hire means he can hire some other dumb guy to kill all three of you. Murder means nothing to Reginald as long as he gets his way. There is no justice.

"I had such plans for my life, you know? I wanted to love someone who would love me back and grow old with me. I wanted children and grandchildren. I wanted to see the West and have an adventure, not live like an animal escaped from my cruel keeper. I couldn't go back to my family. They didn't believe me when I told them how cruel he was. They would have returned me to him. I was alone in the world. Only my grandmother believed me, and she died about six months before I left.

"I'm so confused. I know that they killed me last night but I don't know what happens now. I've been so cold since I died and I don't know how to get warm. Do you know where I go from here?"

"Libby, what year is it?"

"Why, it's 1870. Why do you ask?"

"Just curious, it's not important. Here is a beautiful golden shawl to go with your crimson hair. You'll definitely be warmer now.

"You see, once you died you simply remained stuck in this dark world. I've also brought along a protective and powerful escort, who will guide you across that Light Bridge to the Heaven World you see right over there. Once you are there, wonderful beings will help you to understand this life you have just lived. I know it's confusing."

"It – it is confusing yet for the first time in what feels like a long time I feel safe and now, warm. But if I only died last night. . . I guess I don't understand how this works, how you can help me. I don't even know your name or how you came to help me. I can feel the light and the love that is there. Thank you for finding me and helping me out of this place."

Libby and the Angel smiled at me as they slipped into the light stream that is the Heaven World. I knew that someone loving would meet her and welcome her home.

Quake Country

There were no more ghosts in any stack of time that I could find on that property, however, I was still sensing something unsettling so I continued to look around and analyze what was there. In this dimension, it is relatively easy to look beneath the surface of the earth and see what factors are influencing the energetic frequency of a location. Often it is underground water or slipping sand and sometimes it is an earthquake fault.

That was precisely the case here. Earthquake faults can create a permanent feeling of unease on a piece of property. This land was sitting on a very fractured earthquake fault. This causes subtle energy shifts to take place that create an anxious feeling. Because of this feeling of fractured energy, people and animals do not feel safe here. This area would have been devoid of some of the larger wild animals, and horses would have felt uneasy all the time in any corral. Fractured earth opens up pathways for Lower Realm Intelligences to move from the 4th dimension to the 3rd dimension though these subduction plate tectonics. And they were all over the place here. But the centuries of time that this desolate area has existed did not see many people living on it, which was why there were not more ghosts.

All I can do to balance the energy of a subduction plate or earthquake fault is to etherically add balancing energy to it and seal up as much of the dark entrances as possible.

"I Knew It!"

When I returned to talk to Gerald and Kennedy, they sound much happier.

"You know, we aren't sure what you did on this land, but we can feel a difference. I mean, I'm impressed and that's saying something coming from me!"

Gerald's comments felt like high praise.

"So, what was happening and what kind of difference do you feel? The feedback is important."

"Well, first off, all of our horses and even the dogs seemed skittish all the time. There was an area of the property that they would actively try to avoid and now they have no problem walking in that spot. Kennedy and I are sleeping better. Aren't we honey?"

"Oh yes and even though Gerald still feels that what you do is weird, he can't argue with success. Did you find any ghosts? That was my biggest curiosity. I always felt something happened here."

"Yes, you had a rather gorgeous ghost with long wavy red hair and a beautiful face. Her overbearing possessive husband had her murdered when she tried to escape him. She had made it from Philadelphia to here when his hired guns caught up with her and killed her. My heart went out to her. She thought they killed her last night but she actually died in 1870. She could be buried somewhere on the property but I have no idea where her body might be. It could be where the animals were reluctant to go. Oh, and you had quite a few earthquake faults. I worked to calm that energy."

"I knew it! I'm so glad you could help her. I can't tell you how much better we feel. I didn't realize we had any quake faults but then we didn't look at a geologic map when we bought the property. Hopefully that won't continue to affect us. Thank you so much. Things feel so much better."

Epilogue

Libby Hughes received the help she needed and the area was cleaned and cleared. Kennedy and Gerald went on to build their spa retreat, and Gerald gained a new respect for remote viewing.

I am always grateful that the dead have no idea how long they have been waiting in that darkness. Poor Libby had been there for over 140 years when I remote viewed this dusty spot of earth in Alpine, California.

Terror Through Time

"Hi Tina, so glad we get to chat. Thanks for calling me back. I love all the Feng Shui that we did together. I can tell you, the house feels so much better, more balanced, and happier, and everyone is sleeping well."

"That's great, Valerie. How are your girls?"

"They're doing really well. Ah, mostly they're doing well. There's just one little problem and that's why I called you."

"Okay."

"It's my oldest daughter, Sophie, who's pretty psychic for only four years old. That's why we have done so much to fortify the house against ghosts. We put up all the cures, did all the intentioning you taught us to do, put angel images in her room and my husband and I are diligent in doing our spiritual practices. Our house feels great. Sophie hasn't indicated that she sees ghosts here since the last time you cleared it. We think we're doing all the right things. We've got the green lights going at night, beautiful music, you know, the works."

"Sounds perfect to me. Then something else must have happened."

"Yes, it has. Something must have shifted that I missed because all of a sudden, she won't go upstairs to her playroom. We have this great house where we have lots of open space and there's an upstairs playroom that overlooks the great room, so I can see and hear her playing. She loves that room. Or she used to love that room. Now I can't even get her to climb the stairs without her hyperventilating, crying, and begging me not to make her go beyond the very first step. This is nuts. Makes my husband, William, so frustrated and he and I didn't know what else to do but call you."

"What does Sophie say she sees when she starts to climb the stairs?"

"Oh my God, that's the strangest part. She doesn't see anything. She just feels fear and dread. She seems terrified when she faces the stairs. William is torn between believing her and wondering if she is trying to get attention. But she hasn't exhibited this behavior before. It's as if every time I suggest that she go upstairs I'm creating more fear and anxiety inside of her. We're utterly baffled. I keep going back to the fact that she isn't telling me that she is seeing anything scary. Oh, and this happens day and night. Time of day doesn't seem to matter. We can be playing with her, and she's laughing and talking to us and then ask her to run upstairs and it's as if we asked her to march into hell. This is the weirdest thing. What do you think?"

"This is the strangest thing, you're right. Did you burn Dragon's Blood on the stairs and her playroom?"

"Oh yes, we used lots of it and it felt great afterward and it made absolutely no difference to her. Her terror was still there."

"Can I talk to her? Can we do a video chat?"

I felt that if I could talk to her just a bit, I could gain better insight into her situation. Normally, I just do the remote view, but something about this case was different, needing a slightly altered approach.

Fear in the Morning

"Okay Tina, we can see you now. Sophie, come say high to our friend Tina."

"Hi Sophie, how are you doing?"

"I'm okay."

"How's your day, sweetie?" I can see her soft brown eyes and shiny brown hair as she smiles at me over the computer screen. She's so adorable and so bright.

"It's good. I've been playing with my Legos. Here is my Lego doll. I can build a house. Do you want to see it?" She answers me in her charming little girl voice. Her sunny mood and eager smile are so warm, normal, and natural, as if nothing's bothering her.

"Oh, I love your doll and you know I love Legos. They're so much fun! But Sophie, I want to ask you a question. Your mom is telling me that you don't want to walk up the stairs to your playroom. Can you tell me what you see when you start to climb the stairs?"

As soon as I ask her this question, her eyes fill with tears and her sunny mood darkens as if a terrifying storm is approaching and she is plunged into a scary place. She nibbles her lower lip. She looks at the floor. Then she looks up at me through the magic of our computers.

"Please don't make me go upstairs. I don't want to go up that step." Then she bursts in to sobs and starts hyperventilating. Her mom hugs her and tells her that she is safe, but Sophie is unconvinced.

Tears of fear slip down her face as she begs: "Don't make me go upstairs, Mommy. Please!"

What was Sophie seeing? More specifically what was she seeing that she couldn't describe? I was completely perplexed because this family had worked diligently to raise their personal frequencies and the vibration of their home. They are conscientious with their spiritual practices and their home is loving and wonderful.

Sophie calmed down and she and I stopped chatting. She returned to playing with her Legos. Valerie turned to me, bewildered.

"Tina, what do we do? Do you believe she is genuinely afraid?"

"Oh, I absolutely believe her. I also feel that this emotion is so powerful and is so instantly triggered that we must find it. Let me take a look around and I'll get back to you.

Seeing the Face of Terror

Valerie and William's home is in a beautiful, well-kept, and friendly bedroom community of Denver, Colorado. That night I remote viewed their home – again. It had only been a month since I last scanned it after they moved in and removed two ghosts in their garage. Once those lost souls were transitioned, the rest of the house was fine.

This time as I remote viewed the house, I noticed that there were no ghosts, no lower realm intelligences, and no dark beings. The house felt just great. So, I waited.

I waited for the stacks of time to manifest. There it was: before there were bedroom communities outside of Denver, before there were settlements here and there, a vast open rolling landscape was all that could be seen. As I scanned this stack of time, I could see a Native American encampment, with Braves practicing running a raid on a settlement or perhaps a wagon train as it crossed their area.

Faces painted with black, white, and red lines with black terrorizing circles around each eye made for chilling images as they began their practice raids on horseback against the imagined settlers with whoops and screams. I watched as these men practiced brandishing shock and terror over and over, each time a bit more forcefully than the last.

But in this moment, in this stack of time, no one died. These men were only rehearsing their actions. I shuddered to think of the men, women and children who would eventually face them in their future, which is now, Colorado history. This area of Denver experienced many massacres of European settlers. Seeing these Braves in preparation was an aspect of history unknown to those of us who study American history and the frightening things people faced as they moved into all the lands of what became the United States. There were also massacres of Native Americans by the Colorado Territory militia. There was little mercy as wars saw slaughters on both sides.

European settlers simply took what they wanted. They did not ask the Native people; there was no compensation to these first Americans for the land that was taken. What made this so much harder was that Native Americans did not 'own' land. They respected the land, used its riches but did not deplete it. They wintered in one area and then moved to other areas as the seasons changed. 'Ownership' was not something they could understand or why the white man could not share the land. Native Americans rightly feared the takeover of all of their domains as thousands upon thousands of land hungry people invaded their sacred spaces. They were defending their very way of life. They wanted to terrify their invaders so that they would not linger here but would move on further west or return from whence they came.

Colliding Markers in Time

It used to be that we thought of time as a straight line, and once that 'time' was over, it had no further influence on the present. But Einstein noted that time does not flow like a straight running river. Time moves in eddies and pools, in loops and in ascending and descending stacks. Understanding that all time exists at the same time is still a challenging concept for all of us to understand. So, if all time is operating at the same time barely separated by the distance between specific stacks, then it must be theoretically possible for two moments of time to collide. This concept would then make it possible for one person, or child to see the overlay of that previous time. As I am going over this in my head, I pause and ask myself if this makes any sense. Does this happen more often than we know? Have other people seen this? I have seen it many times but usually I would find it because someone had died in a location and the energy of the method of death would create a powerful marker in time. Dynamic, tragic, or joyous events can leave an energetic signature on a location.

Perhaps the reason that so many famous locations are set aside as historic places is because the energy of the event that created its historic designation in the first place is so powerful that no one should live on that spot on the Earth. Consider Independence Hall in Philadelphia, Pennsylvania where the Constitution of the United States was signed. This location was part of changing the history of the world. Consider also, that battlefields, graveyards, or massacre sites continue to emanate for centuries after the horror has ceased, the bodies buried and the memories forgotten. Think how unhealthy it would be for anyone to live at the site of a Nazi concentration camp. These are places we know of, and we can easily understand the influence of history that they exert. But what about the places that moved unnoticed into the slipstream of history? We may not consciously know about them, but the residual energy of that moment or that stack of time can still influence us.

Can You Manipulate Time?

I think I understand what happened to Sophie. I suspect that perhaps it was near this place and time of year, over a hundred and sixty years ago that these Native American warriors were practicing going on a raid.

Sophie was seeing these chilling men through her subconscious mind, in this overlay of time. This previous moment felt scary to her. Maybe she had a past life and she saw them in that past life, maybe they influenced her during that time or did in fact end her life. Did Sophie die in the raid these Braves eventually conducted? Was the image of their horrifically painted faces, burned into the subconscious of this child? At this point we are never going to know for sure. All I know is that this stack of time was influencing Sophie and I had to figure out what to do about it.

As I am watching this ever-repeating scene before me in my remote view, I pondered the challenge of the moment. I cannot change history. These Braves were practicing in that exact spot where Sophie's house is currently located. How do I stop the action? How do I change some aspect of their situation enough to stop Sophie from seeing these regrettably memorable faces?

When you are considering your options in such a bizarre situation many thoughts spiral though your head. Two factors would seem to come to mind. The first is the fact that during the time that the Braves were practicing, they were not repeating that action forever. Time itself would move past that set of practicing days. Many tribes only camped in areas for a limited time and then moved on. It is possible that had I never looked into this, the problem would have taken care of itself. However, I did look. I did know what she was seeing. I chose to help her.

I decided to do something to influence the land during that time, specifically, this spot of land where Sophie's current house is in this modern age. The footprint of their home is not large, just the house, a tiny front yard and driveway and a very small backyard. Not even a quarter acre. What I chose to do was to clear this tiny footprint of land through that previous stack of time. This would mean that the Braves would unconsciously either move around this small area or avoid it all together. This would not interfere with time and history but would, I hoped, provide some needed relief for Sophie right now.

Confirmed Faith

"Hi Valerie. How did you all sleep last night?"

"We all did really well. Sophie woke up bright and cheerful, and a bit happier than she has seemed to be the last several days."

"I guess the real test is whether or not she's willing to climb the stairs to her playroom."

"She's much better! She is still timid about going upstairs in the dark, probably just from memories of what she's seen or felt. But today she went up on her own! It was a big deal to me, but I didn't let on to Sophie that I was observing her. It was as if she didn't even have to think about it when she climbed the stairs. What a difference a day makes! Thank you so, so much. I'm dying to know, what did you find?"

I related what I found and my challenge in repairing the situation.

"Thanks so much, Tina. I'm so glad this is resolved. I think in a way it confirmed my faith in Sophie. She has never lied to us; it's just not part of her character and your remote view confirmed this for William and me. I think our big take-away from this is that it is important to believe in your child."

"A psychic child cannot help what she sees and she would have no idea, no concept that her own parents cannot see or feel what she is experiencing. I'm sure Sophie felt that if she could see it, surely you and her dad could too. I've seen several parents who actually developed their own psychic ability to be able to assist their children more adequately. That doesn't happen often, but it can occur."

"I'm not sure my psychic ability is developing but I do believe in Sophie and whatever it is that she is able to see. We're so grateful for your help!"

"My pleasure, Valerie."

Epilogue

Believe in your children, especially if your child has no history of lying to you. Psychic children don't always know how to convey to their parents what they are seeing, sensing, or hearing. Even if you cannot find a psychic to help you with what could be a supernatural problem, at least try to work through the situation with your child with respect and compassion. Patiently record what your child says that they hear, sense, see, feel, or even smell. Read and study all that you can to understand more adequately what will often seem unfathomable.

There is so much that we are still learning about time. Accepting what we do not know and learning to work with what we can begin to understand is critical to opening the doors to new frontiers of managing psychic phenomena.

I shudder to think of what could have happened to little Sophie if her parents had not been as wise as they are. They were willing to consider a psychic solution to what appeared to be a behavioral problem. A less enlightened set of parents might have either severely punished this child or taken her to a psychiatrist and put her on drugs. Perhaps those of you reading this story will come to understand that there is no such thing as no such thing and simply because you cannot personally see something does not mean that it is not there or does not exist.

And finally, I spoke directly to Sophie in this case because her mom was right there and I was only asking her about her feelings, not going into any detail about her psychic ability.

Prayers for Sending Ghosts to the Heaven World

The Wall Between Time

Many times we think that because someone lives in a relatively new house, that there could not be something that happened on the property. The destruction of a structure does not erase its energy: there can be an overlay of energies on one piece of ground. Some locations have had horrific events play out on what appears to be merely rural acreage. Green rolling hills, new vegetation fifty to a hundred years old simply cannot erase the energy of a traumatic event, a death, or a massacre.

Time may eventually heal all wounds for mortal people but that same concept does not necessarily hold true for land and/or buildings. That energy can linger for centuries. Sometimes, though, it takes just the right property owner to realize that there is something wrong and seek to repair it. The karmic ramifications, the karmic echo of such a request can then positively affect that property for hundreds of years to come.

The 75-Year-Old 'New' House in Suffolk, Virginia

Miss Ginny was a very Southern Lady. She lived in what seemed to me a huge home for rural Virginia, easily six thousand square feet. She had known my sister for quite a while and, one day, the subject of ghosts came up. My sister asked her if she had ever seen any type of ghost in that big old house and, did she ever mind staying there alone.

Once Miss Ginny got to thinking about it, she decided that she had felt pretty uneasy about things on more than one occasion. While she could not say that she had actually seen a ghost, she occasionally had an uneasy feeling about certain areas of the home. She had decided that was because she had lived there so long and she knew who had died in the house. She told my sister that she was willing to let me see what I could find. She honestly had no idea if it was haunted or if there had been any other events happen on the property.

Through the Stacks of Time to Roughly 1845

Upon remote viewing the house, the first thing I noticed was that there seemed to be two houses, one was the current house, and the other one, which seemed to be overlaid upon it, was a much older home, over 50 years older. What made this story so powerful was one constant element in that house that the owner denied was there when I eventually spoke to her. This particular element was a physical object, and transcended time and space and ironically seemed to connect several different stacks of time.

The energy of this property was toxic. People who had lived here had not necessarily been happy nor were many of them very kind personalities. I saw several ghosts lingering in this house from different stacks of time. Let us begin with the children.

When I began this remote view, I could see a house from roughly 1845. This was a large property, even then, and it took many people to make it work. The backbone of the house was a slave by the name of Sally. I could see the 'scene' open up for me as I watched Sally go from room to room, moving about the kitchen, and helping the other slaves to manage the laundry. And I could see Sally with her two children. But there was no father for these children. I suspected the father was either the homeowner or one of the overseers who managed the slaves in the fields.

As I watched this scene that seemed to show me many months of time, I was able to watch as Sally was lying on her deathbed in a cottage by the edge of the property. Only her two children were beside her, crying. She kept telling her children to be strong. I was unable to see any other slaves there to help her.

After Sally died, I could see that time moved forward several months. I expected to see the ghostly Sally haunting the house but I never saw her there. I was greatly saddened when her daughter, wearing charred, shredded clothes approached me. I could not begin to imagine what had happened to this child and her little brother standing meekly by her side in equally burned rags.

"Hello, children, you look like you could use a bit of help. Are you cold?" I wanted to offer them some help before I encouraged them to share what had led them to be in such horrific condition.

"Yes'um, we's right cold. And we're scared. Is you come to hep us?"

"Yes, I have, honey. See I've got these pretty shawls for you and your little brother. Do you know what happened to you? Can you tell me your names, how old you are?

"I's Evaline and I think I's 'bout twelve years old. I gots my little ole brother Henry here, who I'm a guessen's 'bout six. We was 'aworkin' in da' big house over yonder with our momma. But momma got terrible sick. I misses her so much. Momma was ailin' so much, and I does what I could, I tried. You gotta' believe me, I tried ta hep' her! But she jus' - she jus' up an died! We didn't know how to hep' her. Them people was mean, real mean. I reckon that the Massas in the big house didn't want to spend no money on a slave so no doctor come to hep her. When momma died, they didn't want ta' spend no money to bury her, so dey burned her body up. Henry and me we were 'acryin' so hard watchin' her body burn. We was so scared! What was we gonna do without her?

"They's no grave for us ta' visit. They's no un ta' love us. What was we gonna' do? Momma looked afta' us so much. But she was awful thin when she died. Do you'all know how come our momma die? We jus' love her so much and we be missin' her. We wish she could find us an hep us. We don't know what ta' do now.

"You'all be lookin' so bright! Can you hep' us find our momma? Did momma send you? We be missin' her a powerful lot. We keeps seein' all these bad dark things. Who they'all be?"

"Evaline, Henry, I have come to help you find your way home. However, first, can you tell me how you both died?"

Little Henry was standing obediently next to his big sister, his black, tear-stained face sad evidence of his unending emotional turmoil.
"The Massas in the big house, - well I reckon they plum don't know what to do with us after our momma died. We tried to work real hard but we couldn't no way do all that our momma done fo' them."

I could well imagine that two small children could not do much real work and the slave owners had no desire to look after slave children. They couldn't sell skinny twelve- and six-year-old slaves because they would not bring much at the slave market, so they must have come to a terrible decision. I took a deep breath at this, not daring to imagine what had befallen these distraught children. Evaline continued.

"One night not too long afta momma died, we was asleep in da' shack where we was 'alivin'. I heared someone outside so I holds Henry real close ta' me. I was plum 'afeared of what was out there. Then I hears someone put something against da door. Den I smells fire. Da fire started so quick like that I tried to get me an Henry out real fast – I had ta' take care of him now.

"I worked an worked to get that there door open when the smoke started 'acomin in and den da' door went up in flames and we couldn't get out! I was screamin' and yellin' for someone ta' hep us but ain't no one comin. I tried, honest, I tried real hard to save me an Henry, but we started chokin' and burnin' and then next thing I knowed, we was standing where the shack had been, lookin' 'round at so much darkness. I didn't rightly know what happened ta' us, or where we was or what we was supposed ta' do now."

Revulsion fills my very soul, as I force myself to listen to this child tell me what it is like to be burned to death. The horror of this situation was beyond heartbreaking. It is hard to conceive of a family so cold that they could murder two children in such a cruel, calculating, and heartless manner. I took a deep breath and reminded myself that I had to focus on helping them now. As Evaline is explaining her last horrific moments to me, I quietly bring in children angels to hold each child's hand and to give them additional soft golden colored blankets to place over their cold, trembling, charred bodies.

"I'm so sorry you were so afraid and this terrible fire happened to you. I cannot imagine how terrified you and Henry must have been. Tell me, Evaline, what happened next?"

"We was seein' the massas of da' house looking at da' burnt out shack and kickin' our bones. I was cryin' watchin' our bones be kicked around. No one buried us. I didn't know what it meant ta' be dead, or what I was supposed ta' do next. Where was we supposed ta' go? We couldn't find momma an' then we seed these black things 'acomin at us, pullin' at us. What was we ta' do?"

The plantation owners burned these children alive making sure a burial would be unnecessary. After these children died, there was no physical trace that Sally or her son and daughter had ever lived there. Sometimes, it is a stiff challenge to manage your own emotions when you see savagery on this level.

Death is always a mystery to children, especially when they are even briefly able to see their own charred bodies and bones. They had no frame of reference for understanding where they were. Evaline and Henry saw these terrible dark beings all around them. I could also see these dark, four-foot-tall devil creatures, these Lower Realm Intelligences that are attracted to powerfully negative energetic places. These creatures harass souls who seem to be stuck on that 4th dimensional plain. All these children had ever known beyond their mother's love, was cruelty and fear in that house.

"Where Is Our Momma?

"Once we was dead, we kept a lookin' for our momma. We knowed that she be dead, too, but we don't never see her. We was a hopin' that she was a lookin' afta us even though she be dead. Where was she, Light Lady? How come our momma weren't there for us? Why did God let this happen ta' us? How come nobody come to take care of us? Is you here to hep' us? How is I gonna' take care of me an Henry in this new dark place? He cries all the time and I ain't got no idea how to hep him. What's we gonna' do? Where is our momma?"

Time does not exist in the dimension they are in, and there is a feeling that nothing ever changes for those souls trapped there. I could well imagine the perpetuation of Evaline's fear, frustration, and aloneness in this situation. The angels I summoned to help them begin their transition to the Heaven World seemed like glorious lights in the gloomy, terrifying environs of the 4th dimension.

"Dem folks be so bright and beautiful, is you sure they be for us?"

"Oh, my goodness, yes! These angels are for you so you and Henry won't be alone or afraid anymore. They have come to take you home to your momma. It's okay, you can take their golden hands. Can you feel the angels?"

"Yess'um, I reckon we can. It feels right nice. Thank ya' kindly for both me an' Henry."

Evaline never forgot her manners and I was deeply impressed with her devotion to her brother.

There is always a sense of relief, of letting go when any soul is able to connect to an angel and the angels who embraced these children were each about their own size. My heart went out to them. These poor kids could not believe this comforting and compassionate light was for them. The children angels are now hand in hand with the ghost children and the angels are standing brightly by to guide the children home. Evaline spoke to me one last time.

"Light Lady, they's a squeezen' our hands and guidin' us ta' dat purdy light. Look, look! I sees Momma! There she be, waitin' fer us! I sees her open arms! We's a cryin' and Momma's a cryn'! Thank you, Light Lady, for takin' us home!"

I watched with relief and gratitude as the angels slipped into the light with these sweet children. The reunion with their mother Sally was simply glorious to behold. I sent my love to the angels for their poignant assistance to these traumatized souls. Finally, I felt that Evaline and Henry were at peace.

This is an exceptionally sad story of murder and service. Little Evaline was eternally taking care of her brother, Henry, in spite of their cruel murder. These were brutal times: the children of slaves were not considered human, and as such were a burden. Not all slave owners were this cruel of course, but in this case the sheer brutality of their deaths was hard to stomach. Sometimes that child was a painful reminder of the master's sexual abuse of female slaves. Removing this 'evidence' was not unusual.

In this case, the mother was able to move on because although she died a sad death, she was not murdered and she was an exceptionally loving parent. Her love and care for her children enabled her to cross over and await the time when she could welcome her children home.

The question that begs asking is why she was not a ghost, lingering to look after her children. The only answer we may have is that once the light came for her, she willingly entered it, perhaps feeling that she could do more for her children from that bright place than lingering around the life she had just left. Her life had been so hard, that it would make sense that she would welcome the light when it came.

The Ugly Brick Wall

"Miss Ginny, did you have any idea that those children could have been here? Was there ever any talk of their having lived and died all those years ago?"

"So many people have lived and died on this property that I had no idea that those kids were here. I feel terrible even though it's been roughly 160 years since they died. I didn't see or feel them, but then you did say that they were elsewhere on the property, not in the house. The current house is relatively new, having been built within the last 75 years or so on the same property. I guess I didn't realize that this house was constructed in the exact location where the original house stood back through many decades of time. You know, this is all so fascinatin' to me."

"Yes, it is pretty amazing. Do you know of anyone who has died in the house itself?"

"Oh yes, it appears that many people died here of a variety of types of deaths. One fell down a flight of stairs, another had a long lingering illness and another couple seemed to have died in their bed – together. And these were merely the deaths that I know about. I'm not sure if there were any more. Can you see the rest of these folks?"

"Well, I've only visited, that is, remote viewed the house once so far. I intend to keep working on it. You know, Ginny, one of the many ironies of this big southern mansion, with its huge oak trees outside of it and its high ceilings is that despite the various people who have died in this house, the only people I have seen so far were those poor slave children. When I do this work, I don't get to pick and choose whom I will encounter. Souls are presented to me as they are each meant to be helped, and as their karma manifests for them to move to a different realm.

"I also want to point out that the current house was built over the original brick house and that the original house had at some point, also, at least partially, burned. While this house fire was unrelated to the deaths of these children because their shack was on the edge of the property, the fire energy would indicate that there was a powerful residual element of darkness that permeated all the grounds.

"That much darkness, hate and negativity from those two murders could easily have led to the fire. The only part remaining from the original house was a brick wall that is still there in your current house. This wall seems to be the physical element or connector among all the stacks of time. The energy of so many deaths vibrated out from the ugly red brick and mortar wall."

"Tina, let me assure you that this brick wall does not exist, could not exist. You see, the original house had been totally leveled after the original fire. In fact, I'm absolutely sure that there could not possibly be such a wall in my current house. I just know it's not here. You must be mistaken."

"Well, Ginny, I can only tell you what I see and what I keep seeing is a brick wall that still exists in your current house that is from that original house. It is this lone brick wall that is acting as a time bridge between the past and the present."

"Well, I reckon I don't know about any time bridge but that brick wall doesn't exist. I'm sure of it."

A week passed and then one afternoon, I received a most excited phone call from Miss Ginny.

"Tina, you're not going to believe this, but I found that brick wall you keep insisting is here!

I found it! It really bothered me that you were so sure, so just to prove you wrong, I walked the whole house and as I was walking into the basement, I touched an old brick wall that I remembered, finally, that my daddy told me was from the original house! I don't even want to know how you know that. Then as I continued to walk down the stairs to the basement, I noticed that that stairwell into that basement had always given me a terrible feeling. I got a chill and then I remembered that one of the many people who had died in my house had fallen down those very stairs and passed away right next to that wall! I shuddered. Tina, have you seen that man, I think it was a distant uncle – have you seen his ghost here?"

"Miss Ginny, that soul must have moved on, because I never saw him in the several times I have 'looked' at your home. Some souls do move on or else if they are still lingering, they aren't haunting the location where they died."

But Wait – There's More

However, that was not the only issue on this challenging property. Miss Ginny invited, my sister and I to visit the next time I was on the East Coast.

Over tea, Miss Ginny asked if I would like to have a tour of this unusual house with its huge ceilings, reminiscent of an old antebellum mansion. The house would seem to have been reconstructed sometime before World War II. My hostess explained that this had once been a working farm with slave quarters somewhere on the property. They raised tobacco and cotton, and there are still cotton fields that surround this property.

This house was cavernous. It had that old Greek revival style architecture with enormous columns at the entrance. The three-story brick structure had interior bare brick walls, which added quite a bit of architectural interest. All the floors were hardwood and they endlessly creaked and groaned with every step you took. I could not imagine a better burglar alarm than those profoundly, noisy, slippery floors.

The entry way opened up to a tremendous staircase that took you upstairs to the six bedrooms and several baths that covered three floors. All the ceilings were fifteen feet high with beautiful crown molding. This house had an old-fashioned parlor, not a living room, and it felt like it was far older than 75 years. It also had a spacious sunroom, one of those special rooms filled with walls of windows, floral fabric on the wicker chairs and light hungry plants. The whole house was graced with furniture from an entirely bygone era. The owner herself felt a bit like she was a bit stuck in the past. When you entered this home, you were transported to another time and space, and it was not an entirely happy feeling.

While she was giving us the museum tour, I could hear her dog outside.

"Ginny, have you noticed that your dog is endlessly barking at that second-floor window? He barely even takes a breath; he's barking so insistently."

"You know I might have to put him to sleep. This dog barks so incessantly that I'm at my wits end. Can you, I mean could you possibly 'fix' my dog? Do you know how to get him to stop barking? I have to tell you that I'm so frustrated with him that I just may have to put him down, because he never shuts up."

"Dogs bark for a reason, especially if they are barking in one fixed location seemingly 'at' something. Would you mind if I 'take a look' and see what he's barking at?"

"Honey, you just be my guest."

I remote viewed the room where the dog was directing her barking and there was a ghost couple standing in the window watching. They seemed to take great delight in tormenting Ginny's dog. The dog was trying to tell her mistress that this couple was there, but the owner couldn't understand her dog's impassioned barks. This is not a criticism of the owner. She had no idea she had more ghosts in the house than the original two I had first seen. I removed the couple, helping them to cross over and the dog immediately stopped barking. But there was more to come.

I would have expected a type of graciousness to the house but instead the house still felt as if there was 'a hardness' to it, almost a frustration. We entered room after amazing room. One room was pink, another blue, another with old-fashioned wallpaper. The bathrooms were old, antique almost in their arrangement. The dining room was large, gracious and a reminder of a completely different historical period of time. The living room, or parlor was also outwardly gracious but at the same time, stiff, unwelcoming, almost secretive.

"Tina, y'all come on down here and look at this basement. Here's that brick wall you kept tellin' me was there. And here's where my uncle fell down the stairs to his untimely demise. Do you seem him now?"

I had an immediate and unpleasant reaction to her toxically creepy basement. It was exactly as I had seen it.

"No, I never saw him. He could be somewhere else, but at this moment, he is not here."

"Now, would y'all like to see the attic?"

The Attic

"Really? I can't believe there is more to this house."

"Oh, yes," she said, "it's quite an attic."

So up and up we went, up three creaky, wooden staircases until we reached the door with the attic that went up yet another staircase.

And it was when she opened that attic door that I could feel them, hundreds of them.

"Um, Ginny, do you realize that this attic is haunted?"

"Why, no," she said, "it can't be, you cleared the house and it felt cleared, it felt so much better."

"Well, I surely didn't clear the attic because when I did the remote view, I didn't see this entire population of people, but then that first remote view stack of time was pre-Civil War."

"Alright, what's 'hauntin' my attic?"

"This attic is an underground railroad for Civil War ghosts. There are slaves, soldiers from both sides either passing through or taking up residence here. Sometimes, Ginny, there are locations that just seem to attract ghosts. Some linger and some immediately transition to the Heaven World. In this case, these ghosts looked as if they were waiting for something or someone to help them. With your permission, I'll clear them all. But you have to understand that even though I am removing them, more will come."

"I don't understand, Tina. You're sendin' them all on to Jesus. Why will more come?"

"Because there's something about this house that seems to beckon them in that ghostly time. I don't always understand why these things happen; I can only tell you that they are happening."

"What can I do if you think that more will come?"

"Ginny, you will need to set up a type of doorway or reception center that will enable them to transition to the Heaven World. We need to come up with a location in the house where this can happen.

"You will also need to learn how to keep yourself safe so that the ghosts will not bother you anymore. If you are performing spiritual service, you still have to follow spiritual protocol for managing ghosts. This means that you have to ask for Divine assistance, say prayers requesting help for these transitioning souls and send gratitude to the angels who are assisting you.

"The spiritual service of your work with these souls is critical. I want you to understand that many of these souls died in violence, fear, and intense pain. I know you are such a good soul that you will find great satisfaction in knowing that you have helped them."

"Well goodness, I've been a good Christian woman all my life and I'll do anything I can to help these folks find Jesus, to find God. Just give me the steps to follow and I promise you I'll do it."

Epilogue

This case illustrates an interesting point, which is that because so much was happening on that property, she could have had several different psychics come and see what was there and she would have been told an entire variety of different stories. The irony is that all of them would probably have been correct. I can well imagine how confusing this would have been for any owner. I was fortunate to have been able to visit and to remove all that were presented to me.

I was not called back to her house because she was now ably managing the ghosts that seemed to go through her attic. And she kept her word. She continued helping those souls until at some point, they simply stopped coming. Her sentinel was her now very beloved dog who alerted her to the presence of souls in need of her assistance. She and her dog were teammates, in that unusual job of helping the lost souls of yesterday transition into the bright souls of tomorrow.

Prayers for Sending Ghosts to the Heaven World

Darling Charlotte

How do you talk to a perfect stranger about the death of her child? In the movies, the psychic just knocks on the door or a house where a child has died and starts telling the parent that their child's ghost is standing right there and wants to talk to them. The parent is thrilled and invites this total stranger, this psychic person into their home and then miraculous things begin to happen.

Reality is not always so heart-warming... but I am getting ahead of myself. Having psychic ability is not the only skill required when you must deal with the fragile feelings of the living and the persistent demands of the dead.

A Chance Encounter

My sister Andrea was having her hair done when she had a chance conversation with a woman in the chair next to her. This lady was discussing her neighbor who had just written a book about the death of her child some 30 years prior. This mom's story took the reader into her journey deep within herself to find peace after the death of her child. The family had moved from the location of the accident in California, to Virginia Beach. My sister mentioned how great it would be to offer this author a copy of my book The Light Worker's Guide to Healing Grief©, because this woman was obviously still suffering. The neighbor seemed willing to make the connection to help this grieving mom.

As my sister shared this story with me, and the critical element of the mother's unending grief, I began to have this odd feeling, which grew as the days went by.

My sister began to sense it as well. I slowly came to the realization that this woman's deceased child was coming to me for help. I had no greater connection to her than my sister chatting with this woman at the hairdressers. Yet, the feeling was unmistakable. I realized that I needed to help this little one cross over into Heaven, but nothing is that simple in this nether world in which I live.

Everyone's Worst Nightmare

While my sister was working to get in touch with the mom to offer her my grief book, I could sense the presence of this little two-year-old. I needed to cross her over, and it felt like I should do it pretty soon. But no matter what I did, I kept getting the additional message that I was to help this mom with her daughter directly. Normally, it is no problem to assist a soul, especially a child who is grieving his or her own death and has not made the essential soul transition to the other side.

However, in this case, for some reason, I was supposed to make contact with the mom and assist the mom to help her daughter transition. How was I going to do that? My sister had asked for the phone number of her beauty parlor friend to be able to share the book with her neighbor. In the meantime, I read the book the neighbor had written to see if we could get a better sense of the mother, whose name was Carol. She was still grieving her daughter's death as if it had happened yesterday. Her tremendous grief was due to the child's method of death. We gathered that the family had tried to move on, had done what they thought was the requisite grief work and had even had another little girl. But I realized that no matter where you go you cannot escape the guilt that comes from the loss of a two-year-old child.

That sense of failed responsibility, that staggering guilt of 'I should have been watching her' is going to haunt any parent for a very long time. Forgiving yourself is exceptionally difficult.

Their story unfolded on one lovely summer day, when the family had gone to the beach to celebrate a birthday for a family member. Lots of relatives were there and they had had a delicious picnic under bright red beach umbrellas on the beach at Pacific Beach, in San Diego. They brought a net and had begun to play volleyball. At one point, Carol, handed her daughter to her husband to watch while she went back to the car to care for her new baby daughter's diaper and nurse her. The dad, Victor was watching Charlotte until she went way up on the beach to play in the sand with her beach toys near the other moms and their kids. Victor told her to keep her life jacket on while she played and not to go near the water until he came back for her. She nodded. Unbeknownst to his wife, Victor left Charlotte to play with her toys, assuming that the other mothers would watch his little girl. Victor then went off to play volleyball with the other dads.

But no one was watching Charlotte, so no one noticed that she took off her life jacket. Since she was not playing with another child, and she was unable to see either parent, she decided to return to the water to play. By the time she realized that she had gone too far, she was in way over her head. A stranger pulled her body out of the water and called an ambulance.

As the paramedics were working on her, Charlotte's father returned and discovered that they could not resuscitate his daughter. He rushed to his wife's side and demanded to know why she had not been watching their daughter. Carol was stunned. Why, she asked, what happened? The rest of that heart-crushing day was a blur of accusations, recriminations, and massive doses of grief. And yet despite this severe trauma, this couple had stayed together and worked through as much of their grief and guilt as possible.

How was I going to connect with these parents? How could I possibly broach the subject of the death of their daughter 30 years ago? Whether or not I thought I could find a way to make this connection, I knew I needed to do this. But it is always awkward to tell anyone that you are in contact with his or her deceased loved one. They automatically have a tendency to assume that you are some type of charlatan with a scam up your sleeve seeking to prey on their misfortune. I already sensed that this was not going to be easy.

How Do I Explain This?

My sister had contacted the mother about her book so that when next I visited the East Coast, I could gift her, and her husband a copy of my grief book. Even this ruse was going to be somewhat clumsy, but we really had no other reason to connect with these parents. The more I connected with Charlotte, the more I realized that she desperately wanted to tell her mother and father something private, and personal. In mortal life, a loved one dies at a chronological age, and time; and for the living family time continues to move on. But in the 4th dimension, a soul is frozen at the age of his or her death. I suspected that both parents were holding on to this child so that even if she wanted to cross over, she would have difficulty making the transition to the Heaven World.

Finally, my sister was able to arrange a meeting for the three of us, which turned out, was the very next month. We met at a coffee shop and sat at a quiet table in the back of the room. My sister and I introduced ourselves and told Carol that we admired her writing. She was polite but guarded. She addressed us in a brusque, almost irritated manner.

"Look, you could have just mailed me your grief book. Why the insistence on meeting me, and my husband, about wanting to give us the book in person? What's going on?"

"My sister and I wanted to meet you and your husband in person. I'm sorry your husband was not able to come. Obviously, you have done a great deal to share your story and we were deeply touched by all that has happened to you and your family. However, the truth is that we wanted to meet in person because we had other information to share."

That statement made her even more suspicious, as if we were going to be doing something terrible to her or somehow capitalize on her pain.

"I don't know about this. I should just get up and leave."

"Look Carol, we have a deep appreciation for what it's like to lose a child. I wrote this grief book as a way to help other families deal with such a catastrophic loss since our experience was so profound."

At this point, my sister shared her story of the loss of her daughter at the age of six. We showed her the book and then finally I asked her about Charlotte.

"As you can see, we have some idea what's it like to go through this. Can you tell us a bit more about Charlotte? Please?"

"I don't know; it's so personal. We were at the beach; I thought my husband was watching her and he thought I and other moms were watching her. She went into the water and obviously went too deep and she drowned. It was horrible. Why are you asking me to re-live that day? Charlotte moved on, we moved on. That's it."

"Carol, are you sure your sweet Charlotte moved on? Are you sure she crossed over?"

"Look, I'm pretty certain, but then, how would I really know for sure?"

Finally, I had an entry into this delicate subject of helping Charlotte.

"This is really why we're here. Ever since I read your book, I have felt Charlotte's presence. I have never met your child; have no connection with you or her or your family other than your book. I have to tell you that she has not crossed over and she does want to talk to you. Would you be willing to let me facilitate that process with you? We could do it together."

Carol looked at me dumbfounded.

"You're kidding right? Talk to my dead daughter. How cruel is this? What's the fee for such a thing? What's the angle?"

I knew that Carol's hard outer shell protected fragile feelings.

"There's no charge; there's no fee for assisting a soul in this situation. It's a service that I'm offering you. That's all. It's just that your daughter won't let me cross her over. I can cross her over. Technically, I don't need you to do that with me. But in this highly unusual case, she is adamant that she has to talk to you about something. She won't tell me. It's only for you to hear. Nothing bad will happen. I completely understand your fears. As I'm listening to myself tell you this, believe me, I know how odd this sounds."

"This has got to be some scam." Pauses and thinks. "But since there's no money involved . . . I'm actually curious now. Obviously, you went to some trouble to contact me, so. . ." Carol hesitates briefly. "I guess it would be alright."

We chatted a bit more. I explained the process. Slowly, something began to shift within her and I could tell that she was softening to the prospect on a deeper level.

When I felt she was ready, I began the work.

The process itself is extremely simple but powerful. I asked angels to surround Carol so that she could be fortified for whatever it was that she was going to hear. I was impressed. I could tell immediately when she connected with Charlotte because tears began to trace a steady path down her pale cheeks; her voice softened. She lowered her head.

"Charlotte, honey," I said, "now is your opportunity to talk to your mommy and tell her anything you want her to know. Carol, you can now tell your daughter anything you want her to know as well. I encourage you to each forgive the other for all that happened that fateful day. It's time to heal Charlotte's death. Your conversation is private, only between the two of you. I will not hear it."

Carol's tears were so genuine, so poignant, that her voice was reduced to a whisper. I could feel her having a conversation with her daughter. I watched, as her shoulders seem to release the tremendous emotional burden, they had carried for thirty long years. Grief and guilt never take a holiday: they become your shadow self and this is what happened to Carol. I brought in an angel to comfort Carol and another angel standing by to escort Charlotte to the Heaven World when the time would be right.

"Carol, when you're ready to assist Charlotte to cross over, let me know and we will do this part together."

Carol sat up a bit straighter, took a deep breath and addressed me.

"We're ready. Both of us are ready. We're at peace. I – I can let her go now, finally. It's the right thing to do and I know she'll be all right. I can see the angel is here to escort Charlotte. He's so bright, so hopeful," she said taking another deep breath. "We're both ready to let go."

With that, I nodded to the glowing angel patiently standing by. He then gently lifted little Charlotte into his arms and strode with her into the Heaven World. She waved at her mom one last time, smiling brightly. Then she was gone. A peaceful silence settled among all of us at that table.

No one spoke.

Carol took a few moments to collect her thoughts as she began to wipe away the tears streaming down her face. Andrea, and I were patient with her. This was a powerful moment. Finally, Carol looked up at us.

"Do you want to know what Charlotte said? Do you want to know why she kept coming to you? I feel that you have a right to know."

"Of course, Carol, I would love to know, but I did tell you that your last exchange was private. I will respect your privacy, but yes, I would love to know why she insisted on speaking with you one last time."

"Charlotte told me that she was so guilty! I couldn't believe it! She said, 'I killed myself, Mommy, it was my fault, I knew I shouldn't go back in the water. Daddy told me not to go there, but I didn't listen. I'm so sorry, Mommy, can you and Daddy please forgive me. Please Mommy, I'm so sorry!'

"And, Tina, she was crying. She needed me to forgive her and here it was, all this time it was me who felt that I let her down, that both my husband and I should have been watching her, paying better attention. You never think that your drowned child will be blaming herself. We both cried. I felt like I hugged her somehow. I could feel her presence. I could hear her tiny voice and feel how she used to feel when she was beside me. . ."

Carol swallowed hard. Paused for a few moments and then continued.

"We forgave each other. We forgave each other, Tina. Do you have any idea what this means to me? There are no words to describe this experience. No words. Thank you. I can hardly wait to go home and share this astonishing, life changing experience with my husband, to help him relieve his guilt. Maybe, finally, we can all heal as a family. I feel like thousands of pounds of emotional weight have been lifted from me. I realized that I was holding Charlotte here because I couldn't let her go."

"Maybe, Carol, you were holding on to each other, trying desperately to resolve this guilt when what you really needed to do was to have a few precious moments with each other. Be sure to send Charlotte prayers in the Heaven World. They will help her transition. You did a wonderful job. This was exceptionally difficult but you showed tremendous courage by being willing to talk to her in this unusual situation."

We all got up from the table and hugged each other and then we went our separate ways. Carol's face glowed. There was lightness in her step and she waved at us as we drove away. The entire encounter took no more than 20 minutes: twenty life-changing minutes.

Epilogue

About a week later I got an email from Carol telling me how much better both she and her husband were feeling, how much lighter. They laugh more and although they cried in each other's arms that night, they healed on many levels. Such is the power of assisting a tiny soul who only wants to explain her story.

Any parent can ask angels to assist their child to cross over by saying The Crossing Over Prayer© at the end of this book, playing the audio of it in The Crossing over Prayer Book© on Audible, or playing the video on my website.

Any parent can ask their child for forgiveness for whatever caused that child's death, whether or not the parent was at fault. Parents believe that somehow, they are supposed to protect their children from anything happening. But things happen. We seldom think of asking our deceased loved one for forgiveness, but it offers tremendous healing.

Any parent can forgive their child for leaving them as well. Again, we seldom think that we would even need to forgive a child or loved one for leaving us, but it can make a life-changing difference between healing and hurting for a very long time.

Carol and her husband will always miss their darling Charlotte. You never stop longing for your child. However, you can heal on many levels when you allow yourself to let go, forgive each other, and walk a new path of healing.

Prayers for Sending Ghosts to the Heaven World

When Evil Haunts the Living and the Dead

Is There Such a Thing as Evil?

Yes, absolutely, there is evil, and it exists whether you believe it or not. Evil exists to offer people a chance to choose: be evil or create goodness. It is the challenge and the opportunity of free will. If a parent sexually abused you, will you abuse someone else sexually or will you take a very different path? Will you learn from the evil that was done to you or will you simply follow the same evil path? Often people who had horrific childhoods make heroic strides on their karmic paths simply by leaving that vicious experience behind and showing their loving hearts.

Does Evil Affect Us?

Yes, evil can affect anyone, any living person, whether he or she believes in evil or not. It does not matter what name you put on it, negativity, cruelty, or violence: evil exists. No matter how good you are, or how hard you try to be a good person, you, me, all of us are influenced, negatively or positively by dark deeds. Maybe you saw something that was so dark, so cruel, that you made up your mind that you would not let this happen to someone else, that you would make a difference in the life of another in a positive way. You can choose not to be evil, not to do evil things, not to repeat the past, not to seek vengeance or perpetuate cruelty. Such is the paradox of evil.

If you grew up with a mother who was vicious and cruel, by a parent who beat you or who was emotionally vacant, how will you choose to behave in the future? If your parent or family member sexually abused you, this is an evil action. Perhaps you do not know why one or both parents were terrible to you or allowed bad things to happen to you. All you know is that you may have wanted to love that person but their actions were vicious and cruel. Their behavior was evil toward you. How will you create your future? If you choose to study your family, you can make different choices. You can become a kind and loving parent. You may also choose not to have children until you have learned to heal yourself and fully appreciated the lessons those cruel parents taught you. I have seen many clients take this approach to their karmic path.

We come to each mortal life for a full buffet of different experiences. Each experience is a karmic opportunity to become a more sage personality. If we chose poorly in a previous life, then in the next life, we will be given the opportunity to make different choices in how to handle that same negative situation, or deal with that same toxic person. That which we avoid dealing with in one life will be offered to us to learn from in life after life until we finally learn how to make wiser choices. Once we have truly learned the lesson that evil offers us, then we can move on to more sophisticated experiences.

Once souls cross over into the Heaven World, they are afforded the opportunity to sit down with Counselors of Divine Wisdom to review the life just lived. We all get to see how our decisions affected others, how they rippled out through time and space, and how that ripple was eventually returned to us. We create karma with every thought we think, every decision we make. The more we grow in each lifetime, the more we can become the light that removes evil from our path.

Can Evil Affect the Dead?

Is that even possible? Once you are dead, what does it matter? Who would even know if something dark affected a ghost – right? Wrong! Those who make it a point to help the dead, who hear their plight, know how much they are influenced by the evil darkness that accompanied them in death and prevented them from crossing over.

Perhaps someone you loved took a dark drug path and wound up murdered or she took her own life. It is easy to see how much evil is associated with her death. You can only imagine the evil that haunted her days and nights. But now that the soul is dead, what happens? Can the terrible darkness that surrounded this person in life continue to affect her in death? Yes, this is possible. What that soul is going to see are small Lower Realm Intelligences, creatures around three feet high with (as cliché as it sounds) red eyes. There are other types of animal-like beings who seem to feast on the misery of the dead soul. I wish that none of this were true, that all souls, even murdered ones, and souls who committed suicide, were magically transported at death into the Heaven World, but alas, that is not what happens. These souls desperately need our assistance.

You may have felt frustrated that you could not stop someone in life from going down an evil path. Maybe you tried to help him with his depression or drug addiction but nothing seemed to work because you could never dislodge the evil you found inside him. However, sometimes in death you can be of greater service to him. As soon as you learn of the person's passing, immediately request Angels of Transition to surround the person. Then play the video of The Crossing Over Prayer© or say The Crossing Over Prayer© listed at the end of this book and at TinaErwin.com. Say the prayer at least three times, in a forceful, strong, confident voice.

There is then the blessed possibility that you will feel their transition into the Heaven World. That soul will finally feel the peace of release. You will have rescued this person from an eternity in the lower astral environs of the 4th dimension. You will have facilitated their passage into the Heaven World where they will receive guidance, healing, hope and blessings.

Even if this person committed murder or perpetrated some other type of evil on others, even if he showed no remorse whatsoever, there is still hope for that soul in the Heaven World. The reason is that none of us can stand in judgment of another. Once the soul is in the Heaven World, then higher beings will assign them to the right place for them to work through their actions while they lived that mortal life. If you transition them out of the 4th dimension, you have performed a great service because that person will not reincarnate from the lower astral as the same evil person he was when he died.

This action also begins to heal the person performing this service on profound levels. Perhaps you could not stop someone from embracing darkness, but their death is the time that you can be of service to them. Once the service of assisting them to transition to the Heaven World is completed, you and much of your family may finally feel the dark veil of depression lift.

Emotional Haunting

When Evil Haunts the Living and the Dead

Severe trauma and tragedy do not leave a person at death: these deeply harrowing memories create psychological scars and sometimes, actual fractures within the soul. Past life emotional trauma can arise from abuse, method of death or an experience so powerful, so terrifying, painful, or shocking, that it leaves an indelible mark on the soul.

Emotional haunting is one of the most prevalent, yet not well understood forms of suffering from past life memories. Once the person reincarnates, those subtle scars linger with the soul. The individual will normally not remember anything about her past lives. Yet, the energy of a past life ordeal may 'haunt' her on elusive levels. The person tries to find ways to understand or to heal this 'thing,' this 'emotion' that haunts dreams and influences life in many subtle ways.

What subtle ways does emotional haunting linger with someone? Some men despise the colors red and yellow. When spiritual work is done to find out why anyone would hate such colors, they find that these men suffered through terrible wars trying to help the dying and wounded victims and grew soul weary of the volume of blood and the yellow pus of infected wounds. Those color representations symbolized the tragic loss of life and the brutality of war.

One woman discussed the irrational fear her young son had of water. Bath time was always a fight. Was this a soul who drowned in a past life? Was the haunting memory of water associated with his death?

Another man was terrified of fire. He eventually realized that he had watched a woman burn to death when he was a small boy. The trauma of that image haunted him all of his life.

This subconscious desire to comprehend the towering energy of a past life can manifest in an unusual interest in a particular era, the study of law to overcome a profound injustice, practicing medicine to heal the wounded they could not save in another time and place, or an intense magnetism to a location. Even though the person does not always need to know what happened in that past life, he or she needs to acknowledge the driving or lingering interest and pursue it emotionally to find some level of peace.

What makes this especially challenging is that until the person finds out why this irrational fear, sensitivity to a color, dislike of a location, or a particular person, concept or a belief system exists, he or she is still in resonance with the haunting memory of that previous life. It is critical to do the spiritual/emotional work to heal that past trauma. It is hard to realize that not healing this haunting feeling maintains the resonance with the dead energy of that particular past life. When healing begins, there is a new feeling of freedom from the haunting memory of that previous suffering.

An example of such an emotional haunting is the person who had a severe hatred of several types of organized religion, the country of Spain and virtually all of New England. In her case, past life regressions revealed that in one life, a Catholic Priest running the Inquisition in Spain shoved her out a window as a death sentence. In another life, she was drowned as a witch in New Bedford, Massachusetts. This revelation enabled her to understand why she was never comfortable while visiting Spain and felt chronically uncomfortable in New England. She also found herself filled with rage whenever she entered any type of church. Now she understands and she is no longer experiencing haunting by the energies of those past lives. While past life regressions are not necessarily required, sometimes they do help. She felt compelled to find the truth behind her unusual haunting emotions. She sought out spiritual help to begin the healing process once the understanding of the power of those past lives became clear to her.

How do you know if you are being haunted by an event from a past life or an early childhood memory? You have to explore it, educate yourself about your feelings. If necessary, find a spiritual practitioner to help you work through your thoughts, haunting memories, and feelings. If the behavior is not rational in current context, then the only possible explanation is that something somewhere took place that created some type of fear, rage, grief, or revulsion. Once you can discover that you have these emotions based on a previous trauma, you can begin to heal it by understanding that now, in this moment you are safe and that what happened previously does not have to cause you any further trauma.

Emotional haunting can explain that bad feeling we may get in a situation or location, but what about ghosts that haunt a specific area?

Energetic Haunting

Some real estate agents seem to know when a house for sale is haunted or had something toxic take place there. When they walk into a home, they can instantly feel a presence, or an energy. The agent, having no idea what or who is there, simply knows that something is being felt.

This was absolutely the case for my family when we sold our house in Charleston, South Carolina in 1985. We knew the house was haunted. The entire neighborhood was haunted. We were just one house with our own particular story. However, in 1985, I did not know how to remove ghosts. We never told our real estate agent how profoundly haunted our house was, despite its age of being only nine years when we sold it.

We did not have to tell her; she felt it. Despite the sticky, mosquito infested environs of Charleston in the summer, our agent never spent an extra minute in our house she did not have to during an Open House. She told us the house gave her the creeps. I felt bad about that, but it illustrated the point: she felt the energy of our resident ghost, Jake (see Ghost Stories from the Ghost's Point of View Vol. 1.)

People who do not consider themselves psychic may often feel the energy of the dead. They just sense it. Ironically that same person who felt that a house is haunted house can walk into a hospital and not feel a thing. Yet a very psychic person can walk into a hospital and all of a sudden, feel reduced to a melted puddle of overpowering, grief-filled, conflicting emotions.

Hospitals are locations of powerful events. People experience the full range of emotions in hospitals: relief, grief, pain, shock, and rage. Daily mopping of the floors will not ever fully remove the energy of the tears of gratitude and hope, bitterness and sorrow shed in hospitals. Let us also consider the metal in those hospital rooms, operating rooms, clinics, emergency rooms, hallways, gurneys, and equipment that takes on the emotions of the people who use those facilities. Whether or not you think you are psychic, there is the possibility that those energetic layers of powerful emotions will be felt when using a medical facility.

Another example is a dentist's office. Most people have some fear of visiting a dentist's office. Dental procedures are often painful. The power of that pain and fear leaves an energetic residual energy subtly lingering there. No one ever clears that energy from a dentist's office. There are layers upon layers of emotionally toxic energy applied there over time, and that energy begins to haunt that building.

How difficult and permanent is that energy? Consider the case of a business in Ashville, NC that asked me to remote view their second-floor office and find out why they were having terrible business difficulties. Upon psychic investigation, I discovered that the office below them had been a dentist's office, a very negative one. This dentist apparently caused his patients quite a bit of pain. Subsequently, he went out of business, but the energy of the pain his clients suffered lingered energetically in the floor, ceilings, and walls of the building. Upon explaining this to my clients, they verified that there had indeed been a dentist's office there, but that was 10 years ago. Many other businesses had subsequently occupied that office space – admittedly unsuccessfully.

Some attorney's offices carry the energy of betrayal and rage, fear and sorrow depending on the type of attorney. Consider the focus of various types of attorney offices: litigation, divorce, estate, defense attorneys, and public defenders. Imagine the toxic energy that will embed in walls, floors, metal, and even wooden desks. If you have an office adjacent to one of these types of attorneys, you may find that your office is not harmonious. People may 'take sides' readily and the atmosphere may be adversarial. This is an energetic haunting because you can feel this toxic energy but may not be able to logically explain it.

Energy is neither created nor destroyed so the energy of a previous occupant is going to remain there unless someone does something to shift or change that energy and merely redecorating or burning a cooking herb like sage, will not make a significant enough change. The energy of the previous owners has to be psychically cleared.

Proximity Haunting

There are several stories in these ghost trilogies where ghosts from a hundred years ago, seemed to 'find' a particular living person, because they believed that person could help them. They were able to maintain a close proximity to that living person.

Proximity haunting is a deliberate type of haunting, meaning that someone or something from the past has reconnected with a living person. It can be a type of energy or a ghost who did not cross over.

Does proximity to that past energy matter? Not necessarily. A person can live in another part of the country or even half a world away and still be connected to a past event in another time and place. Time and distance do not matter in the 4th dimension. It is the energy of the traumatic set of circumstances that determines the energetic link.

Ghost Stories from the Ghost's Point of View Trilogy, Vol. 2. has several stories that link one particular person to three completely different ghost stories from the Civil War. The looming question is how could ghosts who died in the 1860s find someone in the 21st century?

I have long pondered this issue. An unnerving number of ghosts do not know they have died. Most ghosts simply continue to exist where they died not realizing the end has come. But in several highly unusual cases, the ghosts not only knew they had died, but they were also aware of who helped them while they were alive. They somehow knew how to stay connected to a person through the stacks of time, space, and reincarnation.

One possible explanation for this phenomenon is that in some unusual circumstances, souls know how to find each other. It could be that the aka cord connections that exist between human beings continue after death within the memory banks of the soul. Because these men had been soldiers and slaves in that lifetime, the shared experience of the trauma of their life kept their frequency lowered preventing them from transitioning to the Heaven World. When the living person reincarnated and lived somewhere near where they had previously lived and died, these men reconnected. Thousands of Civil War dead reconnected to this one person repeatedly.

If you find yourself haunted by a location or memories of a location, this could be proximity haunting.

Deliberate Haunting

When Evil Haunts the Living and the Dead

There is a difference between ghosts on a property who have no idea that they are dead and no idea that their presence is creating a haunting situation, versus ghosts who are deliberately haunting a property. Ghost Stories from the Ghost's Point of View Vol. 2 shares a very unusual story where there were both, and they came from very different periods of time.

A ghost who is deliberately haunting a property or a person knows that he or she has died and has made a conscious decision to haunt a particular person or family for a specific reason. Even if the person doing the haunting has a positive purpose, the end result ultimately creates a negative karmic situation because the soul is not moving into the Heaven World and is actively interfering with the free will actions of a living person.

Assisting ghosts to move on stops the clock on their karmic debt because they incur karma with every action they take as ghosts. That clock only stops when they take that first glorious step into the Heaven World.

The ghost we had in Charleston was deliberately haunting us. There is no doubt that he knew what he was doing, despite the fact that several of his actions were actually quite helpful (see Ghost Stories from the Ghost's Point of View Vol. 1) he deliberately frightened us and that fear created negative karma for him.

Charleston has so many actively haunted houses, mansions, and plantations, businesses, battlefields, farm fields, riverbanks, and slave quarters: the ghost population is tremendous. The ghosts on our old Archdale Plantation neighborhood were very active, knew they were dead, and knew they were haunting dozens of homes in the area.

It is critically important to move on any ghost, but especially those ghosts who are deliberately haunting a location. In Ghost Stories from the Ghosts' Point of View Vol. 1, the story of The Rocket Scientist provides a classic example of a tired female ghost from the 1860s, who fell in love with a modern-day, living person. Moving her on was critically important because her karmic clock was constantly ticking, meaning she was still earning negative karma as a ghost even though she was not malicious. Once she crossed over, she finally stopped earning karma and she could begin her healing process after the ravages of the Civil War.

Ghosts from modern times who realize that they are dead and seek to 'look out for' living people do so with awareness. This is deliberate haunting. Living people have to move forward with their lives. 'Looking out' for a living person will never be helpful to them. It can cloud their minds and prolong their grief.

Other ghostly souls seek to 'harass' their living family or friends because their controlling natures do not cease with death. These people are focused on their desire to control. Some souls decide to haunt their families before they are even dead. These are very conscious beings with a personal agenda and moving them on to the Heaven World is imperative, for example:

One extremely controlling and domineering mother-in-law, told her son on more than one occasion that upon her death, she intended to haunt he and his family. She was not kidding. The day she died, as soon as the wife was informed, she contacted me and I immediately found her, assigned an angel to her and he firmly escorted her into the Heaven World. In another powerful case, a mother died and took fiendish delight in haunting her grown daughter. This vicious controlling ghost sought to completely manage her daughter's life and was successful for ten years. Finally, her daughter called me and asked that I help her to cross her mother over into the Heaven World. Once this was done, the daughter had her first night's sleep in a decade, as her mother had haunted her the most at night.

Inadvertent Haunting

Inadvertent Haunting means that a ghost does not realize that their presence is haunting a location or that his or her presence can be felt. These souls do not comprehend that their presence can affect living people.

All ghosts on any piece of property are occupying the same space as living people, separated by stacks of time and dimension. Many ghosts from decades or centuries past do not see or sense the modern occupants nor are they consciously interfering with the current owners, even if living people can sense or even see them. Ghosts from current time may also not be aware that death has come to them. These examples would be inadvertent or unintentional haunting.

A few illustrations would be the kitty ghosts from a 1920s apartment who had no idea that they were haunting the modern-day cats currently living in that apartment, in downtown Hollywood, CA. Another example would be the souls of people who commit suicide still regretfully lingering around the location of their final moments. Their mournful presence can set up a suicidal resonant energy field and can actually attract people to that location who want to end their lives.

Current owners whose homes are near cemeteries may find that they keep running into someone and/or feel someone's presence. There is nothing deliberate about this type of haunting. Graveyard ghosts frequently wander among the headstones and if homes are built over old burial grounds, the dead of centuries past can inadvertently be haunting the living. The stacks of time are simply colliding with each other usually because one of the home's occupants has some level of resonance with one or more of the ghosts. Everything is connected; even our pasts are connected, whether or not we are aware of it. Here again, helping them to cross over will be imperative as we cause them to cease the turmoil they are in as death comes to them, over and over. This is a great act of compassion.

Residual Haunting

"If the walls could talk . . ." they would tell us all about the predecessor energy of the souls who occupied that space through the recent moments of time. Residual haunting is slightly different from Energetic haunting because this is more the energy that is left behind by the emotions of daily life, rather than the powerful Energetic energy that has become imbedded in large institutions.

Human beings are constantly shedding energy. Imagine the energy expended in an argument. Walls and floors will hold that energy for longer and longer times the more arguments are screamed there. Entering that type of room will cause us to inwardly cringe, the residual haunting of that toxic energy soundlessly impacting us.

We smile when we think of the many warm happy birthday greetings sung over sweet cakes and candles in a family dining room. Think of the lullabies, sung in children's rooms: rooms with these events will feel sweet, safe, and happy for a very long time. We would say that the energy is wonderful in these places.

Think of the happy energy of being promoted to a new office because the previous occupant was also promoted. That residual energy will be positive. However, if you got the promotion because someone was fired, that residual pain, humiliation, and anger are going to haunt you until you can imprint your own energy signature on that office. If you did not know what happened in that office when you got there, and discovered that you found yourself feeling constantly angry, or frustrated you would want to inquire about the circumstances of the previous employee's departure. This would also tell you that you would need to do a thorough cleaning and clearing of that desk space to begin to feel better about your job and your new office.

Sometimes, ghosts travel with the souls they are haunting – that soul shadow of sadness. The energy that ghosts and/or previous owner left behind will impact you. But sometimes the energy of the owner alone can haunt you. When we moved into our current home in San Diego, I remember quite clearly feeling like I was in the home of the previous owner. Granted, I had some level of sensitivity, so it was logical that I could feel her energy in the floors, the walls, even the shower. I continually felt like I was living in someone else's home. I had to perform quite a few spiritual practices to shift the energy and make this house feel like ours.

A real estate agent asked me to help her with the office space of her two assistants. The problem: both of them were chronically sick. Upon closer inquiry into the history of the building, it was discovered that a spa/massage business was directly below them. Clouds of negative energies were often released with each person who received a massage and that energy lodged itself into the walls, floors, and ceilings of the building. Both assistants' desks were directly above that business. The quick fix was to place several mirrors (we used Feng Shui mirrors but plain mirrors would also work) facing down to confine that energy to the massage business. The result: the assistants found that they were seldom sick anymore. Normally massage businesses are wonderful places, providing a beautiful, positive service, but you never know how a person will react to the energy given off by a massage client and in this case, it was not as beneficial as the assistants would have hoped.

Residual Haunting is acknowledging the energy we all expend in our day-to-day lives. But we can change the energy of that past haunting by changing the energy that we are emitting. We can clear residual energy by many spiritual practices, including prayer, the use of flowers, burning the resins of Frankincense, Myrrh, dragon's blood and thoroughly cleaning the spaces. Sometimes if the energy is particularly awful it will take a bit of time, but it is possible to rid a home or other space of toxic residual energy.

Portal Haunting

"Mirror, Mirror on the Wall . . ." The fairy tales of magic mirrors that can talk to evil castle characters pervade books and movies. Are magic mirrors merely in fairy tales? Can mirrors affect us in our ordinary 3rd dimensional lives? Absolutely, what were those fantasy mirrors really? They were doorways to darkness. The concept of mirrors being doorways or portals to the 4th dimension has long been imbedded in fairy tales, adventure sagas and romantic stories. Perhaps that is why people wrote about them: these things were real to them.

And they are still real to this day. I was once asked to clear a house, because the owner told me that she was having so much difficulty sleeping. Once I remote viewed the location, I could immediately tell that a mirror above her bed, was the offending element. It was almost as if someone would emerge from that mirror and create problems for my client. I immediately suggested to the owner that she remove the mirror because I knew that I could never clear her room with that mirror in place.

"But I paid several thousand dollars for this very special mirror. It's supposed to have great energy, which is why I put it above my bed!"

"Then why aren't you sleeping well below it? I suspect that whoever sold you this piece of questionable art simply used it as a vehicle to access your energy field during the night. Let's do an experiment: take the mirror down, wrap it in aluminum foil, shiny side in, to contain the energy and put it in your garage. Once you have done that, let me know and I will continue to clear your room."

"Fine," she said, "I'll do that as an experiment to prove to you that it isn't the mirror. It must be something else."

But it wasn't anything else. Once that mirror was removed, I cleared the room and the client finally slept well. But you must be wondering what happened to that mirror?

Well, after several days, my client returned to her garage and what she saw caused an icy chill to race down her spine. The aluminum foil wrapped mirror was sitting in a box. The foil should have been smooth, but it wasn't. An imprint of an angry fist was clearly visible in that aluminum foil coming from inside the wrapped mirror. It was from whoever was using that mirror as a portal. This negative entity was unsuccessfully trying to push past that shiny foil. The foil acted as a reflective surface returning the energy, effectively checkmating whoever was trying to harass my client. The reflective, mirror-like nature of aluminum foil is a wonderful tool to contain and/or to return negative energy. She threw the mirror out and slept well ever after that.

Another client had 35 mirrors in her home. Several were so toxic that simply looking at them was enough to clue me in that they were portals. One particular mirror was so negative that I felt like I was being choked when I looked at it. Once this information was shared with the homeowner, to my utter astonishment, she ripped that one and several others off the wall, put them in a black plastic bag, got out a hammer and shattered the mirrors. This action instantly broke the magic access and those portals were forever closed.

Have you ever been in a location and you felt as if there was a doorway to darkness? You might be wise to look around you and see if you find any mirrors that make you feel uneasy. Sometimes, images of bodies of water can create that same portal energy. Also scan for photographs or paintings, which contain images of water. Examine how you really feel about these pieces of art; you may be surprised at how negatively you look at that piece.

Another way to close a portal if you are absolutely unable to destroy it is to change the energy access. This means that on the back of the mirror or painting, write the words: love, blessings, hope, God, Christ, joy, or any other extremely positive word. Words all by themselves carry a very specific energetic frequency and can close a portal. If you cannot remove the portal object from the wall, or if it is a circle or an oval shape, you may want to write in tiny letters, these words in the corners. If the mirror, painting, or photograph is a rectangle or a square, put lines in the 90° angles of the object creating 45° angles. This will immediately alter the energy as well, because changing the angles to 45° changes the mirror shape to a 'bagua' or 8-sided shape. This octagonal 'bagua' shape is sacred.

If you are in a hotel and cannot do those things to a hotel room mirror, simply cover it with a towel. You may find that you sleep significantly better.

Object Haunting

Any object can be haunted, especially if that object is metal. Metal holds on to the vibrations of people, places, and things. Metal holds personal vibrations so well, that this is often how some psychics are able to locate a body or a person: the psychic can tap into the person by the energetic residue left on the metal object (this is called: Psychometry).

This is one of the reasons that I discourage people from purchasing antique jewelry. Vintage jewelry may look beautiful, but unless you are especially sensitive, you are unlikely to be able to discern the history of that piece of wearable art. Yet you may find that whether or not you can discern a past problem with the piece, you can still immediately be influenced by that piece of jewelry, whether you believe in this type of situation, or not.

If you think about it, you would never want to wear the engagement ring of a woman who died during her engagement, or who deliberately broke the engagement. The energy of death or rejection would be firmly imbedded in that metal.

Would you want to wear on a daily or even infrequent basis a piece of jewelry worn by someone while he or she was being murdered?

The energy of terror, grief and tragedy would emanate from that ring.

Jewelry worn by people with fatal illnesses also takes on the energy of that illness, in effect, haunting whoever wears it and possibly causing the person to take on the same illness.

The metal in the jewelry and if there is a stone in the jewelry, both will take on the personal vibration or frequency of the previous owner. This is why people believe that some pieces of jewelry and stones are 'cursed.' The jewelry piece is not cursed as much as it is emanating the energy of all of the negative things that happened to previous owners of that piece. Your vibration/frequency can begin to take over the energy of the piece but you would have to wear it a long time for that to happen. It is better to clean the object in salt water or plain salt, in the ocean or by another spiritual method. Some jewelry does not do well with salt, so you will want to be careful with the clearing method you use.

Furniture can also emanate toxic energy depending on who previously owned it but not to the same degree that a metal object would. If you are using it every day and have not cleared it, then you may have a problem with how you feel when you use those pieces. Overtime, your frequency will begin to take over the frequency of the furniture. But if it feels terrible to begin with, then it is better to clear it or not own it.

Whenever you receive or inherit something from someone else, even if you know the person, it is an important spiritual practice to automatically clean and clear the object.

Karmic Haunting

Karmic haunting means that you can often carry the burden of sin or share the light of hope. Used objects not only carry with them the energy of their previous owners, but they also carry with them a much heavier level of energy: the karma those owners created when they used that piece of jewelry or object. Most of the time, you will not feel that karmic burden unless the object has a tremendous level of karma attached.

Karmic haunting is among the most dangerous and chilling types of hauntings anyone can experience. This may appear to be an esoteric and vague concept, but this is where people come to believe that an object is cursed. Objects are not cursed. Objects carry with them the residual energy of their owners. However, some owners may have done wonderful humanitarian acts or hideous, murderous acts and a myriad of actions in between. The more significant those actions are, the larger volume of human beings they have affected the more intense will be the karmic burden.

Karma affects all of us and attaches to objects associated with certain events. <u>If you own that object, you are now directly connected to the karma of that event,</u> whether you intended to be connected to it, or not. Let us look at several powerful examples.

A woman was shopping at a flea market and came across a pin with insignia from one of the deadliest elements of the German High Command in World War II. She bought that pin and instantly became karmically connected to the murder of millions of Jews. This pin, worn by high-ranking German officers directly connected the modern-day wearer to the karma of mass murder. Needless to say, this woman's life became very negative.

In another case, a man was offered an 'outstanding deal' on a 1940s era yacht and the previous owner told him why he had to sell it at such a rock bottom low price. The previous owner had been a highly successful businessman. Everything he touched turned to gold – until he bought this yacht. Then, not only did he almost lose his business, but he also suffered several deaths in his family. He also related that the man who sold him the yacht died while he owned it and his heirs were anxious to unload what they believed to be a 'cursed' vessel. The new owner scoffed at all this talk of 'curses.' Ridiculous, he thought. But soon, things began to happen to him as well. He fell ill, his business suffered, relatives began to die and finally someone explained the karmic ramifications to being connected to the German General, who was the original owner of the yacht. The German General was Heinrich Himmler, the architect of the 'final solution' and (again) the murderer of six million

Jews and other people throughout Europe. Here again, owning this yacht connected the owner to the karma of one of history's worst mass murderers.

Consider the karma of owning weapons involved in anyone's death. Perhaps the real question to ask before receiving or purchasing anything that has any connection to World Wars I or II, the Civil War, slavery, or any other tremendously negative event, is this: do you really want to now carry the karmic connection/responsibility of owning that piece?

Yet karma works both ways. Consider the story of the woman who happened to sit on an airplane next to Mother Theresa. The air traveler was feeling chilly, so Mother Theresa gave the woman her own personal shawl. From that moment on, the woman felt healing move through her body. This woman was extremely perceptive and realized that what she had was so precious that she began sharing it with anyone she knew who was ill. So now this woman is connected with the karma of Mother Theresa, and the karma of healing. In this case, the woman's life took a positive turn and continued to be positive because with every healing encounter, she was furthering her own karma and the karma of Mother Theresa and her mission of offering compassion to any soul who crossed her path.

Can you be influenced by the karma of an object if you do not know the history of the piece? Yes, of course you can. It is important to always seek to discern the history of any piece that you purchase and if you cannot do that, at least make an effort to clear the object. Then ask that the object be blessed, that this object be filled with light and finally say a prayer releasing the object from any negative connections. These actions begin to separate you from the karma of the object and shift whatever negative energy may have been associated with this object. If you do all of this and still feel a powerful negative energy, you may have to release ownership of the object. In this type of case, the sheer volume of negative karma attached to it may be far powerful more than any well-intentioned clearing can accomplish.

Mortal Haunting

"I return often to my childhood home in my dreams. I roam the halls. I stare at my bedroom and I play in the backyard. I'm not sure why I return there so frequently, but it seems to bring me some sort of comfort."

When my client told me this, I shuddered a bit. The current owners of that house possibly see her at night, roaming the halls of their home. They do not know she is not dead. They would not be able to imagine that a living person can haunt a home.

But a living person can haunt a home. All right, you cannot be in two places at once – or can you? If you daydream about a location often enough and it becomes real to you, are you not in two places at the same time in your mind?

Most of the time retracing our steps in a place that brings us peace is harmless, but this is a situation where a person is obsessed with a particular location. Can the person's presence, the energy expended to constantly visit that location actually impact living people? This is different from residual haunting because with residual haunting, if you are living there, eventually, your own vibration, your energy begins to replace the energy of the previous owner. In this case, the previous owner's energy keeps imprinting on the house. The living person is just strolling through the past and has no idea that that very active, very real daydream or night dream is haunting a home. They would not believe that the current owners of the house could feel their presence and would not understand what is happening to their house.

If this situation happens to your home, what can you do? There is no ghost to remove. What you can do is to ask that an angel firmly remove the person from your house right now. Eventually the living person will cease wanting to psychically return to your location and you can be at peace. You can also have a qualified Feng Shui practitioner help you to provide greater psychic protection. Mortal haunting is a real phenomenon, although relatively rare.

Thought Forms, Lower Realm Intelligences or Ghosts?

What is the difference between a Thought Form, a Lower Realm Intelligence, and a ghost? The world of the 4th dimension is populated by many different beings. Many of us know what a ghost is, but there are other forms of non-visible energy that ply the ether of the 4th dimension that can impact us. This knowledge will also help you to understand the importance of keeping a positive outlook on life and focus on positive spiritual actions.

Thought Forms

Have you ever heard the concept that thoughts can become reality? Where does that idea come from?

A Thought Form can be a manifestation of someone's thoughts that can take a physical form. Native American lore describes beings or 'shape shifters' that can take on any shape, especially animal shapes, birds, wolves, snakes. Black magicians created black cat thought forms or demonic types of shapes to harass people in the sleep state. Beings that exist in the Lower Astral, also known as the 4th dimension, can shape energy into forms that appear to people in the 3rd dimension. But other supposed 'beings' are simply the thoughts of one or a group of (usually seven) people focused on creating a temporary energy form. Usually that form is not for the benefit of the 'targeted' person. The number seven is an ancient magic number used by both light and dark spiritual workers.

Discussed in books of magic, dark magicians are seen 'conjuring up' something to influence another person. They supposedly use all kinds of devices to create a mixture that would have some imagined power to negatively influence a living person. These things created an energetic connection to the person selected for torture.

However, karma, being equal, keeps all things in balance. If the person was in resonance with goodness and light and often wore many symbols of this goodness, then the person would very likely not be influenced by the maleficent energies of these dark personages. They would literally have hardened themselves as a target. Many dark magicians look for easier marks or targets.

However, in some remarkable cases, very beautiful thought forms can be created by the energies of unconditional love. These can range from the appearance of a very bright light, or powerful streaks of white light that show up on photographs, to a light that seems to emanate from an individual. Everything is energy. Thought forms are powerful energies, either negative or positive that can take visible shape.

Lower Realm Intelligences

A Lower Realm Intelligence is a being that roams the 4th dimension. Some psychics call them shadow people, others refer to them as demons, or little devils. In the 1990 motion picture "Ghost," Patrick Swayze plays a man murdered by a business associate. There are two scenes where these horrible creatures, these Lower Realm Intelligences, were accurately portrayed. In one scene, the murderer of Patrick Swayze's character, Sam, was hit by a car. These red-eyed creatures immediately came up to terrorize the murderer. In another scene when the architect of Swayze's murder died by accident, again these terrible creatures appeared.

Who you are, what you have done in life and how you died, determine your vibration or frequency at death. Lower Realm Intelligences torture the dead based on that soul's frequency at death. If a mass murderer dies, he is not magically whisked into the Heaven World. Based on the powerful darkness that surrounded the soul in life, that same darkness will accompany him into the terrifying environs of the lower astral or 4th dimension. There his frequency will instantly attract these horrific creatures that will automatically begin to torture this killer. These dark little beings will feed on the negativity of the mass murderer's death energy. Perhaps these are the eaters of the dead often described in more esoteric literature by psychics of old who could also see these nasty beings.

If the mass murderer died in a shoot-out, then the psychic called in to clear that location, must be very skilled to be able to fully remove not only the toxic ghost, but also these Lower Realm Intelligences. If the psychic only removes the ghost and leaves the Lower Realm Intelligences, then the toxic energy will remain in that location. To fully clear such a darkness-saturated spot, you have to close the doorway or portal to the 4th dimension that was created by the murderous act, in addition to removing the ghost and the Lower Realm Intelligences.

If a location is over-run by Lower Realm Intelligences, mechanical things will break down, people will have trouble sleeping, they will quarrel, will become ill. Animals may also become sick and often die when these beings harass them. Animals do not have a 'belief system.' Animals know if a location is energetically toxic to them or not and if it is, then these creatures will try to tell their owners through their chronic illnesses and/or endless barking or meowing or running away from home.

These vexing little beings can also appear to people who are sensitive and to very psychic children in certain dark/negative locations. If a child tells you she sees or feels something, pay attention. Believe what they are saying, even if you personally do not 'see' or 'feel' it.

Ghosts

Thought Forms are temporary forms of energy created by a person or a 4th dimensional being. Lower Realm Intelligences are little devils who inhabit the 4th dimension and who can harass the living and the dead. Ghosts are souls who have left their mortal bodies. The energies that originally animated these people are still there, and the energy of these souls can become visible to living people. A ghost can disappear and reappear repeatedly. Usually, a Thought Form can only manifest once or perhaps twice at the most. Lower Realm Intelligences can only manifest if the frequency of a location is low enough for them to appear, and then briefly.

Despite what you may have heard, souls do not necessarily linger because they have 'unfinished business.' Ghosts are ghosts because that soul did not cross over into the Heaven World. Ghosts linger for thousands of different reasons. The primary one is that 99.9% of souls have no idea what to do when death guides them out of their physical body. Even those who think they are prepared find that death is still a confusing shock.

These souls are stuck in the 4th dimension and often find themselves desperately trying to speak with a living person to find out: what do I do next? But you can help them by saying The Crossing Over Prayer© at the end of this book or playing The Crossing Over Prayer© video on TinaErwin.com to help any soul to cross over into the Heaven World. This will be the compassion that you will want for yourself.

Once a soul has made his or her way into Heaven, then they cannot return to haunt you or anyone else. The most they are allowed to do is to briefly make an appearance at their funeral or visit a loved one in their dreams. They do not return to haunt the living – ever. Why would they? They no longer require mortal help. They are receiving the wisdom and guidance of the Heaven World and can provide far more assistance to the living from Heaven than they ever imagined.

Opening the Door to Darkness

Is it possible to open a doorway into darkness and not realize it?

Do certain actions perpetuate the energies of evil?

Is it possible that a doorway to darkness may actually be in the very ground upon which a home is built?

Is it possible to tell in advance if a piece of property has negative energy running through it?

If you could avoid purchasing a piece of property because it has the potential for a literal stream of toxic energy to course through it, you would do that, because the knowledge of how the natural world works is a balance of the positive and the negative.

In the past, when Native Americans evaluated a piece of property, they looked for signs of negativity. These could which trees that were diseased, stinging vicious insects, like yellow jackets or wasps, vines of poison ivy, oak, or sumac. These signs told them that this area had a toxic energy. They would not camp there.

But when homes are built in subdivisions, when the warning signs of negativity are erased, it would seem impossible to determine whether or not that location is toxic. But there are things you can do when you are about to purchase a home: speak to the neighbors about the house and area. You would be surprised to learn about the things that happen in a house. Take the story of the woman who was considering purchasing a home in an upscale neighborhood. She discreetly asked neighbors if the current owners were happy in the house. Two out of three would not say anything. The third neighbor told her bluntly not to buy the house. She explained that the house had had 3 previous owners and all of them had gone bankrupt while living there, in addition to having health and marriage problems. Needless to say, the prospective buyer did more research and discovered that this neighbor was correct.

Sometimes there is nothing wrong or out of balance with the land. The issue becomes the toxic actions of previous owners. It is in this way that a doorway into darkness may have been opened. People do not realize that when they perform certain actions, they are 'practicing magic." Saying positive prayer and sending healing to the world is white magic. Playing with the Ouija board or dabbling with Tarot or Angel cards enters the realm of gray magic. Going beyond dabbling with Tarot cards by doing 'readings,' and holding Séances or performing spells on someone is practicing black magic.

Playing violent video games is also a form of working black magic because you fill the house with terrible violence.

Houses can also become filled with darkness due to vicious actions by previous homeowners, which can include physical, sexual, emotional, or spiritual abuse, as well as illegal and prescription drug abuse. These types of energetic violence open a door to darkness, which is often challenging to close. If methamphetamines have been used and/or manufactured on a piece of property, it cannot be cleared. The house must be torn down, destroyed and the land given healing treatments. Even with physical and spiritual healing treatments, no one should ever live on that land because the toxicity can last decades.

If someone was murdered in the home, this action can create a cavern of terror. Ironically, you can clear a home where a murder took place but not a home where there was a meth lab. Methamphetamine labs use toxic chemicals that permeate walls and floors and even the surrounding earth itself. This toxicity shreds the auric field of people who breathe any part of it. This type of area cannot be cleaned or cleared by any method or by simply clearing the property. Only time and nature can ultimately heal that toxic physical and psychic load.

If a house burned down and was rebuilt on the same property, there is also the potential that a new fire can return on that same property. Sadly, illustrating this point is the story of a piece of property in Virginia Beach. The first big box store had a mysterious fire and burned to the ground. The previous building was torn down. It sat vacant for several years. A second, different big box company built a beautiful new store. Within a year that store also burned down. Time passed. Finally, after a third big box store also burned down, no one would put another business on that land.

That space was vacant until someone built a park on the property with fountains. The energy of the fountains will help to cool and clear that property.

The energy of fire comes from an originating event that may be lost in the mists of time. This causes the land to be in resonance with the angry energy of fire, making future fires more likely than property that has never burned. Land must be properly cleared and/or the frequency of the home or business increased if there has been any kind of fire event. These actions will remove tremendous darkness. (Remember: sage will not clear any of these situations.)

My Own Spiritual Service

Ghosts or Spirits?

A ghost is a human being who has died, entered the 4th dimension, and not crossed over into the Heaven World. Once someone has left their body, they become a ghost. However, most people have no idea how to help a ghost. Many families sense a soul around them or hold on to a loved one preventing them from even trying to cross into the Heaven World. This is why The Crossing Over Prayer© was written, as well as the other prayers included at the end of this book. They are all designed to open up a doorway to the Heaven World to provide service to the dead.

I strongly encourage anyone who can sense a ghost to help them to cross over as soon as that soul is encountered. This is tremendous spiritual service and those souls, afforded this Divine assistance, often return prayers of gratitude from the Heaven World to the living.

It is also important to remember that <u>ghosts never become spirits.</u> Spirits are other intelligences that exist in the 4th dimension. There are positive or beneficial intelligences in the 4th dimension as well as dark and evil beings in this dimension.

Understanding the Veil

The 'veil' is the spiritual separation between the 3rd and 4th dimensions. This separation exists so that souls can have a spiritual experience on Earth. The 3rd dimension is the Earth plane, a place of time, space, and gravity. The 4th dimension is the 'ether' a place of no time, no space, and no gravity. Souls move immediately to this location after death and they can linger here for hundreds, even thousands of years before crossing over into the Heaven World. Some souls do cross over into the Heaven World because they are prepared in some way for their death and welcome the light when it comes for them.

When a psychic talks to the 'other side' are they talking to 'a' spirit, spirits, angels, ghosts, devils, or Divine beings? How does the psychic know with whom they are speaking when they are 'listening' or 'channeling?' Most of the time the psychic has no way of knowing for sure who is on the other side of the 'veil.' Only an extremely experienced psychic can tell the difference and this type of psychic would never channel or work with any type of 'spirit' in the 4th dimension. She would understand the danger of doing that type of thing.

People use the term 'spirit' as a catch-all phrase to describe all beings in the 4th dimension, as if all these intelligences were the same. They are not the same. Differentiation is critical here.

Who's Who in the 4th Dimension

Ghosts are people who have left their body.

'Spirits' is a term for alcohol and really has nothing to do with beings on the other side of the veil.

Angels and Divine Beings are just that, beings from the 5th dimensional Heaven World: they do not reside in the 4th dimension although you can ask an angel to help your loved one in that dimension.

Devils, lower realm intelligences, black magicians and dark thought forms reside in the 4th dimension.

When someone talks to or channels 'spirit' there is no sure way to know exactly to whom they are speaking or listening: the being could be a ghost, a black magician, or an angel (on assignment from Heaven). It is wise to remember that any clever black magician can appear to be an angel or Divine being. Performing due diligence in the 4th dimension is challenging. Another way to look at it is to consider that people in the 3rd dimension are not always what or whom they appear to be. A police officer may be abusive, a priest or clergyman may be a pedophile, and the head of the PTA may be an alcoholic. The 4th dimension is no different. Few beings are quite what they appear to be here.

If someone is doing Tarot or Ouija and he or she believes that they are positive and comfortable with the being communicating with them on the other side, perhaps they should think again. These two ancient tools of black magic will never be for anyone's higher benefit, no matter how competent a psychic someone thinks they are. Often times, the more you use these tools of the dark side, the more financial, legal and health problems you encounter. A woman who had 50 Tarot decks claimed to her last breath that these dark tools had no effect on her. But she died of cancer, penniless, and homeless. What made this all the more heartbreaking was that she was a lovely person who only wanted to help people. She may have been fogged by the sooty energy of the cards, which ended up affecting all aspects of her life in a negative way. Even very good people can be tricked into believing in these tools of the dark side. The truest spiritual process has no need for these questionable crutches of dark magic. <u>Loving kindness and service are the best tools anyone can use on their spiritual path.</u>

The Spiritual Path

We are all on a spiritual path, be it religious, emotional, or psychic/intuitive. This path is not for the faint of heart. Walking the spiritual path is like tiptoeing through a minefield in an earthquake and a thunder/lightning storm. You must tread cautiously, thoughtfully, and wisely.

Read, study, and apply all the lessons you are learning. Suppose you did dabble a bit with Tarot or Ouija. That may very well be part of your path. However, once you realize that you have a greater understanding of the hazards of those dark tools, you can choose to wrap them in aluminum foil and throw them out, or you can burn them to break the magic. Then bathe with salt, clean, and clear your home using the powerful resins of Dragon's Blood, Frankincense, Benzoin, and Myrrh, spray your home with sweet orange oil, play the music of Mozart for several days and then move on with your learning journey.

The stories you have just read share a bit more about my own spiritual path and some of the more memorable psychic experiences of my own. I sincerely hope that you have enjoyed them!

Prayers for Sending Ghosts to the Heaven World

Prayers for Sending Ghosts to the Heaven World

The following prayers are excerpts from The Lightworker's Guide to Healing Grief and are provided to help anyone with difficult death situations.

The Crossing Over Prayer©

This prayer will assist any soul to cross into the Heaven World. Once a soul has made this glorious transition from this transitory world of darkness into the glorious light of God, the soul will be restored, physically, emotionally, mentally, and spiritually. This prayer will also work on ghosts whom you may not know. This prayer offers all souls the peace of release into the arms of God.

Prayers for Sending Ghosts to the Heaven World

The Crossing Over Prayer©

Dearest Lord above,
I humbly request that you take
any and all souls, who have found
my divine light of service, into
the Heaven World,
right now.

I ask that an angel wrap each
soul in a blanket of healing light,
right now.

I pray that every single soul
will use the Light Bridge provided
by my angelic team to transition into the
Heaven World,
right now.

I send love and healing to all souls
no matter how they died, no matter
their level of guilt, without any judgment
or prejudice whatsoever,
right now.

May the light of your love, Father,
embrace and keep all of these souls
now and forever.
Amen.

A Prayer for Understanding

This prayer will assist you in seeking answers to the often, unfathomable question of why someone you loved has died. The more you say this prayer the more you open yourself to the insight that can come from God.

A Prayer for Understanding©

Dearest Lord,
I most humbly pray that I may understand the
loving ways of perfect order.
I pray that I may understand the
cosmic view.

I pray that I may find meaning in my
pain and hope in my yearning heart
at the transition of my
precious loved one [Name].

Please grant me strength and insight
so that in my healing path,
I may be of service
to others.
Amen.

The Compassion Prayer for Suicide

This prayer offers assistance in healing and understanding. Suicide is so painful for family members left behind. There are endless unanswered questions. Often there is a subtle level of guilt that some friends and family members feel because they are convinced that there is something they could have said or done that would have prevented this event from happening.

However, sometimes, we cannot know the pain and sorrow, anger, and internal turmoil that a person was feeling as they left this world. Sometimes, we are not meant to know these things. Sometimes, all we are left with are the questions for which there is no resolution.

Sometimes, all that we can do is pray to God and ask for assistance in healing the soul who so suddenly left and for healing our own bewildered hearts.

Eventually, it is critical to understand that it is important to provide assistance to the soul so that he or she can find the Light of Transition, and the hope of healing.

This prayer can be read completely, or you can read only the sections that are healing for you in this particular moment

Prayers for Sending Ghosts to the Heaven World

The Compassion Prayer for Suicide©

Heavenly Father,
my precious one has ended his (her) life.
Therefore, I most humbly ask
that your gentle Angels of Transition
guide my beloved one to the Heaven World
right now.

I request that forgiveness be given, Father,
for whatever events or circumstances
led to his (her) decision to leave mortal life.
I ask, Father, that you embrace my dearest one
with the depth of your compassion.

I humbly request, Father, that you provide
healing to fill the dark, angry, or profoundly sad
places of his (her) very soul, with the powerful
restoration of the Light of your Divine Love.

My heart is aching, Father, with deep despair.
I pray that you will help me to understand
His (her) death with your light of compassion
and without judgment.

I humbly pray, Father, for love and healing
for my entire grieving family.
Please help us to understand and accept this
heartbreaking moment and the days ahead,
with your Divine Grace.
Thank you, Father, for loving [person's name].

Prayers for Sending Ghosts to the Heaven World

Thank you, Father, for loving me.
Thank you, Father.
Amen.

The Healing Prayer for a Murdered Loved One

This prayer is a difficult one to read if you are facing the death of a murdered loved one. Families facing this type of grief often feel betrayed by God, by the concept that God would allow such a terrible thing to happen to someone they love so dearly. Anger at God is not unusual in these times. Families feel that they are also victims of such a tragic situation. Sometimes, individuals find that they disconnect from anything spiritual including the concept of prayer or of healing in this way.

And yet, there can be no healing without God, without reestablishing that divine connection. Sometimes in the darkness of grief and tragedy, this connection helps each of us to hold on and move through each challenging day of dealing with police, detectives, courts and the often, endless unanswered questions.

Assisting the soul to cross over is critical to the soul's ultimate healing. However, letting go of someone who died this way is profoundly difficult. It is normal to want to hold on to the soul. However, releasing the soul to the divine will ultimately help all parties to heal. Souls who are released to the Heaven World, find that the Divine can restore them.

If this entire prayer is simply too difficult to read all at once, then simply read the section that works at the time for you. Each stanza is designed to stand alone.

The Healing Prayer for a Murdered Loved One©

Heavenly Father,
My precious [name of person]
has been violently taken from me!
Therefore, I most humbly ask that your gentle Angels of Transition immediately wrap my beloved in a blanket of your healing light and then guide my them to the Heaven World
right now.

I ask that they receive profound
healing on every level, for the fear, pain, and trauma he (she) may have suffered as death came.

I pray that now and always,
you will embrace him (her) with the
restoring Light of your Divine Love.

I am heartbroken that I did not get to say
goodbye. Please, please tell him how much I
love him now and forever.

He didn't deserve for this to happen.
Please tell him how much I will miss him,
and that I will pray for him every night.

Letting go is so hard. But I know I must do this.
I want him to heal in every way.
And I need to heal too. I am so angry!
I am so hurt that this could happen
to someone I love so much!

We are all suffering and do not know how to
heal. Please help us to cope with this unending
pain, and the anger in our hearts.

Please help us to find the strength to fill our
hearts with your Divine Grace,
a bit more as each day goes by.

Above all, please help us to face the difficult
days ahead without him.
Please fill us with the Light of your Divine

Grace, to help us to understand and cope with
this heartbreaking moment.
Thank You, Father,
Amen.

A Prayer for my Beloved Animal

We all love our pets and yet when their light leaves our lives, we are often embarrassed to admit how heartbroken we are. Sometimes, we are made to believe that we should somehow just quickly 'get over' the loss of this creature that graced our lives for such a long time. Grieve your pet. Pray for your pet. Honor the love you shared.

A Prayer for My Beloved Animal©

Heavenly Father, I most humbly ask that you guide my sweet [name of animal] to the Heaven World
right now.

I ask, Father, that you provide love and healing to my loyal companion, my most beloved creature,
my precious [animal's name].

I ask, Father, that this valiant animal be embraced with the healing Light of Divine Love. I send gratitude to you, Father, for the time I had with this wonderful gift you sent me, this sweet and loyal creature.

I pray that my beloved animal will know how much I love her (him) now and forever. I miss my friend, Father. Please help me to heal my own aching heart.
Thank you, Father.
Amen.

Glossary

Affirmation

An affirmation is a positive statement that we say to ourselves to reinforce our sense of self and to heal some part of us that has been wounded.

Aka Cords

Aka cords emanate out from your solar plexus—the area just below your breastbone. This is the place where the cord extends out and makes attachments to everyone you have ever met, to every place you have ever been, and to everything you have ever owned. The longer you are attached or connected to something, someone, or someplace, the stronger your aka cord is. Your thoughts also flow along these fine, filament-like energetic cords. This is why when you are connected to someone and that person is thinking about you, you often sense it. This is also why if you have powerful cords attached in a strong love relationship, you often feel it immediately when the person dies. There are many ways to understand how these cords are eventually cut. The more profound the relationship, the thicker are the aka cords of attachment.

Angels

Angels are divine beings from the Heaven World who work in the 4th and 5th dimensions to help mortal souls. Human beings are not and can never become angels. Any mortal person can call upon an angel for assistance; this is not imposing on any angel. Angels incur positive karma when they are called upon for assistance by a mortal person.

Angels of Transition

These are specific angels who assist souls to cross over into the Heaven World. Anyone can request their assistance as well.

Appropriate Realm

This is a location that people who commit terrible acts of violence are sent. It is a realm within the Heaven World where the fractured soul can find guidance, soul healing, and methodology for balancing the karma of the violent life previously lived.

Archangel

These are a group of angels who oversee other angels. They are considered significantly more powerful than perhaps the lower ranking angels. All angels are on a path of soul evolution. Archangels are simply at a higher stage of spiritual evolution.

Astral Plane

This is the area of the 4th dimension, the land of no time, space or gravity, the dwelling place of ghosts and other lower realm beings.

Aura, Auric Field

This is the protective bubble, force field, immune system that surrounds the human body. This 'field' can be enhanced or corrupted based on what is happening to a person. The aura can change colors depending on the person's emotional state or condition. Some psychics and psychic children can see auras.

Clearing Resins

Frankincense, Myrrh, Benzoin and Dragon's Blood are powerful resins from Sumatra and the Middle East. When burned on charcoal disks these resins will clear a tremendous amount of predecessor energy, lower realm intelligences and ghosts. Neither sage bundles nor any type of incense will do this, only these resins.

Dimensional Doorway

We live in the 3rd dimension, a dimension of time and space and gravity. However, in the 4th and 5th dimensions, time, space, and gravity do not exist. The ability for ghosts to move between dimensions is greatly facilitated by a doorway between each dimension as well as the assistance of angels who act as emissaries to facilitate the transition.

Divine
The divine is a connection to God and a location where God can be found. It is the powerful, positive energy of the Heaven World. We all access the divine when we pray, send love and healing, and assist ghosts to transition to the Heaven World.

Divine Beings
These are Intelligences who inhabit the Heaven World and who assist mortals in the 3rd, 4th, and 5th dimensions.

Emotional Haunting
The feeling that a ghost or a location is haunting you because of how you are reacting whenever you are there. This can also be an experience from a past life that haunts you, appearing in your dreams or causing you to focus on a particular subject matter throughout your life.

Ether
This is another term for the 4th dimension, where ghosts among other beings, exist.

Frequency
Negative energy, guilt, grief, depression, drugs, alcohol, and toxic people lower frequency. Hope, love, healing, joy, and delight

raise frequency. All positive efforts raise frequency. This concept of frequency or vibration at any given moment may determine your level of health.

Ghosts

These are mortal people who have died and who have not transitioned into the Heaven World. They are now souls inhabiting the 4th dimension.

Healing Blankets

A tool any mortal person can request to assist any ghost. These blankets are infused with the essence of the divine and help raise the frequency of any soul to facilitate transition into the Heaven World.

Heaven World

This is the 5th dimensional dwelling place of God, Jesus, angels, and Divine Intelligences. This is the location a person reaches when he or she crosses into the Heaven World. This location also includes various appropriate realms where even violent souls can receive healing for the extreme fractures in their soul that precipitate terrible violence. They also are provided ways to work through the karma of the life just lived.

Intelligences

These are spiritual beings who can inhabit the lower astral or the Heaven World.

Karma
This is the spiritual law that states that for every single action there is an equal and opposite reaction. What you do comes back to you.

Ley Lines
These are the electromagnetic grid lines that cover the entire planet. These lines are critical because they define the migration routes that animals and insects use. All beings depend on these ley lines to help find their way on Earth. Ghosts are often found in greater quantities along the intersections of some of these types of lines.

Light Bridge
This is the term used to describe the divine pathway, which connects the 4th and 5th dimensions to the Heaven World.

Light of Christ Consciousness
This is 'an energy' of light, which any mortal person can request to help a situation, themselves or a ghost who is lost, alone and afraid. This light facilitates transition into the Heaven World and soul healing, regardless of any person's belief in Christ, their particular religion or lack of religious belief.

Light of Compassion
This is a divine light that has the potential to live in the hearts of mortal people as well as in the essence of angels, Divine Intelligences and God. This light spreads love and care, hope and the promise for redemption, forgiveness, and healing for all souls.

Light Lady
This term primarily refers to the author of this book. This is how ghosts generally refer to the author when they see her in their 4th dimensional realm. She appears especially 'bright' to them, literally full of light, hence the reference to 'light lady.'

Light of Transition
This is a unique form of light that comes to a soul who is ready to transition into the Heaven World. This light is the bridge between the 4th and the 5th dimensions. Additional terms meaning to cross over into the Heaven World include:
Appropriate realm
Heaven World
Light Bridge
Moving on,
Crossing over
Bridge to the light
Crossing into the light
Light of the divine

The other side

Light Work
This is spiritual work that helps others in a loving, gentle, nonjudgmental, and non-prejudicial manner, regardless of that person's religion or belief system.

Light Worker
This is a mortal person who seeks to assist the living and the dead in any karmically correct, spiritual manner possible.

Lower Astral
This is an aspect of the 4th dimension, which is the home of very dark intelligences, lower realm intelligences and spiritual vermin. Some people and religions refer to this as hell.

Lower Realm Intelligences
These are beings who are also referred to as little devils, torturers, dark guys who inhabit the lower astral. These creatures can bring great torment to some ghosts stuck in the 4th dimension. These being can also torture living people during the sleep state.

Metaphysics
This is a two-part word: 'meta' meaning beyond or expanding upon, and 'physics' meaning the study of matter in space and time.

Literally, metaphysics is the study of physics beyond what we currently think we know and understand.

Predecessor Energy

This is the energy of past people, structures and events that have existed on a particular piece of land or location. This energy can have a powerful effect on those currently living on that property even if the dwelling is brand new. The following types of energy will make any area especially toxic: violent weather, fire, murder, death by almost any method, war, prison/prison camps, meth labs, assault, abuse, bombing – literally any violent act will have an impact on the land or location. The energy lives in the wood, the minerals of the earth and in any structure(s) on that site.

Psychic

This is a person who has at least one of many spiritual abilities beyond what science can reasonably explain. This person may see and hear ghosts. He or she may see into the future, sense things by holding on to an object or be able to 'know' things not routinely expected.

Psychic Protection

Psychic/spiritual protection can include performing spiritual practices including blessing and prayer and requesting Divine protection. A person can wear specific stones for protection such as black tourmaline, tiger eye, kyanite, howlite, quartz crystal (which is continually cleaned and cleared after each use) and other radionics devices (see below).

Psychometry

Psychometry is the psychic ability to sense the energetic information of a location or an object.

Radionic Devices

These are devices a person can wear which changes the frequency of their body and is reflected in their auric field, making it stronger. A Radionic device can be a stone, or series of stones, a platonic solid, such as an octahedron, or tetrahedron, sacred shape, such as the Fibonacci spiral, the cross or star.

Reincarnation

This is the concept that we live thousands of lives for experiences. We gain the required experiences, die by some method, get stuck in the 4th dimension, or cross into the light, review those life experiences, choose a set of parents and then we are reborn again. A person can reincarnate from the lower astral which explains the source of violent people.

Remote Viewing

This is the psychic ability of being able to physically be present in one location and project your consciousness to another location anywhere in the world, transcending time and space. Once in that location the remote viewer may be able to scan the energy of an area and determine what is happening in the present and/or what happened in the past.

Resonance

In metaphysical terms, the simplest explanation is that you attract who and what you are. You will attract experiences to you based on who and what situations you are in resonance with at any given time. You attract to yourself others who are like you: The Law of Resonance.

Sage

This fragrant herb is wonderful for ceremonies and sausage. However: sage will never remove a ghost, a Lower Realm Intelligence, clear a space or remove predecessor energy.

Shadow Lands

This is the 4th dimension, the place you may find yourself if you are knocked out of your body and end up in an unconscious state and cannot find your way back to your body.

Shaman

The Shaman for any tribe is the spiritual advisor for the entire tribe. He or she may also be the Medicine Man or Woman, helping the tribe to heal physical and emotional wounds. The term Shaman is one of great respect. Usually, these men and women are very proud, peaceful, and wise.

Soul Frequency

Every soul has a specific frequency that defines him or her at death. The higher the frequency of the soul, the easier it will be for that soul to transition to the Heaven World. However, often the method of death or level of guilt and shame will cause a soul's frequency to be much lower inhibiting their transition to the Heaven World

Spiritual

When we say that someone is spiritual, we assume that this means that they are on a positive path. However, being 'spiritual' does not mean that all 'spiritual people' are doing positive light filled things. Some of the people considered to be the most spiritual can be doing some of the darkest acts.

Spiritual Beings

These are beings who exist in the 4th and 5th dimensions. The higher realms of the 5th dimension of the Heaven World offer us the most positive spiritual beings you can imagine, angels, Counselors of Divine Wisdom, Divine physicians and so many more. However, the 4th dimension also includes spiritual beings who are black magicians, lower realm intelligences, wraiths, tormentors, and other beings best left undescribed. We would be wise to be circumspect and specific when we refer to 'spiritual beings' because they are not all the same.

Spiritual Laws

This is the theme and variation of the energy of karma at work. Each law operates in every dimension. Examples:

For every action, there is an equal and opposite reaction.

You attract to yourself others who are like you: The Law of Resonance.

You attract what you fear the most.

Stacks of Time

All time exists at the same time in a specific stack of time. A 'stack' is a specific window or layer of time where something tremendous happened. The energy of that stack of time will keep vibrating out. To heal the current era of time, you often have to heal the past. When remote viewing a specific location, the psychic must sift through what are called stacks to find the specific stack of time that is currently influencing present events.

The 3rd Dimension
This is the dimension of mortal time and space and gravity. Mortal, living people reside in the 3rd dimension. Gravity anchors people in this dimension so that they can experience life because time and space exist here.

The 4th Dimension
This is the dimension of ghosts where time, space and gravity do not exist. People who are ghosts, exist in this dimension. It is an existence because they never change the clothes, they died in. They are not aware of the passage of time, even though hundreds of earth-timed years can go by, and they travel at the speed of thought.

The 5th Dimension
This is the dimension of the Heaven World, God, Jesus, Angels, and Divine Intelligences. We cross into this dimension as we enter the Heaven World. This dimension also has many, diverse aspects and when any soul crosses into this dimension, they are immediately routed to the correct are based on their frequency and the totality of their life experiences and karma created. So even if a murderer is crossed into the Heaven World, he or she will go to the realm of the 5th dimension commensurate with their karmic ledger.

Thought Forms

All thoughts are 'things' and these things are forms of energy, even if you cannot see them with your physical eyes. Some thoughts are so powerful that they can physically manifest as semi-visible objects and, in some cases, can manifest as physically visible to anyone. You may see them as orbs, or they may seem to be ghosts, or scary apparitions. Psychics who are well schooled can see them in the 4th dimension. Who creates them? Sometimes white magicians create them, and they can look like shafts of bright light. But the more common type of thought form is the type that is created a black magician and can appear to be something terrifying, either in human or non-human animal-like from. Visualizing salt raining down upon them, readily removes them for they do not have strength in their shape but before you remove them, it can be unnerving the first few times you see them.

Vibration

Please see Frequency.

Wraiths

These are intelligences, energies, and manifestations from the lower realms, from hell. They are dark, evil and can be terrifying. They may appear in a room, a home, or on a piece of property. They have made appearances in many movies about magic, castles and evil. In the movies they appear as hollow beings, wearing shredded clothing which floats through the air behind them. Scary music is always played when these beings are present. These wraiths are evil, spiritual beings. This is why simply labeling spiritual beings as only good would be incorrect. Spiritual beings can exist in many different realms and walk both the evil side as well as the angelic side. I suppose in all realms, it is important to understand just exactly which 'side' you are on. They are, however, quite fragile and sending them a prayer, or the Light of Christ Consciousness will almost immediately cause them to disappear.

About the Author

Tina Erwin CDR USN (Ret) has studied metaphysics for many years, gaining insight into the interpersonal relationships at the heart of everyday living. Her writing comes from an intense desire to know and understand the unseen world of action and reaction combined with a sincere desire to share this understanding with other knowledge seekers. Her first book, *The Lightworker's Guide to Healing Grief©* is a treatise on how to help yourself or someone else to heal grief. Her second book, *The Lightworker's Guide to Everyday Karma©* is a lighthearted look at applying the principles of karmic law to everyday life.

Her next books: *Ghost Stories from the Ghost's Point of View Trilogy Volumes 1, 2 and 3©* introduced to people what it is like to be dead, what it is like to discover that the life you thought you were going to have is never going to happen. Literally you see the ghosts' point of view.

Soul Evolution, Past Lives and Karmic Ties© and **Karma and Frequency©** are both fascinating tools to understanding the more esoteric elements of who we are, why we are here and how we can build better lives.

The Crossing Over Prayer Book© offers the reader 88 amazing prayers to help themselves and others, including the dead. This is an invaluable tool.

Her lifelong studies into the deeper meaning of events and actions were further enhanced by the experiences of a dynamic 20-year career in the Navy, working for the U.S. Submarine Force, retiring at the Commander level. Commander Erwin found the Navy to be a tremendous schoolhouse in which to study all the facets of behavior, from the worst to the finest levels of humanity.

You can learn more about her books, and her videos on her website: **www.TinaErwin.com** or connect with her at **Tina@Tinaerwin.com**. You can also reach her at **GhostHelpers.com** or **Contact@GhostHelpers.com**

BONUS MATERIAL: I Get Questions

Over time, I have received many questions about being psychic, how I learned to live with it and why I do it and do I have a choice. So, I thought I would take a few minutes and offer some insight into what this type of life is like for me.

I love what I do. Yes, it's difficult sometimes because I deal with so much death, but the thought of helping the millions upon millions of souls who have found the light is what keeps me going. It has taken me all of my life to develop this ability, to get to this point where I can be of tremendous service to people, living and dead. The journey was not easy but then no one's journey is easy. I've never met anyone who would say they have had a perfect or charmed life. We all have challenges and lessons. Perhaps at the end of the day, at the end of our lives, how we were of service to others is the most important question any of us can ask and be hopeful that the answer is that we did a lot of good work and brought light into the world.

1. Question
    a. Are you ever afraid when you are doing a remote view?
    b. Do you ever just "trust spirit?"

Answer

I was at first. Entering the realms of the unknown can be dicey at first but I have been studying all the elements of psychic ability, magic, death, life in the other realms and how to work in those realms for close to 50 years. There are some very obscure texts that discuss some of these more esoteric elements and after you have reads hundreds of these pages, you begin to learn more than just the basics.

And no, I never "just trust spirit." A spirit can be anything you can imagine, from a black magician, a wraith, an angel, or a higher realm being and a ghost. Without performing due diligence, you have no way of ever knowing who you are really speaking to or who you think you are speaking to. And I don't share my method of performing that due diligence – of validation of the reality of who I am working with.

2. Question

How do you know you are going to know how to deal with what you find in another dimension?

Answer

That's such a powerful question and the answer is that you are not going to know that answer going into any psychic situation. What you have to trust is your own intuition, your own psychic sense of reality, your own confidence and above all the power of your more elevated personal frequency. You cannot expect to do any psychic/spiritual work with a low frequency. My book *Karma and Frequency©* fully explains this issue of maintaining a high/elevated frequency. It becomes a lifestyle.

3. Question

Have any of the experiences deceived you, meaning that you weren't really fearful when you started, but you ended up being terrified in the middle of a situation – on the other side?

Answer

Yes and no. I have had some exceptionally violent ghosts think that they could intimidate me, and one even tried to strangle me, but then I remembered how spiritual law works, my own personal power level and the fact that I have tremendous help from the higher realms. I always ask for help.

4. Question

Why don't you become depressed dealing with so much death and often horror that you find in these remote views?

Answer

When you have the opportunity to be of such tremendous service to the living and the dead, it lifts you up emotionally. People don't come here to live a perfect life. Souls enter mortal life for the opportunity of experience and that includes all kinds of experiences, both the wonderful and the horrific. Helping them to cross over enables them to better understand the life just lived. It is huge spiritual service.

5. Question

Seeing the evil people do to other people, do you ever become really angry or enraged at the injustice of what happens to souls?

Answer

Much of what I see has already happened. No country or group has ever been immune from the atrocities of war, famine, disease, totalitarianism, dictatorship, or medical genocide. I help people after they have died, so I am offering solace, pain relief and upliftment in a way that makes a huge difference to the soul. I can't change what happened to them, but I can change how their soul receives healing and processing for the *next life.*

6. Question

Do you ever cry in the middle of a remote view? Are the conditions or situations so tragic that you want to burst into tears and give in to the emotion of what is in front of you?

Answer

Sometimes, yes. Sometimes I have to steel myself against the horrors of what I'm seeing and have to deal with. But the overriding mission of helping the living and dead, precludes me thinking of myself and requires that I focus entirely on the soul and/or souls in front of me. Providing the very best service helps me to cope with the horrors that I see.

7. Question

After you work on the "other side" as you call it, are you ever tired, for hours and days?

Answer

Yes, this work is exhausting. You have to build up your stamina to face the mental requirements required to stay absolutely laser focused on the job at hand. It may seem that you haven't 'done' that much but the fact is that it takes a lot of brain power to do this work, especially if you work at night and you have to allow time to rest and recover. Psychics who say that they just ask spirit to help them and feel great after a session have always baffled me. Where is that energy coming from? The psychic has to process the energy from the higher realms to be able to use it and that is where the biggest use of physical/menta/emotional energy comes in to play. And yes, sometimes I am very weary for a full 24 hours after the job is done, especially if it takes several days or nights to finish the work. Working in the garden, walking in nature is how I or anyone can restore themselves. I also allow myself extra sleep and I eliminate as much drama from my life as possible. I deal with plenty of it on the other side. Connecting to the natural world is visually and mentally healing. I also have a tremendously supportive family and I rely on them for a source of love and happiness.

8. Question

How did you learn how to do this? Who taught you?

Answer

How I learned to understand and use this unique skill, is very complicated and would take up an entire book all on its own, to be able to explain it. Sometimes, when you have growing ability, other forces step in to help guide you in your process and your future. The simple answer is that study every day – still. You can never learn enough about this field and I often re-read many powerful texts just for the added info I might glean.

9. Question

Do you ever teach other people how to remote view and cross over the dead?

Answer

I never teach other people to remote view. The karmic responsibility of this process is way too great to be able to share this process. I once had an individual who did learn to use remote viewing and although she seemed to understand all of the spiritual laws attendant with it, she did not follow all of them and ended up violating many serious elements of karmic law. The ramifications were not kind to her. The lesson was quite clear: if you are going to do this level of psychic work, you can never, ever compromise your spiritual ethics for even a moment of mortal time in either dimension. If you do, the karma that comes back to you is magnified because *you cannot say you did not understand the karmic ramifications of your actions.*

10. Question

How do your kids feel about what you can do? Is it weird for them to have a mom like you?

Answer

I taught my children to understand how powerful and important intuitive ability is and how to use it. We are all psychic and whether or not we think we are psychic is irrelevant. You cannot make it through a day without using some level of psychic ability. The easiest example is driving a car. You have to sense/feel the traffic around you all the time to be a safe and effective driver. I also did not do 'weird' things to freak them out or their friends. Judicious use of your ability maintains your credibility with all of your family members and garners respect on a daily basis.

11. Question

How hard is it to be married to someone like you?

Answer

".... Someone like me" I would say that it is challenging to be married to a psychic. It takes a special kind of partner to embrace my level of ability. At the same time, I do not abuse this level. I don't 'cry wolf'. I only share information that I feel is valid. You cannot protect all of your family members from everything in their life. You also have to remember that your spouse may not have your level of ability and often what you can do is incredibly unnerving to them. Again, judicious use of the ability will keep your marriage and relationships in balance. It is never enough to 'just have psychic ability,' you have to seek the wisdom to use it wisely in every situation which means that your responsibility is significantly higher when you have this level of psychic ability.

12. Question

Do you ever wish you didn't have this skill, this ability to see these horrible things?

Answer

You develop psychic ability over lifetimes of experiences. You 'graduate' to each next level based on past life experiences. See my book *Soul Evolution, Past Lives and Karmic Ties©,* which helps to explain what comprises a soul and how we have the experiences we have for the lessons that we need to learn. So yes, while it is always difficult to see horrible things and hear tragic stories, it doesn't diminish the job that has to be done.

13. Question

Do you ever wish you were normal and could just be a mom, a wife, sister, grandmother?

Answer

Yes, sometimes that would be great. But then I remember, that for some people, I enable *them to be normal* because I can remove something that is causing them great stress in their lives.

14. Question

How hard was it to explain to the people your kids married, who you are and what you can do?

How did they respond to you when they 'learned what you can do?"

Answer

This question makes it sound like at some point we, as a family, sat each prospective in-law down and said, you need to understand that your new mother-in-law is a psychic and sees and talks to ghosts. It was not that way. It was becoming part of the fabric of our family, of our lives and having discussions just come up and talking about the topic openly and honestly that helped each of them understand what the situation was/is and how they fit in. Eventually, each of them used the service I provided and then used the tools that I made available, like The Crossing Over Prayer© to be able to handle things themselves.

15. Question

You don't seem shy in talking about your experiences. Do you ever get weird looks or people who automatically dismiss your ability as not being real or thinking you are a real weirdo?

Answer

In *Ghost Stories from the Ghosts' Point of View Vol 1,* there is the story of The Rocket Scientist. The client was a rocket scientist from

NASA, Langley and he didn't believe in what I did and bluntly told me so but he also needed my skill set. Eventually, he believed me and gained a new perspective on "there is no such thing as no such thing." I do welcome those who deny that ghosts exist. I love explaining the physics of metaphysics and ghosts to them: energy is neither created nor destroyed, so the energy that animates a physical body has to go somewhere, become something else at death. This is the Second Law of Thermodynamics. This is hard science.

16. Question

Did you have these abilities when you were a kid? How did your family respond to you? Do other family members have this skill set?

Answer

I believe that all children come in with some natural psychic ability.

They don't realize that not everyone can see and do what they can see and do. So yes, I could see the ghost of my cat when she died and sense things. My siblings had their varying senses of psychic ability. We each evolved to use them differently based on what our life path turned out to be.

17. Question

Did you use this psychic ability when you were in the Navy?

Answer

Technically, overtly, no I didn't use it when I was in the Navy. What I did use was my ability to sense things about people, locations, and situations. If you can feel what your crew needs, what they are feeling on a fundamental level, you can avoid problems before they become difficulties. If you can hear what someone isn't telling you but you have a powerful feeling that they should be telling you more but for some reason they are not, then you can ask more probing questions, get to the bottom of a situation before it becomes a drama, or a nightmare.

18. Question

Did any Navy people know you could do this, weird thing, seeing ghosts?

Answer

No, only a handful of people knew I had any psychic ability, when I was in the Navy. Several people suspected it but could never be sure because I never discussed it with my command.

19. Question

Have you learned all you can learn about being a psychic?

Answer

You never stop learning how to improve your skill and ability. This is why you must constantly study and learn and apply what you have learned to all the unusual, and challenging situations that confront you on a continual basis.

20. Question

How did you get other people to believe in your psychic ability?

Answer

It just happened naturally. When I was a child, I could remote view but I didn't know that this is what it was called. My parents thought it was 'cute.' I tried to share what I could see such as the ghost of a cat or ghostly child, but my mother said that there was no such thing as ghosts and she would dismiss what I saw or was trying to explain. After that, I didn't share anything else with her. I think it upset her. Some families punish their children for having and/or displaying their psychic ability or choose to put them on drugs. It's horrible. It's like punishing someone because they can see or hear.

21. Question

Is it lonely having this ability?

Answer

Sometimes, but mostly I am working so much that I don't have time to worry about loneliness. You have a skill set. You use it. You move on to the next job. I also have a powerful relationship with my family so I am not lonely.

22. Question

Do you consider your psychic ability a gift?

Answer

A gift is something that someone gives you for your birthday, a holiday, or an occasion. You can choose to accept it, return it, or put it away and never use it. Psychic ability is not a gift you can 'give back' or 'reject.' It is just that, an ability that you develop life after life, after life, after life. It lives within you and you have to learn how to use it or consciously choose not to use it.

You earn karma either way: use it or not. If you 'use' your psychic ability to tell futures, flip tarot cards, give readings, conduct seances, or read palms, you are doing what are called parlor tricks. This is not responsibly using your intuitive abilities for the greater good. This use of the skill set earns neutral or negative karma, especially telling someone's future. That is a violation of spiritual law because you have an infinite number of futures and telling someone just one of those potentialities creates a reality where one may not necessarily manifest naturally. You are 'interfering with that person's future' *even though the person asked you to do it*. The reason this is so serious is that to a person without your level of ability, you appear 'all knowing' even if you aren't.

This creates a reality for a person and that person weirdly works to create that very reality because your words are always in the back of their head – and they believe you. *They want to believe you.* If you use your ability, hone it through spiritual service to the living and the dead, or find a different way to be of service., then you earn positive karma. If you study for many years, even privately, as a hobby, you may find that you are gently guided to a way to use that ability for the greater good.

Another reason that psychic ability is not a gift is that no one wants to see the horrors of someone's death, the massacres you see when you clear a battlefield or invasion location. You can't 'unsee' those things. They are there in your memory, making your skill a responsibility, not a pretty package you happily anticipate opening.

23. Question

If you can see the future of a person and it is horrible, do you tell them?

Answer

There is no easy answer to this. It's just a hard question and it depends. If it's a 'don't get on that airplane' kind of vision, then yes, but if it is vague, you have to be careful about sharing anything at all. It's very difficult.

24. Question

Why don't people know what to do at death?

Answer

No one knows what to do at death because for centuries we have expected organized religion to tell us what to do, but all religions are sorely lacking in this area. It's as if they are whistling in the dark, hoping no one will notice that this huge event that will affect 100% of us won't really happen, happens! And when it does, we feel cheated that we were not given direction on what to do.

The only faith that does tell you how to die and what to do after death are the Buddhists. Their direction is clear. They enable their believers to no longer be fearful of death but embrace this normal cycle in a soul's existence.

25. Question
How did the Navy prepare you for your life as a full time psychic?

Answer

I was a terrorist expert for the US Submarine Force, among the many jobs I had in the Navy. This taught me how evil works, how it takes layers of protection to create a viable shield from this darkness and how raising your frequency and hardening yourself as a potential target pays huge dividends.

Evil exists in all dimensions and it exists in all walks of life, in families many times, of course in corrupt governments, agencies, organizations and military services.

But alongside this darkness there is also the goodness that also exists and mitigates, dilutes, and destroys the darkness. Every positive effort someone makes toward the light of justice, balance, love, and compassion, raises all of us up, even the unwilling bad guys among us. It's just how it works.

The Navy provided an opportunity to gain greater insight into the very nature of the darkness and what it takes, how much effort it takes to dilute it. It also shows how powerful the rewards are as well.

26. Question

When you communicate with spirit, who are you talking to?

Answer

What is 'spirit'? I hear psychics talk about talking to 'spirit' all the time and in truth I suspect they have no real idea whom they are speaking to in that 4th dimensional realm.

I don't use that term because I specify who I am speaking to: ghost, black magician, angel, wraith, or higher realm being. Knowing for sure, performing due diligence is critical to being able to safely work in those realms.